Luce Irigaray's Phenomenology of Feminine Being

SUNY series in Gender Theory

Tina Chanter, editor

Luce Irigaray's Phenomenology of Feminine Being

VIRPI LEHTINEN

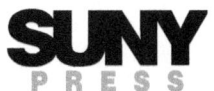

Published by State University of New York Press, Albany

© 2014 State University of New York

All rights reserved

Printed in the United States of America

No part of this book may be used or reproduced in any manner whatsoever without written permission. No part of this book may be stored in a retrieval system or transmitted in any form or by any means including electronic, electrostatic, magnetic tape, mechanical, photocopying, recording, or otherwise without the prior permission in writing of the publisher.

For information, contact State University of New York Press, Albany, NY
www.sunypress.edu

Production by Eileen Nizer
Marketing by Michael Campochiaro

Library of Congress Cataloging-in-Publication Data

Lehtinen, Virpi, 1970–
 Luce Irigaray's phenomenology of feminine being / Virpi Lehtinen.
   pages cm. — (SUNY series in gender theory)
 Includes bibliographical references and index.
 ISBN 978-1-4384-5127-5 (hc : alk. paper) 978-1-4384-5128-2 (pb : alk. paper)
 1. Irigaray, Luce. I. Title.

B2430.I74L44 2014
155.3'33—dc23   2013021966

10 9 8 7 6 5 4 3 2 1

I dedicate this book to the memories of my grandmothers Aili Flinkman and Siiri Lehtinen; to my mother Terttu; and to my daughter Tuuli-Titania.

Contents

Preface	ix
Acknowledgments	xiii
Abbreviations	xv
Introduction	1

Part I Body 13

1	Feminine Existential Style: An Operative Concept	15
2	The Philosophical Discourse and Canon, and Femininity	21
3	Irigaray's Activity of Productive Mimesis: Opening of the Possibility of Original Feminine Expressivity	39
4	Phenomenology of the Body: the Methodological and Conceptual Framework for Irigaray's Investigations of Lived Embodiment and Expressivity	53
5	The Feminine Lived Body	69

Conclusions to Part I 87

Part II Desire 89

6	Irigaray's Account of the Beloved Woman as a "Man's Woman"	91

7	Opening up the Possibility of Woman's Self-Love and Love among Women	99
8	Male Phenomenologists' Promise of the Uniqueness of Woman in Carnal Love	105
9	The Continuum of Caressing Gestures in Accordance with the Holistic Conception of Sexuality	109
10	The Philosophical Discourses of Carnal Love: Obstacles and Openings for the Becoming of a Woman Lover	113
11	The Male Lover, the Feminine Beloved One: A Specific Way of Understanding (Carnal) Love	139
12	Irigaray Writing, Speaking, and Acting as a Woman Lover	145

Conclusions to Part II — 163

Part III Wisdom — 165

13	Original Aspects of Woman in Philosophy: Intermediating between Materiality and Spirituality, Nature and Gods	167
14	Irigaray as a Midwife for Diotima's Daimonic Philosophy of Eros	177
15	Writing: An Intervention into the Neutrality and Absoluteness of the Subject and a Model of Sensible Ideality	183

Conclusions to Part III — 205

Conclusions — 207

Notes — 211

Bibliography — 221

Index — 227

Preface

At its most promising, Luce Irigaray's work is an exemplification and catalyst of the dynamic forces of change and transformation. From the perspective of phenomenology of the body, persons and their works such as (philosophical) writings constitute a complex network of dynamic relations and are constituted by such relations. These include relations to oneself or to itself, to other persons or writings, and to the world, all formed in embodied, affective, and spiritual dimensions of subjectivity. In our written works these constitutive relations can be made explicit and elaborate or they can remain implicit, even hidden. Similarly, these constitutive processes, with their inherent dynamism and potentiality for truthfulness, can be recognized, cultivated, and developed to varying degrees in our individual and communal lives. On the basis of these ideas, this book maintains that change and transformation are inherently anchored in Irigaray's philosophy in its focus on these constitutive relations and their inherent dynamism with regards to topics, themes, style, and potentiality for truthfulness. The aim is to provide means for perceiving Irigaray as a radical philosopher of change and transformation in the following six respects.

1. Irigaray's work offers both the impulse and means for **personal growth and flourishing**. Irigaray's work demonstrates that the perspectives of women have not been traditionally included to the philosophical investigations of the sense of being, and the lives of women have thus not gained elaborate and self-defined expression in the spiritual sphere of being. In response to this, Irigaray's work is consciously written from the first-person perspective of a woman. In so doing, she invites the reader to more fully assume her/his own first-person perspective in reading, speaking, writing, and acting, i.e., to participate more fully in the process of the constitution of the sense of human existence. This process entails the observation of the continuities and discontinuities between one's own experience, Irigaray's first-person expressions with reference to feminine pre-discursive experience, and the relation of both to the "general" structures of experience. Moreover, Irigaray's opaque way of writing invites us to continue completing, questioning, and offering alternative ways of manifesting and acknowledging feminine being, be it in thinking and writing or in acting and living. On the basis of these observations I suggest that Irigaray's work exemplifies feminine being in its bodily and spiritual generative potentiality by opening up the possibility of an infinite process of differentiation.

2. This work presents Irigaray as a philosopher of love and desire par excellence. In Irigaray's daimonic conception of eros, **desire and love** are understood as the most **intense transformative forces** in human life. Love and desire are oriented toward future, which is opened up in the way we inhabit the here-and-now of our becoming. In their intensity, love and desire reveal the affective element inherent in our perception and in our attitudes toward ourselves, others, and the world. Moreover, detached from the metaphysical presupposition of the hierarchical dichotomy of the soul and the body, love and desire appear as permeating all the dimensions of subject—embodiment, affectivity, and spirituality. Understood in these ways, love and desire are prone to open us not only more fully to the actual but also to the potential in our relations to ourselves, to others, and to the world.

3. Philosophical discourse and practice can become more truthful in its investigations of being and the sense of human existence if the first-person perspectives and expressive acts of women are included. At its best, philosophical thought that has culminated in speeches and writings can exemplify the generativity inherent in love and desire. Irigaray's work shows how we, by returning to the daimonic origins of eros through sexual difference, can become conscious of and more fully realize the philosophical practice as thinking, speaking, and writing as gendered human beings who are both incarnate and spiritual. Irigaray's own work, in its materiality, affectivity, and spirituality, is exemplary here, but she also detects such potentiality in the classical philosophical works. Her works address the reader as a woman and a philosopher with no contradiction between the two, in contrast to the philosophical culture in general. In this way, her work also establishes a model of a woman-woman relation (in philosophy). Irigaray's philosophical work also demonstrates that any philosopher is necessarily connected to the other spheres of life, and all dimensions of subjectivity, even when these relations remain unrecognized.

4. Irigaray's work provides means to become conscious of **our habitual ways of living and thinking gendered being.** As such her work contributes to renewing, developing, and cultivating these ways and becoming better aware of them with both their restrictions and potentialities. An example is Irigaray's explanation of how the sense of woman and femininity has been traditionally male-defined, and she also shows that the effort of forming the self-defined feminine being, each doing her own part, is still needed and meaningful. This task of rethinking femininity and masculinity is in principle unaccomplishable, and is significant also in respect to reconceptualizing gender-blending identities. This is because gender-blending identities are more often than not articulated as a variety of relations to masculinity and femininity; also from this perspective, masculinity and femininity seem to constitute the sense-forming basis of gendered being in its variety. The sense of femininity and masculinity, however, can be conceptualized and lived as open to differences or with a tendency toward similarity, and herein lies the decisive point of the actualization of sexual difference/indifference or sameness, as Irigaray's work urges us to recognize.

5. Irigaray's work as a whole also opens up a possibility to perceive and transform the motivational, gendered basis of the **destructive tendency of our way of living as culture**. These destructive tendencies consist of the reduction of persons to instruments and nature and animals to resources at the risk of seriously damaging our living conditions. This is done in forgetfulness of our lived embodiment, which constitutes necessarily in relation to the elements and the environment (breath, movement, nourishment), but also in forgetfulness of the basic sense and perception of human beings as irreducible to any predetermined instrumental purposes. As Rachel Jones (2010) shows, Irigaray's efforts for the recognition of our maternal origin, and coming to terms with it, is a task of the utmost importance in philosophy, and also in our culture more generally. Mapping out the implications of this recognition in thought and in cultural and social practices is also an urgent task in our era: human generativity is restricted to human beings, on the part of women, and to cultural artifacts. These acts of generativity do not entail reproduction of the Earth and the elements on which we depend, even if we think and consume as if they would. So, both the possibilities and limitations of human generativity should be recognized, and Irigaray's work provides as yet undiscovered resources for such a task connected to the ideas in this book.

6. In all of the above-mentioned potential modes and means of recognition and transformation, and in becoming aware of ourselves as gendered beings, the **dialectics of dependency and integrity** are crucial. Irigaray's work offers perspectives and tools for perceiving and developing these dynamics. We can only strive for our singular and communal flourishing within the network of relationships that are constitutive of and constituted by of our being and becoming. Because of this, the identification of these relationships, their order of primacy and the figures, roles, and positions available to us as persons, philosophers, and as members of (professional) communities, is crucial. Irigaray's work offers a paradigmatic example of the dynamics of change and development inherent in such a process: it constitutes a dynamic unity in a constant process of change and transformation, yet it maintains its cohesion in its mode of changing. However, the very same paradigmatic example also demonstrates the risks of blind spots and the constant threat of freeze, stabilization, and halt. The identification of these is impossible without other readers, writers, or persons in pursuit of truthfulness, and herein lies the core of Irigaray's, or any work's or person's, potentiality as a dynamic and changing whole: in its openness to others in interaction and dialogue.

Acknowledgments

This book is the result of research work that was carried out at the Department of Philosophy in the University of Helsinki. Sara Heinämaa's insightful and precise comments and criticisms have played an important role in developing the manuscript that this book is based on. The manuscript has been commented on in a supportive and critical way also by the following professors and scholars: Morny Joy, Debra Bergoffen, Pirjo Lyytikäinen, Sigridur Thorgeirsdottir, and Eva Maria Korsisaari. The book also benefited from the helpful and generous comments that were made by anonymous reviewers of the SUNY Press.

I would also like to thank the following institutions for funding the research work: the Academy of Finland, Finnish Cultural Foundation, the Oskar Öflund Foundation, the Ella and Georg Ehrnrooth Foundation, and the Emil Aaltonen Foundation.

Parts of Chapter 15 have been published in the article "On Philosophical Style: Michèle Le Dœuff and Luce Irigaray." In *European Journal of Women's Studies* 14, No. 2, (2007): 109–125.

Abbreviations

Works by Luce Irigaray

S	*Speculum de l'autre femme.* Paris: Les Éditions Minuit, 1974.
SO	*Speculum of the Other Woman.* Translated from the French by Gillian C. Gill. New York: Cornell University Press, 1985.
CS	*Ce sexe qui n'en est pas un.* Paris: Les Éditions Minuit, 1977.
TS	*This Sex which is not One.* Translated from the French by Cathrine Porter and Carolyn Burke. New York: Cornell University Press, 1985.
AM	*Amante Marine de Friedrich Nietzsche.* Paris: Les Éditions Minuit, 1980.
ML	*Marine Lover of Friedrich Nietzsche.* Translated from the French by Gillian C. Gill. New York: Columbia University Press, 1991.
PE	*Passions élémentaires.* Paris: Les Éditions Minuit, 1982.
EP	*Elemental Passions.* Translated from the French by Joanne Collie and Judith Still. London: Athlone Press, 1992.
OA	*Oubli de l'air. Chez Martin Heidegger.* Paris: Les Éditions Minuit, 1983.
FA	*The Forgetting of Air in Martin Heidegger.* Translated from the French by Mary Beth Mader. Austin: University of Texas Press, 1999.
E	*Ethique de la différence sexuelle* Paris: Les Éditions Minuit, 1984.
ESD	*An Ethics of Sexual Difference.* Translated from the French by Carolyn Burke and Gillian C. Gill. New York: Cornell University Press, 1993.

SP	*Sexes et parentés*. Paris: Les Éditions Minuit, 1987.
SG	*Sexes and genealogies*. Translated from the French by Gillian C. Gill. New York: Columbia University Press, 1993.
QEL	"Questions to Emmanuel Levinas." Translated from the French by Margaret Whitford, 178–189. (Originally published as "Questions à Emmanuel Lévinas sur la divinité de l'amour" in *Critique* (November) 522, 911–20). In *The Irigaray Reader*. Edited by Margaret Whitford. Cambridge, MA: Blackwell,
JTN	*Je, tu, nous: Pour une culture de la différence*, Paris: Grasset, 1990.
JTNT	*Je, tu, nous: Toward a Culture of Difference*. Translated from the French by Alison Martin. New York, London: Routledge, 1993.
JAT	*J'aime à toi: Esquisse d'une félicité dans l'histoire*, Paris: Grasset, 1992.
ILTY	*I Love to You: Sketch for a Felicity Within History*. Translated by Alison Martin. New York, London: Routledge, 1996.
ED	*Être deux*. (Originally published in Italian *Essere due*, 1994). Paris: Grasset & Fasquelle, 1997.
TBT	*To Be Two*. Translated from the Italian by Monique M. Rhodes and Marco F. Cocito-Monoc. London, New Brunswick: Athlone Press, 2000.
OO	*Entre Orient et Occident: De la singularité à la communauté*. Paris: Grasset, 1999.
P	*Paragraph: Luce Irigaray Presents Dialogues Around her Work*, (25) No. 3, Edinburgh University Press, 2002.

Interviews of Luce Irigaray

JLI	"Je—Luce Irigaray: A Meeting with Luce Irigaray," with Elizabeth Hirsch and Gary A. Olson. Translated by Elizabeth Hirsch and Gaëton Brulotte. *Hypatia* 10, No. 2 (1994): 93–114.
TLR	"Thinking Life as Relation: An Interview with Luce Irigaray," with Stephen Pluhàček and Heidi Bostic. *Man and World* 29, (1996): 343–360.
JM	"Luce Irigaray," An Interview with Alice A. Jardin and Anne Menke. In *Shifting Scenes: Interviews on Women, Writing, and Politics in Post-68 France*. Edited by Alice A. Jardin and Anne Menke. New York: Columbia University Press, 1991.

Plato

Symposium. In *Plato in Twelve Volumes*, Vol. 9. Translated by Harold N. Fowler. Cambridge, MA, London: Harvard University Press William Heineman Ltd, 1925.

Merleau-Ponty Maurice

PP *Phénoménologie de la perception*. Paris: Gallimard, 1945.

POP *Phenomenology of perception*. Translated by Colin Smith. London, NJ: Routledge, [1962] 1994.

VI *Visible et l'invisible*. Edited by Claude Lefort. Paris: Éditions Gallimard, 1964.

VIE *The Visible and the Invisible*. Edited by Claude Lefort and translated by Alphonso Lingis. Evanston, IL: Northwestern University Press, 1968.

Sartre Jean-Paul

EN *L'être et le néant: essai d'ontologie phénomenologique*. Paris: Gallimard, 1943.

BN *Being and Nothingness: A Phenomenological Essay on Ontology*. Translated by Hazel E. Barnes. New York: Washington Square Press, 1992.

Levinas Emmanuel

TA *Temps et l'autre*. Paris: Quadrige, Presses Universitaires de France, [1979] 1983.

TO *Time and the Other*. Translated from the French by Richard A. Cohen. Pittsburgh, PA: Duquesne University Press, 1987.

TI *Totalité et infini: essai sur l'extériorité*. The Hague: Kluwer Academic, Martinus Nijhoff, 1971.

TIE *Totality and infinity: An Essay on Exteriority*. Translated from the French by Alphonso Lingis. Pittsburgh, PA: Duquesne University Press, [1969] 2003.

Introduction

The debate on Luce Irigaray's essentialism and the dismissal of her thought as heterosexist have obscured her work as a manifestation of open and dynamic feminine being with great generative potential.[1] This book establishes an original reading with such an accent with the help of methodological and conceptual tools of phenomenology of the body.[2] It explores Irigaray's work with the help of the Husserlian and Merleau-Pontian idea and perceptual unity of *existential style* (i.e., dynamic essence), and daimonic conception of *eros* that is congruent with it. Interpreted and framed in this way, Irigaray's work appears as (1) a phenomenological description of previously unarticulated feminine experiences and their ideality, (2) a process of detecting and identifying discursive openings that facilitate articulating, cultivating, and instituting such experience and ideality inherent in it, and (3) a process of manifesting and developing feminine modes of expressivity and of renewing (philosophical) discourse.

One reason that experiences associated with femininity or rooted in feminine lived experience are easily forgotten is that the vague, fluid, and ambiguous characteristics of these are difficult to grasp through the available conceptual means. The most readily available concepts have accentuated the thing-like and stabile mode of being rather than the temporal, dynamic, and changing relations within and between beings. The phenomenological relevance in exploring the feminine being is not restricted to identifying and elaborating new experiences or new types of experience but extends to (a) exploring and developing feminine experience with the conceptual tools appropriate to its characteristics, and through this process (b) can open up the realms of experience and ideality in fresh ways.

From the perspective of phenomenology, experience is never fully given, but always open, partial and perspectival, and this also holds true with regard to the articulation of experience. Accordingly, this book argues that the inherent aim of Irigaray's work is to open and elaborate the sense and significance of feminine being in its temporal and spatial variety. The aim is to liberate feminine being from the fixed and biased notions of femininity. In its bold and radical way of accounting for, and identifying with, the feminine with her name and identity in the cultural and disciplinary context, which associates femininity predominantly with the inferior and the devalued, Irigaray's work is unique.[3] Additionally, the feminine existential style of Irigaray's work is special in its capacity to find ways of showing and opening up the hidden generative potential of the feminine. This book aims to demonstrate that her philosophy still holds undiscovered resources for further elaborations and developments of such potentiality. However, in order for the generative potential of the feminine of Irigaray's work (and more generally) to be actualized, we as readers and persons have a significant role as the origins of our own acts and works.

Methodology

Phenomenological description aims to disclose how things exist for us as "objectively" as possible. This is done, first, by accounting for subjectivity, which is considered to be inherent in all perception and experience. Second, by abstaining from different types of presuppositions, including common sense, theory, empirical science, and all positings of being and value. Third, by striving for greatest possible ideality (in the sense of the perfect and the universal) in the process of describing. Positings of being to be abstained from must be distinguished from being understood as sense and as processes of sense-constitution, which form the "object" and, in their verbally articulated form, the result of phenomenological inquiry. Phenomenological description, documented in writing and/or conveyed orally addresses us in the first-person, and also in our personal being, in its aim "to evoke the phenomena in such a manner that others might more easily see/experience for themselves" or invites us "to read or hear the descriptions so that we might see or hear for ourselves," as phrased by Anthony Steinbock (2007, 34).

Phenomenological investigation into the phenomena or sense of gendered being can help us to distinguish between the biased and the "objective," as well as between the contingent and the necessary. Conversely, the elaboration of the sense of gendered being can help in comprehending the constitution of sense in general, as the embodied and perspectival subjectivity of the phenomenologist is included in this process in a very special fashion. For example, Irigaray's work shows that the sense of gendered being is symbolically laden and temporally sedimented in a way that fails to articulate and express the lived reality of half of the potential "seers or hearers," i.e. potential readers and writers, and accordingly omits and bypasses great resources of symbolization in the pre-discursive experience. As Irigaray's predecessors, female philosophers from Christine de Pizan to Simone de Beauvoir have emphasized, in their own philosophical terms, in detecting the sense and value of feminine being, no disinterested party exists. The identification of the biases and omissions resulting from the unrecognized and unacknowledged features of our discourse and experience is an urgent and continuous task, assigned to *each of us* in our own lives and works.

In Irigaray's view, the model of the structure described above can be found in the philosophical discourse. The feminine speaking subject rooted in lived female-embodied experience is omitted in the philosophical discourse, and has instead been misrepresented from the male perspective. In order to dismantle this bias, Irigaray has introduced an idea and "method" of mimesis. According to Irigaray, in order to gain the position of a speaking subject as women rather than as neuters (i.e., men), we should proceed indirectly and occupy the positions attributed to women by the dominant discourse. Against the background of the idea of existential style, Irigaray's idea of mimesis, in its imitative and repetitive functions and as a conscious, creative activity, appears in a new light, as partially constitutive of a fully-fledged feminine existential style. In order to illuminate such an evolution of the generic feminine, or Irigaray's or any woman's feminine style, I have sought out figures which exemplify different respective proportions of mimetic and self-defined elements and ways of becoming. To this end I have aimed to identify also woman figures who are not explicitly mentioned by Irigaray herself or by the commentators in the (meta)discourse on her "method" of mimesis, but who still can be found to be operative in her *acts of speaking as woman* in the context of philosophy. I have done this by detecting woman figures available in the philosophical writings she focuses on, and with the help of her remarks on figures of feminine genealogy. This process of identification has also been aided by works by other feminist philosophers (Le Dœuff, Whitford, Shapiro, de Beauvoir, and Songe-Møller).

The discursive positions which I have disclosed in Irigaray's work should be understood as continuous with, yet not exhaustive of, the internalized roles and detectable figures of ourselves that are constituted in and by lived experience; herein lies the point of connection between the pre-discursive experience and the discursive formations, on which Irigaray's work focuses. These positions, roles, and figures delineate the possibilities that are given to us in our cultural imagination and also in our conceptions of our own possibilities as philosophers and persons, but they can also be broadened, questioned, and transformed with the result of modifying and broadening our cultural imagination.

Material

Irigaray finds allies in her substantial critique and pursuit of transforming the Western metaphysical tradition, which culminated in Platonism, in phenomenology of the body. The crucial issues include the relationship between (feminine) essence and existence, soul-body dualism and the task of the philosopher. Irigaray's writings, which this book focuses on, connect in the aim of rethinking these topics and themes by reconsidering love and desire, also in respect to wisdom.

Of Irigaray's works, the emphasis is on *Éthique de la différence sexuelle* (1984) even if the relation between *Éthique* and another of Irigaray's major philosophical works *Speculum, de l'autre femme* (1974), and her later work are also considered. In my view, *Éthique* forms an open and dynamic work *par excellence*, a spectrum through which Irigaray's early and later work show their most dynamic and transformative features. *Éthique* focuses on topics of love and desire, but it is also a manifestation of a specific and especially fruitful amorous modification of Irigaray's philosophical style. This amorous mode of her style is crystallized in relation to Plato's *Symposium* and its alternative conceptions of *eros*. More contemporary interlocutors of Irigaray are phenomenologists of the body (Merleau-Ponty, Levinas, and Sartre, and, indirectly, Husserl). The explorations and writings of these philosophers offer constitutive possibilities for the feminine subject manifest in Irigaray's work by developing anti-metaphysical and anti-Platonic accounts of essence/existence. These accounts include the embodied spiritual unity of a person, a philosopher, or a work, and anti-Freudian, holistic, account of sexuality and amorous relationships. Moreover, the works of all these philosophers, Plato included, also offer, a position for a female beloved, and ultimately for a female lover, teacher, reader, writer, and philosopher in their inquiries into the topics of love and desire.

Gender as an Existential Style

Because of the dominant role of accusations of essentialism and biologism in the reception of Irigaray's work, we still lack a comprehensive explication of her conception of woman and her idea of essence more generally. In feminist discussion, the idea of dynamic essence or existential style inherent in Irigaray's work has been confused with several other types of accounting for essence/existence in contemporary philosophy and feminist theory. The idea of existential style operative in Irigaray's work, which originates from the phenomenology of the body, also needs to be explicated and distinguished from two classical, metaphysical conceptions of essence: the Platonic and the Aristotelian.

Let us first explicate the idea of gender as dynamic essence or existential style as it can be found described and operative in Irigaray's work. Due to the inherent openness, dynamism, and temporality of the existential style, the potentiality of change regarding the constitutive relations to oneself, to others, and to the world is constitutively more fundamental than stability. Despite trans-temporal evolvement and change, however, style preserves its unity in its transformations, which can influence either the constituents of the style, their mutual relations, or both. The unity of existential style, however, is given not only by a concept or idea but also in pre-conceptual perception and sensible experience: the two are intertwined (*sensible transcendental* in Irigaray's terminology).

As a perceptual unity, a style is based on embodiment in several ways. The stylistic unity of the *lived* and expressive body is given, i.e., can be perceived, from different, yet interconnected, perspectives: from one's own personal viewpoint but also from the point of view of the other. Moreover, a style does not separate the soul from the body, but connects them in expressive embodiment and corporeal spirituality.[4] According to phenomenology of the body, also affectivity is an inherent characteristic of perception, and for this reason the subjectivity of all perception and experience is at stake when (gendered) being is inquired into.

Existential style is constituted in and by singulars; and singular styles in their embodied, affective, and spiritual dimensions take part in the constitution of a generic, existential style. In this way the concept of existential style applies both to singular women and to the open and dynamic unity formed by singular women: the generic feminine. The singular styles of individual women repeat, imitate, question, recreate, and affirm the generic feminine. The feminine styles of men have a different relation to the generic feminine, and they also contribute to the constitution of the in-between regarding the generic feminine and the generic masculine. In addition to individuals, we also can detect feminine existential style in perceptual entities that are found in the environments of persons, i.e., in nature and in the cultural world. As such, the feminine style can be more-or-less anchored in the first-person lived embodiment of women in its feminine mode.

Style as an existential, perceptual unity is an open and dynamic form, and as such has no predetermined end-point or perfection. In contrast, the Aristotelian idea of metaphysical essence has a predetermined end-point (*telos*). Aristotelian essence is understood as a potency striving for its actualization in a foreseeable manner. Also the Platonic concept of essence is a metaphysical postulate. This metaphysical concept of essence refers to non-worldly entities that can be grasped by pure intuition rather than to the perceptual unities manifest in our lived reality. These non-worldly entities are best understood as non-temporal and static forms. The Platonic essence is characteristically unchanging and is only completely instantiated by individuals or particulars. So, also the relation between singulars and the generic is different in the case of existential style compared to essence in the Platonic sense.

Woman in Philosophy

For Irigaray, both the "method" of mimesis and the selections of writing which she discusses tackle the ideal and actualization of the philosophical discourse. In her view the philosophical discourse has to be focused on if we want to understand the profundity of the bias in the constitution of the sense of femininity. This bias has been temporally formed predominantly by male acts of speech and writing. Women have not actively contributed to the most authoritative acts of speaking the "truth," not even the "truth" of woman. In Irigaray's view philosophy, as the mother of all sciences, crystallizes the sense of femininity due to its ultimate authority of defining what ultimately exists (ontology), how we can know about it (epistemology), and what its value is (ethics). However, it is not sufficient to transform the sense of woman in this discourse. Also, the task of the philosopher should be reconsidered if we want to abstain from metaphysical presuppositions and explore the perceivable as objectively as possible. In Irigaray's reading, the eros of Plato's *Symposium*, inherent in our philosophical pursuits as a love of wisdom, offers both avenues. As such her reading also invites us to think and assume our own responsibility in (re)defining the sense of philosophizing, and also to be vigilant regarding the tension between our inherent tendencies to similarity and difference.

So, while Irigaray, on the one hand, states that philosophy is a master discourse which "sets the laws for all other discourses," she also aims to redefine it as dialogic practice, as a love of wisdom which cannot be distinguished from other fields of existence by its structure but rather solely by its materials. The truthful way of life is intensified in philosophy as Irigaray redefines it, but it is not restricted to it: rather, it potentially runs through all areas of existence. This holds especially true of the pursuit of unprejudicious attitudes toward gendered being in all its variations including the ones which remain indefinite in terms of femininity and masculinity. Feminine being has remained philosophically inarticulate (especially from a first-person perspective), which means that feminine being provides a "new" realm of pre-discursive experience. This realm is relatively uncontaminated by metaphysical presuppositions, and as such is especially prone to phenomenological inquires into experience. Inquiries into the unarticulated, indefinite pre-discursive realm of experience associated with femininity also pave the way to elaborating and distinguishing between the different types of indefinite experiences and perceptions.

Irigaray's readings of both Plato and the phenomenologists of the body are very nuanced and sophisticated. So, her relationship to the writings of the phenomenologists as well as to the writings of Plato, corresponds to Irigaray's idea of love relation in the sense that she both points at the blind spots and biases but also identifies and highlights the promising strands of the chosen writings. This approach, performed from the exceptional rather than standardized position of a female writer, teacher, and philosopher, helps the writings to achieve more ideality, i.e., truthfulness. This occurs through the constitutive role of the reception. Reception, especially when documented in writing, should be understood as constitutive of the ideality of any piece of writing.

Alternative Accounts of Essence and Irigaray's Essentialism

On the one hand, Irigaray's work indicates that the phenomenological tradition is a valuable resource in rethinking human embodied existence. On the other hand, her readings of the male philosophers' texts and her way of selecting the texts arises from her project and her own motivations, which are radical. The starting point, after all, is her—or any woman's—nonexisting position in philosophy, a realm of truth and ideality, as a speaking subject. This is a problem which compromises objectivity and cannot be avoided even by the phenomenologists, despite their critical attitude to the metaphysical tradition and its positing of metaphysical essences.

The feminist debate on Irigaray's essentialism includes four main positions. A group of critics have interpreted Irigaray's position as being motivated by the tradition of feminist thought which celebrates woman's specificity. This feminist approach holds that a woman's nature consists of sharing certain biological, psychological, or metaphysical characteristics. These characteristics are shared by all women and as such they form the criteria for being a woman. This first main position in the debate on Irigaray's conception of woman attributes to her the idea that essences are non-temporal and unchanging ontological and/or conceptual structures. As such the essence can be grasped once-and-for-all by pure intuition. Accordingly, this conception of woman's essence—the Eternal Feminine or Woman—does not allow cultural or political variations and transformation. Neither does it account for the differences among instances of the essence, e.g., among individual women. In her influential early critique, Toril Moi, for instance, attributes the idea of metaphysical (i.e., stabile and fixed) essence based on woman's anatomy to Irigaray's conception of woman. (Moi [1985] 1995, 139). The first mode of essentialism attributed to Irigaray is *metaphysical essentialism*.

An additional problem is that the essence of woman, whether it is based on assumed universal biological, psychological, or metaphysical characteristics, seems to correlate with certain characteristics that are traditionally attributed to women and the feminine by male writers. Traditionally, women have been characterized as emotional, embodied, and irrational, while men have represented the intellectual, the spiritual, and the rational. These "essential" characteristics have been used to justify the separation and categorization of human life into the different spheres of private and public, and human activities into "feminine" and "masculine." Moreover, traditionally, the masculine and the feminine are taken to form a hierarchy in which the inferior term is feminine and the superior term is masculine. Some critics explicitly maintain that Irigaray reproduces and affirms this traditional division and associates woman exclusively with embodiment and emotionality and the activities of reproduction and nursing, which in the traditional view do not include any spirituality (Moi [1985] 1995, 142; Le Dœuff 1998, 14, 118–119; Nagl Docekal 2004, 121). According to this form of feminist critique, Irigaray's idea is to reverse the hierarchical order rather than dissolve the hierarchy altogether (Le Dœuff 1998, 14, 118–119; Nagl Docekal 2004, 121). I will trace the source of these misunderstandings, and will show how Irigaray herself examines and attacks the hierarchical order and the fixed and stabile notion of Woman, and in so doing opens up a space to reconsider and transform the sense of feminine being.

The positive and general nature of Irigaray's descriptions of woman and the proposed neglect of differences among women, which formed the starting points for accusations of essentialism, also form a starting point for a sympathetic reading of *strategic essentialism* (see e.g. Grosz 1989, 112–113; Braidotti 1989, 99). Elizabeth Grosz (1989, 112–113) denies that Irigaray tries to construe a "theory of woman" as Moi claims. According to Grosz, Moi's accusation of essentialism is based on the mistaken identification of woman's anatomy and woman's morphology, i.e., the body constituted through cultural and linguistic meanings. Grosz argues that Irigaray's work concerns the morphological and not the anatomical. This common criticism of biological essentialism is based on a mistaken understanding of Irigaray's account on embodiment, and implies that we should not speak about women in any general sense (Grosz 1995, 55; cf. Stone 2006, 18). As Grosz convincingly shows, however, the category of women is indispensable for the feminist project as a whole (Grosz 1995, 55).

Strategic essentialism understands Irigaray's idea of *mimesis* as a textual and discursive strategy which takes ironic distance from the traditional discourse on woman and claims that this is her principal method. In this understanding, mimesis means that women assume those definitions of woman that have been imposed upon them by men for centuries, and that they use these definitions to serve their own critical ends (Grosz 1989, 111). In this view, the critical distance from the prevailing conception of woman and of the associated hierarchical conception of sexual difference makes the development and conceptualization of differences between women possible and opens up a space for a multiplicity of differences.

Another sympathetic reading of Irigaray's philosophy of feminine being is the deconstructive one, informed by psychoanalysis and Derrida's critique of logocentrism. The *deconstructive reading* is based on the idea that all philosophical conceptions of woman and the feminine are metaphysical prejudices stemming from a certain understanding of unity and presence (see e.g., Schor 1994;

Butler 1993; Weed 1994). Thus, woman and the feminine stand for that what discourse does not and cannot include in itself and in its self-image: incoherence, gaps, and the neglected materiality of writing. Woman and the feminine form the constitutive "outside" of discourse. In deconstruction, this constitutive and systemic lack of woman is inversed and transformed into a "sign of becoming" which stands for everything non-fixed and ungraspable (Braidotti 1989, 99).[5] This understanding of woman and the feminine motivates a methodology, used also by male writers, in which the subversive power of the concept of woman is used to disturb the discourse.[6] The idea of mimesis is important for this line of interpretation in the same way as it is important for strategic essentialism. These readings also share the inability to account for Irigaray's emphasis on feminine-embodied and expressive specificity, an emphasis that characterizes the whole of her works (cf. Stone 2006, 28, 33).

The fourth position, *realist essentialism*, is advocated by Alison Stone in *Luce Irigaray and the Philosophy of Sexual Difference* (2006). Stone maintains that a duality of male and female bodies, with their inherent dual and natural forms to cultivate, exists independently of how we represent and culturally inhabit these bodies (Stone 2006, 18, 49). This interpretation leads to the idea of a natural differentiation of bodies which, when connected to Irigaray's strict emphasis on sexual difference in her works from *Éthique* onward, means that there is an "original, fixed sexual duality in nature," even if natural bodies "are really" multiple (Stone 2006, 49). In order to avoid a dualistic and fixed philosophy of nature as the last word on the issue of sexual difference, Stone is compelled to synthesize Irigaray's philosophy through a German philosophy of nature, with social constructivism.

Irigaray's Work as a Paradigmatic Example of the Constitution of Feminine Identity

This book suggests that Irigaray's work offers a paradigmatic example of how a feminine person and a philosopher comes into being in a network of relations, and how she is both constituted by and constitutive of these relations. As such, Irigaray's work offers an account of the origins, sustenance, and generation of the oppressive structures both in our personal and communal lives. In Irigaray's examples oppression is not understood as one-directional and univocal, rather it is intertwined with the very constitution of our gendered being. However, Irigaray's work also shows how these structures can be disclosed, dissolved, and restructured in our lives and works and, accordingly, in the lives of our communities and institutions.

Along the lines of the descriptive tasks of a phenomenologist, the starting point for Irigaray is the first-person perspective in which truthfulness, responsibility, and agency do or do not become rooted. Accordingly, it is the other person or reader in her or his first-person perspective that is addressed. In her work, Irigaray elaborates the fluid borders between the external figures and their desires, and external expectations and the internalized roles, as well as positions of speech that are congruent or incongruent with these. In so doing, Irigaray's work is also able to point out openings for agency and freedom. She also operates through these openings in favor of change in the status and value of the feminine, both as it is experienced and as it is described from the male perspective and included in the positing of being and value that are found in the metaphysical and phenomenological tradition.

With the support of my expositions of the idea of the analogous structure of embodied subjectivity and writing (Husserl and Merleau-Ponty), I argue that this tradition offers us a way of understanding Irigaray's corpus as an exemplification of feminine style, which is structurally analogous with the feminine embodied subject as Irigaray understands it. By detecting Irigaray's idea of woman in her practice of speaking as a woman in the temporal continuity of her work, we can fully "grasp" her dynamic account of the way of being of a woman. In other words, Irigaray's writing is continuous with feminine embodied being and manifests its generative potential. In this way Irigaray also demonstrates that the potential of feminine generativity is not restricted to giving birth and upraising children of flesh and blood, but extends also to activities of giving birth to other types of embodied-spiritual unities, such as pieces of writings.

On one hand I find that the idea of existential style characterizes Irigaray's conception of woman in particular and gendered being in general, but I also find that her work as a whole exemplifies this idea. Two diverse, though interconnected, modes of temporality can be found when investigating existential style: an individual style in its temporal unity and an individual feminine style as an instance of the generic feminine. These modalities are reflected by Irigaray's work so that on the one hand, Irigaray's *work in its temporal continuum* is an exemplification of a feminine style of a feminine person in its temporal continuum or *personal history*. On the other hand, the habits and motivations formed in the past and the opportunities left open for the future are included in any instance of style in its constitution, in *a piece of writing or at each moment of a person's becoming*.

My study unfolds primarily the latter mode of the constitution of feminine style as an instance of the generic feminine, but also touches the former one. The idea of existential style is the organizing concept of my book, but in a different way than it organizes Irigaray's singular works and her work as a whole, a choice, which I hope will further illuminate the existential style manifest in her work. Moreover, my work offers another manifestation of feminine existential style in its way of exploring Irigaray's work and reporting the process of research in the way it does. In other words, I have aimed to institute one more modification of feminine style into a piece of writing that tackles the fundamental issues of being and becoming.

The Exposition of the Book

To summarize, to understand Irigaray's idea of woman, we must clarify the conception of stylistic unity as it can be found in the phenomenology of the body and relate it to Irigaray's idea of feminine style and its operative function in her work. I will do this in two steps: by analyzing and discussing it as a theme and a topic, and by studying Irigaray's work as a manifestation and institution of the feminine style. The main dimensions of existential style, of a person, of a subject, or of femininity (or masculinity) are embodiment (Part I, Body), affectivity (Part II, Desire) and spirituality (Part III, Wisdom). As already emphasized, all these three dimensions are constituted as relations, relations to oneself, to the other, and to the world, and can be more or less truthful, or "objective."

With diverse emphasis—embodiment, affectivity and spirituality—each part of my work builds a tension between the two extreme ends. These are the habitual and self-deceptive ways of experiencing, acting, and thinking and the task of striving for wisdom, objectivity, and renewal. More precisely, the tension is between the habit of turning toward oneself and toward that which is one's own or similar, and the possibility of opening toward that which is new and surprising or unexpected. Both tendencies are inherent in the discourse, in the person, and in the subject, but their mutual relation can be more or less truthful and fruitful. The dynamics between these two basic tendencies potentially occur in all the dimensions of subjectivity and in all its relations. The distinction between the habitual and that which is new is not clear-cut but is rather a matter of continuity and proportion. We can be more or less aware of ourselves in these relations and the potentiality of awareness and self-reflection adds a dimension to a person's or to a subject's being and becoming.

The crucial role of desire and love with the inherent ideal of truthfulness in all inquiry into essences is also the reason for why the most important and fruitful mimetic woman-figure in Irigaray's work is the figure, role, and position of the beloved woman, who contributes crucially to Irigaray's attempt of developing new feminine figures with characteristic new roles and positions: the woman writer, the woman lover, and the woman philosopher. Irigaray establishes and develops these roles with several types of articulations and modifications of the love relationship. In these ways, Irigaray develops her writing as a work of thinking with a feminine style and, in so doing, opens up the possibility of a feminine subject. She liberates, develops, and extends the mode of expression associated with and attributed to the feminine—the gestural, the poetic, and the "senseless"—and gives a new interpretation to these modes of expression. Irigaray does this from the new speaking positions that she creates by actualizing and developing the constitutive possibilities included in the discourse, by feminine and masculine expressive and affective embodiment. Thus Irigaray is able to establish a creative dialogue between two integral subjects: masculine and feminine.

Part I

Body

> In my case, it was [. . .] a question of inverting myself. I was the other of/for man, I attempted to define the objective alterity of myself for myself as belonging to a female gender. I carried out an inversion of the femininity imposed on me in order to try to define the female corresponding to my gender: the in-and-for-itself of my female nature. This process is extremely difficult to carry out and explains most of the misunderstandings about my work and thought.
>
> —ILTY, 63/JAT, 108

Luce Irigaray's characterizations of woman and her nature as well as Irigaray's ways of bringing the feminine into the discourse through the *speaking-woman* (*parler-femme*) and the *writing-woman* (*écriture féminine*) are well-known but also broadly disputed among feminist philosophers and theoreticians. Indeed, Irigaray's work entails tensions which offer fertile ground for such disputes. On the one hand, Irigaray characterizes woman as inexistent, on the other hand, it seems that she postulates a feminine essence. For example, in her early work *Speculum de l'autre femme* (1974) Irigaray writes: "Theoretically there would be no such thing as woman. She would not exist. The best that can be said is that she does *not exist yet*. Something of her a-specificity might be found in the betweens that occur in being, or beings" (SO, 166/S, 207). I take this citation as a leading clue for my examination of how the two seemingly contradictory ideas—woman's inexistence and her existence—can be reconciled.

In my view, Irigaray explores the problem of woman on the basis of two realities. One is woman as she already can be found in the discourse or theory as a resource and object (of research). The other is the expressive feminine body which, in Irigaray's view, is omitted from the discourse or else denoted in terms foreign to it. In both cases, the meaning of woman is constituted "in the betweens that occur in being, or in beings" (SO, 166/S, 207). In the first case, however, the sense of woman's being is constituted dominantly by a masculine norm, foreign to the feminine becoming itself. In the second case, the unity of feminine embodiment forms a still unexplored perspective from which the masculine norms and their dominance can be questioned, and its sense transformed. The feminine body *in its own terms* can only be brought into the discourse by a *variety* and *multiplicity* of the first-person acts of (feminine) expression. This is why expressions stemming from the lived male body, even if they are sometimes considered as "feminine," do not suffice.[1]

Through discursive *mimesis*, on the one hand, and the first-person pre-discursive experiences and expressions of a woman on the other hand, Irigaray creates a new position of exploring, speaking, and writing. From this new position she is able to invert the masculine, disintegrated and/or fixed conception of woman's nature or essence coined by the dominant discourse and to replace it with an open and dynamic unity of feminine experience—a style of her own not yet accounted for by the discourse. This idea of existential stylistic unity has a specific relation to the idea of feminine becoming.

1

Feminine Existential Style

An Operative Concept

This chapter explicates the existential concept of style and gives a preliminary characterization of the sense which Irigaray explicitly gives to feminine existential style. In addition to this preliminary characterization of feminine existential style, I will also explore it by putting it into operation. In the course of this book I will show how feminine style is gradually unfolded and developed throughout the temporal continuum of Irigaray's work in a manner which is structurally similar to personal history. But I will also demonstrate the significance of feminine existential style by organizing that process of temporal constitution of Irigaray's work into another, genetic order of constitution. The subject's genesis can be detected in any instance of style in its process of being constituted, in a piece of writing or at each moment of a person's becoming. This is because the habits, intentions, and motivations formed in the past and the opportunities left open for the future are included in any instance of an existential style.

∽

Irigaray characterizes sexual difference by several related terms. She speaks about the feminine (*le féminin*), the maternal-feminine (*le maternel-féminin*) and woman (*la femme*), but she also uses the concepts of feminine style (*le style féminin*) and woman's style (*le style de la femme*).

In Irigaray's terms, for the feminine existential style to become actualized, we must, rather than interpreting or repeating the feminine figures and function acceptable within the confines of the masculine discourse, modify the feminine "as an excess that exceeds common sense" (TS, 78). According to Irigaray, the feminine existential style only can actualize "on condition that the feminine

[does] not renounce its 'style'" (TS, 78/CS, 76). In other words, in Irigaray's view it is the feminine "style," which forms the excess of that which is defined as comprehensible by masculine discourse.

Irigaray distinguishes between two senses of style by marking one with quotation marks: she speaks about "style" (or "writing") on the one hand and style on the other. In my view this is a distinction between an experienced and gestural unity of the lived feminine body on the one hand, and a subject constituted by first-person acts of expression in all their modes from gestures to writing on the other hand. In discourse the experienced and perceptual unity of gestural expression obtains a more structured articulation.

Irigaray seems to maintain that in the current situation the only mode of being recognized and acknowledged is the masculine one. Moreover, lacking articulations of alternative existential style(s), the masculine mode of being is not even recognized as a style but instead forms a general norm for coherence. For this reason Irigaray thinks that the feminine "style" is not perceived nor experienced as a style: "[it] is not a style at all according to the traditional way of looking at things" (TS, 78/CS, 76). Furthermore, woman's "style" is not only excluded from the "traditional way of looking at things" but it also questions the already established forms in a radical manner: "This 'style,' or 'writing,' of women tends to put the torch to fetish words, proper terms, well-constructed forms" (TS, 79/CS, 76). Irigaray continues: "This 'style' resists and explodes every firmly established form, figure, idea or concept. Which does not mean that it lacks style as we might be led to believe by a discursivity that cannot conceive of it" (TS, 79/CS, 76).

Instead of lacking style, Irigaray argues, woman's "style" or "writing" has a *figure or form of its own* but this is not acknowledged. Hence, according to Irigaray, while the feminine style is possible, the prevailing discourse does not account for nor does it provide means for the development of feminine self-expression. Moreover, the discourse does not allow us to perceive the potential *gestalt* and style of the gestural unity of the feminine lived body experienced and perceived in our life-world. The gestural unity of the feminine body can challenge the absoluteness of the dominant discursive formations, but only if it is developed in all the dimensions of life and subjectivity.

Irigaray explains that women's "style does not privilege sight; instead, it takes each figure back to its source which is among other things *tactile*. It comes back in touch with itself in that origin without ever constituting in it, constituting itself in it, as some sort of unity. *Simultaneity* is its 'proper' aspect—a proper(ty) that is never fixed in the possible identity-to-self of some form or other. It is always *fluid*, without neglecting the characteristics of fluids that are difficult to idealize: those rubbings between two infinitely near neighbours that create a dynamics" (TS, 79/CS, 76). This quotation shows that in Irigaray's view, woman's style is not a substance, an essence, or an entity for which movement and change would be external. It cannot be experienced insofar as experience is identified with or reduced to reflective experience, "[woman's] 'style' cannot be upheld as a thesis, [it] cannot be the object of a position," writes Irigaray (TS, 79/CS, 76). So, Irigaray does not want to repeat the metaphysical distinction between form and matter or the distinction between idea and appearance. Rather than constituted in binaries or oppositions, the feminine is constituted by proximity, touch, contact, and contiguity (Jones 2010, 84). Moreover, in Irigaray's view, woman's "style" does not emerge from the positings of objects and thesis (*noemata* and *noesis*) as correlates of the meaning-giving consciousness, but rather originates from a pre-discursive source that precedes and escapes these distinctions and positings[2] (Heinämaa 1996).

The feminine style cannot be fully controlled or totally grasped. It cannot be circumscribed nor described exhaustively. This means that concepts which we need to characterize the feminine way of experiencing must be nonstandard and take into consideration the non-graspable character of this way of experiencing and its position outside, or in the margins of the prevailing discourse. If the feminine "style" could be brought into the discourse, it could also indicate another expressive style which does not yet understand itself as a style, but sees and presents itself as an absolute.

According to Irigaray, the feminine style is best characterized by the features of contact, proximity, fluidity, tactility, contiguity, and simultaneity, but still it forms a unity, like that of writing understood as a spiritual-embodied unity, which, in phenomenology of the body, is considered as structurally similar to the lived body. Also for this reason, I will argue that the different concepts of style that Irigaray uses can be best understood in the framework of the phenomenology of the body. The phenomenological concept of style refers to dynamic and relational unity which is constituted in relations, connections and disconnections between different unities and inside singular unities. Thus, rather than being a closed, substantial unity, an essence or an entity with stable features, style is a dynamic, open, and temporal becoming (Heinämaa 1996, 158).

The style at issue here is not a style in the linguistic or literary sense, nor restricted to writing and speech, but is an *existential* style and thus concerns the being and becoming of things, the birth of sense. Existential style is intentional, motivational, and changes in time, but preserves its unity in these changes, or, in other words, changes in ways characteristic to it (Heinämaa 1996, 158). The intentional relations of action, thought, volition, emotion, remembering, and even motility, perceiving, and sensing are constitutive for a style (Heinämaa 2003, 31, 41).

This existential style can be either disclosed as my own style or as an expressive unity of another person. Thus, style is an essential structural feature of the person. Through style a person can be identified both from the point of view of the person her- or himself and from the point of view of others. Style expresses personality to others in different, intertwined ways: it is exemplified in bodily movements and gestures as well as in speaking and writing. In these gestures the relations to others are formed in an individual manner. For their part, relationships with others can effectuate gradual changes in the temporal constitution and motivational structure of subjectivity and in the subject's ways of relating to others (Heinämaa 2003, 31–44). Moreover, style can also be detected in artifacts, such as philosophical writings or works of art.

In all these cases (own, alien, and artificial style), style means a way of relating to that which exists: to the self, to others, and to the world. With respect to the world, a person's style is constituted in the subject's relations to enjoyment and production. With respect to the other, a person's style is constituted in relations to interaction and communication. In our relation to ourselves, the capacity to focus attention to oneself concerns both singular acts and their connections. Thus, the style of a person concerns his or her current state but also his or her past and future, as the lived present opens in both directions.

Past activities, and passivities as well as affectivity, constitute habits which give direction and motivation for future actions and lived experiences. The motivational force of habits and sedimented experiences depends on the capacity for self-reflection and are thus tied to individual and cultural practices and ideals. The possibility of self-reflection is based on the reflexivity of the self: we can be aware of ourselves in our activities and passivities. Depending on the capacity of self-reflection in the three interconnected relations—self, others and the world—personal style can develop more or less fully. This process also includes the process of becoming aware of one's own pre-conceptual experience and its motivational force.

According to the phenomenologists of the body, I cannot experience the other's activities and passivities directly but can only capture them indirectly by his or her expressions. The style of another person is constituted in conscious life on the basis of his or her bodily positions, movements, postures, gestures, facial expressions, and vocal expressions. I can identify the other person as such, i.e., as another self with his or her unique and ungraspable stream of experiences, on the basis of the similarity between my own bodily style and his or her style. The other person is also identified by me as similar or different with respect to my own acts which are constitutive of my style.

Gender as an existential style does not mean to apply to a preexisting norm. Rather, each existential style is constitutive of a norm of its own (Heinämaa 1996, 162). This means that this conception of existential style also includes a new way of conceptualizing the gender-blending phenomena as a confusion or a distraction of the dual tendency in the constitution of gender identities, as stylistic variations of existence (Heinämaa 1996, 162). Merleau-Ponty's holistic conception of sexuality, on which the idea of gender as an existential style is based, does not draw sexual identity from any particular (sexual) organ, acts, or characteristics. Neither can it be localized merely in one field of existence or activity: existential style runs through all these (Heinämaa 1996, 156). This means, for example, that reproduction or sexual act cannot be thought as the origin of sexuality understood as holistic.[3]

Heinämaa describes the development of sexual identities as existential styles in terms of imitation and mimicry, repetition and modification rather than in terms of inheritance or properties (68). So, existential style is formed *partly* by mimetic acts and repetition but is not reducible to them. Because of its temporality it necessarily consists of changes and modifications between bodily and sensuous of experiences. This temporal dynamics of change also opens up the possibility for change within certain confines, namely our nature as embodied and temporal beings, which belong to a certain time and place (43–44).

Being comprehensive, and running through the life of an individual as a whole, style also covers intellectual, even philosophical, activities such as reflection and critical and self-critical inquiries. It is worth emphasizing that this conception of style covers writing but is not restricted to writing. With regard to scientific work it refers to the whole of scientific activity. This whole includes ways of posing questions, applying and choosing methods, constructing interpretations, and presenting the process of research in writing.

As mentioned, depending on the capacity of self-reflection in the three interconnected relations—self, others, and the world—and in their dimensions—embodied, affective, and spiritual—personal style can develop more or less fully. This means that a person, man or woman, can become more or less aware of him- or herself and the relationality by which she or he is constituted. This holds also for women and men as genders or as general styles. The capacity of self-reflection, however, is not only dependent on individual potentialities, capacities, and restrictions but also on the means and obstacles provided by close and distant others, as well as by the dominant culture and discourse. By different, individual and collective, means, an existential style can be consciously cultivated and developed into an explicit form if it is perceived, identified, and recognized rather than used, bypassed, and neglected. This is possible, even if the feminine existential style has come to mean "that which does not exist, or that which hardly exists according to the dominant norms of conceptualizing the sense of being. The feminine existential style, or its partial manifestations, can even be subjected to strategic demands within a particular field of existential activity. The interpretation of strategic essentialism, which is the dominant way of reading Irigaray's work sympathetically, accentuates this option. Yet, I will argue that the (feminine) existential style, originating from the feminine pre-discursive experience, is not reducible to such narrow or crystallized forms or pre-posited aims.

2

The Philosophical Discourse and Canon, and Femininity

According to Irigaray, a variety of prejudicial ideas and preconceptions must be attended to if we aim to establish and make sense of the possibility of the feminine style of acting and reacting, and even to actualize it as constitutive of (philosophical) discourse. These include thematization and description of two modes of self-deception: the masculine and the feminine, which are both operative in the establishment and sustenance of the traditional roles of the male subject and the feminine other. This chapter explicates the sense of the feminine figures and roles as representing and affirming the masculine norm of woman, and as they comply with the traditional understanding of essences as conceptual and ontological structures according to Irigaray (reproductive mimesis). However, Irigaray also maintains that these figures and roles overflow the masculine norm constitutive of "man's woman" and male expectations in several ways. This excess makes possible (Irigaray's activity of) productive mimesis.

∼

Irigaray's mimetic activity is based on her exploration of the dominant idea, and status of the philosophical discourse, the related conception of essences, and the positions attributed to woman in it. Irigaray argues that for a woman only imitation, *mimesis*, provides an *access* to masculine discourse: a woman, exemplified by Irigaray herself, can enter the discursive field only if she assumes the speaking position of a woman defined by and in relation to man.

Irigaray's "methodology" of mimesis leads us to the original source of the partial and biased notion of woman and her essence and its different manifestations. This source is the Platonic doctrine of ideas and in a related understanding of the soul-body dualism.

The Metaphysical Origins of the Philosophical Tradition

In Irigaray's view, the solidity of masculine discourse and the (masculine) subject is based on a system of oppositional and hierarchical differences. The basic opposition is that between soul and body. Furthermore, in this frame of philosophizing, thought as the essential activity of the soul is taken to be independent of embodiment and expression. Thus, expression, which is necessarily embodied, seems to form a surface that is secondary in respect to the depth of soul, which is primary. According to this way of thinking, meaning is at its "purest" in the interiority of the mind of the solitary thinker.

In this traditional way of thinking, the body and expression, if recognized at all, are taken only to obscure pure meaning rather than making it available in the first place. Without a recognized connection to expression, neutral discourse appears as absolute instead of being perceived as constituted by diverse layers and perspectives. This absolute does not need external readers or interlocutors, it only allows other consciousnesses which are assimilated into it by lack of differences. This is because genuine differences can only stem from the perspectives anchored into the concreteness of expression, and these different perspectives have their motivational source and constitutive origin in embodiment.

Irigaray thinks that within the framework of traditional metaphysics the hierarchically inferior is implicitly associated with the feminine, as we will see, in Platonism we can find these ideas explicated: the hierarchically inferior term is embodiment (cf. Songe-Møller 2002, 113–114). This subordinated role of embodiment, as I see it, implies that expression stemming from the body is subordinated to thought. Thought originates in the soul, and traditionally, e.g., in Plato's *Symposium*, woman has been considered to lack a full soul.

In Aristotle's metaphysics woman lacks the rational part or authority of soul and is associated with passive materiality presupposed in reproduction (Witt 2003, 111). In Aristotle's metaphysics the feminine is intrinsically connected to the incompleteness and imperfection which covers both the feminine (reproductive) bodily functions and the rational activity of the soul (Witt 2003, 110; cf. Easlea 1980, 48, 49). In Aristotle's metaphysics "women's existence, [. . .], has a cosmic teleological role: to keep the better principle [male] away from the worse [feminine]" (Witt 2003, 110, 111; cf. Easlea 1980, 48; cf. ED 101). Thus, even in Aristotle's metaphysics, which is traditionally established as an alternative to Platonism, a hierarchical difference between women and men, the feminine and the masculine, is posited (see also Jones 2010, 95). Appearances or passive materiality are associated with women and femininity, and ideas or the functions of the rational soul are associated with masculinity.

According to the structure of interrelated hierarchical dichotomies with mutually exclusive parts, coherence, sense, and perfection exclude femininity. This makes it hard, if not impossible, to conceive of a woman as the subject of thought. This idea has led to the division of activities into masculine and feminine ones. According to Irigaray, instead of writing, theory, morality and politics, the minor arts, which "do not currently make the rules," are left to women. Among these arts which should be revalued and rethought in relation to sexual difference are "cooking, knitting, embroidery, and sewing; and, in exceptional cases, poetry, painting, and music" (ESD, 7/E, 14; cf. Heinämaa 2003, 34).

The Male Philosopher's Authority

According to Irigaray, the most *authoritative* acts of speaking and writing are those that deal with philosophical questions concerning the nature of Being (CS, 72, 146, 155/TS, 74, 149, 159). In addition to the authority related to the importance and fundamentality of the topic, authority is further affirmed by a canonization effectuated by the interpretative tradition.

Irigaray attacks such a philosophy and the self-understanding of philosophy as a discipline which "sets forth the law for all others [discourses]" (TS, 74/CS, 72). In my view the Platonic doctrine of ideas exemplifies this conception of philosophy for Irigaray. Philosophical discourse and its self-image have become a "lawgiver" to the other discourses, scientific and political, theoretical and practical. The Platonic doctrine of ideas is also exemplary because no fundamental differences are allowed in it on the level of the ideal, to which the philosopher has privileged access. Instead, the ideal appears as unitary and solid. Correlatively, what is most "ideal" in a person is that which is stable and unchanging: the intuition of the ideas to be had by the immortal soul of the philosopher. Moreover, in the dominant version of Platonism philosophical discourse and its self-image are based on a strict distinction between modes of speech and writing and modes of language which exemplify unity of expressed and expression, such as fiction or poetry. The sense of a specific work of fiction or poetry cannot be intermediated by abstracting its content, but the sense of a scientific work can be. This is not to say that all the philosophical works categorically apply to this norm.

These conceptual structures posited by the expressive acts of the philosophers do not restrict themselves to the activity of academic philosophizing, but also mark the limits of the possible—in a wider sense. This dominating role of philosophy in Western culture and imagination is an additional reason for Irigaray to start her critical investigation of the meaning of woman with the philosophical canon, with the works of Plato, Aristotle, Plotinus, Spinoza, Hegel, and Kant and continues by inspecting the canonical figures of nineteenth- and twentieth-century continental philosophy: Nietzsche, Heidegger, Merleau-Ponty, Levinas, and Sartre.[1]

Philosophy as a Discourse

In contrast to the main philosophical tradition Irigaray argues that, despite its self-image as an absolute, philosophy though understood as a lawgiver is also constituted and reconstituted by creative and repetitive acts. As such, philosophy is a discourse, *a fabric* or *texture* (*tissu*) (ESD, 120/E, 116). If philosophy is understood as a discursive formation like that of a fabric or a texture, it means that the concepts and conceptual structures are formed, articulated, and sedimented in repeated acts of speech and writing. The relations of these acts and their temporal sedimentation constitute the discourse as Irigaray sees it. It is discourse in interaction with the experienced reality—instead of an ideal reality beyond the sphere of experience and expressions—that produces concepts and conceptual structures. I explicate the idea of discourse which Irigaray wants to disclose here in order to show how, in Irigaray's view, the sense of woman's being has been constituted in it. This idea of discourse as a texture forms the basis of my exploration of Irigaray's (amorous) style of writing. This idea of discourse is structurally similar to the perceivable world conceptualized and perceived by us as sensible transcendental in Irigaray's terms, or as an intertwinement of the ideal and the sensible or as a "texture of beauty" as it can be found in Merleau-Ponty's eidetics and in Diotima's philosophy of eros.

In Irigaray's view, discourse consists dominantly of and is formed by the masculine acts of expression: "It has always been men who spoke, and, above all, wrote: in science, in philosophy, religion, politics"[2] (ESD, 121/E, 117). In discourse dominated by the masculine norm, the feminine is difficult to represent since it is constituted by styles not accounting for themselves as embodied or perspectival: "In other words, the articulation of the reality of my sex is impossible in discourse, and for a structural, eidetic, reason. My sex is removed, at least as the property of a subject, from the predicative mechanism that assures the discursive coherence" (TS, 149/CS, 145).

These ideas explain why the investigation of the meaning of woman has to start from "man's woman," the representations of woman made by man, and take into account the mimetic nature of the male-defined woman, also with respect to her self-identity. The next four sections will explain the key concepts of reproductive mimesis, "man's woman" and woman's essence and discusses what is left outside of these discursive formations.

Reproductive Mimesis in Platonism

As feminine acts of expression have been excluded from philosophical discourse, so the style and subject constituted by them are not actualized in this discourse. Irigaray argues that in order to actualize their feminine style woman writers and thinkers must proceed through a certain *mimesis*. Irigaray's conception of mimesis has been a crucial theme, especially in the reception of her work, and commentators have interpreted her idea and "method" of mimesis in different ways.[3] In *Ce sexe qui n'en est pas un* (1977) Irigaray writes: "There is, in an initial phase, perhaps only one 'path,' the one historically assigned to the feminine: that of mimicry" (Irigaray TS, 76–77/CS, 73–74). By mimesis Irigaray means a partial repetition, occupation, and modification of the representations and speaking positions fixed and stabilized within discourse.

For Irigaray, mimesis can be either dominantly *reproductive, repetitive and copying* or it can be dominantly *productive and creative*.[4] Mimesis as a term depicts a *relation* between that which is mimicked, imitated, or replicated and that which mimics, and thus it is about agency, activity, and skill (Kuisma 1991, 1) According to Irigaray, both modes of mimesis can be found described in Plato.[5] Yet, it is only the reproductive or repetitive mimesis which has gained a dominant position in the history of philosophy, due to the dominance of a certain interpretation of Plato's metaphysics titled as Plato's doctrine of ideas (TS, 131/CS, 129).

While reproductive mimesis, in Irigaray's view, allows women access to discourse, it also creates a serious problem about actualizing the feminine style. The problem is that reproductive or repetitive mimesis has been the *only activity* assigned to women in the history of the Western discourse (TS, 76/CS, 73). Furthermore, the figures and characters that women can imitate in the discourse are either ideals of woman constituted on the basis of masculine needs and desires—*woman as she is experienced or idealized by man*—or else, predetermined ideals of humanity which, according to Irigaray, are forged for man and the masculine. These are two possibilities for activity in reproductive mimesis and both are dominated by a masculine norm. Irigaray writes that she, as a woman, does not have her own model or ideal to reproduce.[6] Because of this, Irigaray writes "I must be quite inferior to someone who has ideals or models on his own account—or else my utterances are unintelligible according to the code in force. In that case they are likely to be labeled abnormal, even pathological" (TS, 149/CS, 145–146).

When the aim is to create space for the actualization and development of feminine style, then reproductive mimesis as the only accepted mode of activity for women, and "man's woman" as the norm for women, has to be questioned. This questioning can only take place in the discourse, where the conceptualizations of that what truly exists are made. The discourse, however, presents itself as neutral, unitary, and solid. Yet, Irigaray argues, the discourse is dependent of materials of expression, such as embodiment and language.

The discourse presenting itself as neutral, unitary, and solid not only excludes women and the feminine, it also hides this exclusion, and as such might appear as impermeable. However, as mentioned earlier, according to Irigaray, access to discourse is available to woman through mimesis. This is explained by the fact that all coming in to language is necessarily mimetic, to some extent for all, but especially so for a woman, since she has no language of her own and no position as a speaking subject which could be acquired from her "place," formed by her bodily being and specific mode of relationality (TS, 85/CS, 81–82). In the current situation, in order to obtain language she has to assume either a position of "man's woman" or the position of man: "I can [. . .] speak intelligently as sexualized male (whether I recognize this or not) or as asexualized. Otherwise, I shall succumb to the illogicality that is proverbially attributed to women" (TS, 149/CS, 145). In order to understand what Irigaray means by this, we must explicate the two modes of reproductive mimesis, explicate the concept "man's woman," and explore the expressive possibilities of "man's woman."

The first case of reproductive mimesis means that women assume a position and a character that already exists and is allowed for women as expressive within the discursive order. These are the roles of the hysteric, the mystic, the beloved woman, the female teacher, the philosopher's wife, and the oracle.[7] In this first case of reproductive, repetitive, mimesis woman is constituted according to her image/ideal formed in (masculine) discourse.

The second case of reproductive mimesis is the following one. If a woman attempts to obtain access to discourse by directly bypassing the positions of "man's woman," she would by necessity end up in the position of a man (AM, 117, 125 /ML, 109, 117). As Irigaray writes, "a direct feminine challenge to this condition means demanding to speak as a (masculine) 'subject,' that is, it means to postulate a relation to the intelligible that would maintain sexual *indifference*" (TS, 76/CS, 74). Thus, an attempt to directly occupy a position of a speaking, writing, and thinking subject leads to the assumption of thought in a masculine manner. In this setting, the cost of operating in the discourse is the denial of one's womanhood, of which Irigaray also has been accused of (Moi ([1985] 1995, 143; cf. Mortensen (1989, 38–39). As Irigaray phrases it: "*either you are a woman or you speak-think*" (ESD, 138/E, 131).

Neither one of the positions of reproductive mimesis described allows a (discursive) change in the constitution of the meaning of woman or challenges the male-defined idea or ideal of femininity. Neither questions the traditional modes of women's discursive constitution, or the dominant idea of discourse which pretends that it is absolute or sexually neutral. Yet, in Irigaray's work the first option of reproductive mimesis, "man's woman," is the one that, when assumed in *awareness* of one's identity as a woman, can open up an access to language and discourse in a manner which makes possible the perception, from both one's own perspective and from that of others, and the development of feminine style.

As already pointed out, the concept of reproductive mimesis belongs to and stems from a certain metaphysical tradition. Reproductive mimesis has, according to Irigaray, been dominant in the history of philosophy, including the constitution of the sense and significance of sexuality and the sexes. Its effects are experienced in "latency, suffering, paralysis of desire as encountered in hysteria" (TS, 131/CS, 129). Reproductive mimesis is always "already caught in the process of *imitation, specularization, adequation* and *reproduction*" (TS, 131/CS, 129). These conceptions of "imitation," "specularization," and "adequation" disclosed by Irigaray belong to a specific theoretical structure: *the Platonic doctrine of ideas*. This doctrine claims that all reality is in non-material ideas. This means that concrete persons, events, and things are merely reflections of this non-mundane ideal reality.

The Outcome of Reproductive Mimesis: Woman's Essence

On the basis of Irigaray's account of mimesis explicated in *Ce sexe qui n'en pas un* and the fact that she quotes Plato's words on the idea and ideal of woman in *Speculum,* it seems that for her the dualistic conceptual structure of Platonism is still operative in Western philosophy but also in theoretical thinking more broadly. It is even operative in "common sense," when the feminine is understood as that which "exceeds common sense" (TS, 78/CS, 76; S, 188–199/SO, 152–159; JAT, 155/ILTY, 99; cf. Songe-Møller 2002, 113–114).

The disclosure of this conceptual structure makes understandable why it is so difficult to identify and articulate feminine style and to articulate it as a temporal, perceptual unity. The Platonic doctrine of ideas includes a concept of essence according to which particulars participate as equal instances in the general essence. This general essence can be characterized by saying that it exists in advance, and is graspable once and for all. The paradigmatic model for this kind of essence is an ideal object of geometry, grasped in the activities of contemplation and abstraction and "localized" in the nonmaterial realm above sensible reality. The perceptual object, for its part, does not disclose itself at once but does so procedurally by perspectives and thus it lacks such ideality. These Ideals[8] become muddled and obscured as perfect forms when found in embodied persons, perceivable nature, or concrete artifacts. All of these are only inferior copies of the perfect forms.

The ontological and conceptual structure of *reproductive mimesis* is exemplified by the Ideal or essence of Woman in the following manner. Woman's essence, when conceived within the confines of the Platonic doctrine of ideas, means that each particular woman participates as an equal instance in the eternal—atemporal—and universal essence or Ideal of Woman. Yet, the Ideal of Woman is itself a deviation from the (masculine) norm of humanity. So the Ideal to which woman participates is in all cases dominated by the masculine norm. Thus, as the Ideal of man is external to her humanity as a woman, she only can imitate this Ideal, without participating in it directly. Thus, both as a human and as a woman, woman lacks her own ideal; she only has a possibility of participating in real humanity through the Ideal of masculinity. If the Ideal (of Woman) understood as an abstract and disembodied entity works as the inherent presupposition operative in our acts of perceiving, it obscures the dynamism, openness, and temporality of becoming. This holds equally for women (or any other temporal and embodied being) experienced and perceived both by women themselves and by men. This way of conceptualizing and perceiving means that a reified essence is shared or copied by each woman, and is possibly included in her self-understanding. So this Platonic understanding of essence implicitly conceptualizes the differences between singular women as insignificant and unreal, and is thus also unable to provide proper means of differentiation between women by the temporal means of (self-)perception and (self-)development.

This assimilation by a reified feminine essence occurs in the following manner. Insofar as women apply to this norm, the differences between women are taken as mere "appearances"; all women are taken to be essentially the same in participating equally in the Ideal or norm of "man's woman." If a feminine person does not subject herself to the norm, she can only be conceptualized or categorized as a deviation from womanhood. The neglect of the differences between women for what is thought to be an identical core of women correlates with a conception of an atemporal and unchangeable idea or essence of Woman. Such an essence cannot be changed by its instantiations, the singular women, not even in principle. Thus, neither the temporal nature of feminine becoming, the need for development of their mutual relations, nor the multiplicity of women can be acknowledged in this framework.

An Obstacle in the Pursuit of Truth: Platonic Conception of Essence

A French phenomenologist of the body, Maurice Merleau-Ponty, argues that this conception of essence has to be destroyed, since it does not allow any account of the temporal and perceptual-sensuous constitution of meaning, but rather *prevents* us from conceptualizing it in an appropriate manner (VI, 153/ VIE, 116). Instead of disclosing the openness of the variations characteristic of the perceivable world, it points to a uniformity which is possible only in the realm of mathematical idealization. Essentialist thought in this sense, as Merleau-Ponty's sees it, refers to meanings postulated independently of experience, to the idealization of lived experience, not to lived experience, or the articulations of it. This Platonic conception of essences has to be distinguished from phenomenological thought (VI, 117–118/VIE, 87). The idealizing results of essentialist thought have lost the "flesh" of experience and have become abstractions or stereotypes, detached from their material and sensible roots.

Yet, from the phenomenological perspective, the material and sensible aspects should be understood as "vehicles of truth" as Irigaray writes in *Marine Lover*, commenting on Nietzsche's relation to Platonism:

> One turn more and Socratism is set up. Despising appearance for its mere beauty, Socrates will yet use its forms and fill them with meaning. He places art in the service of truth, which amounts to saying that he takes hold of it as such and gives it another teleology than the perceptible one it had. He claims to curb those corrupting veils into the 'proper' sense, failing to realize that those very wrappings take the place of vehicles (of truth) for him. (ML, 97–98/AM, 104)

Another possibility, faithful to the lived experience, is opened up when the perceptual unities are taken as starting points of exploration in themselves, and are not neglected as inferior copies of perfect forms. The roles of embodiment and expression in the constitution of femininity have to be reconsidered within this new alternative.

Male Authority in Defining the Sense of Femininity

As said, the idea and ideal of Woman is dominated by the masculine norm rather than by women themselves. This is partly because men have been assumed to act as "impartial" agents with regard to the metaphysical problem of Woman's essence, and defined the Ideal of human being (see also Jones 2010, 101). This founding act is intertwined with male philosophical authority, but also strengthened by male authority in defining what is counted as philosophising.

So, Man's, and men's, authority and assumed objectivity—in the task of defining woman—is strengthened by the conception that he exemplifies best the Ideal of humanity, representing spirituality and rationality instead of embodiment and everything associated with it: sensations, instincts, drives, affections, emotions. In this framework of thought, men are closer to the Ideal and truth, that which exists as real. Women, for their part are associated with appearances and illusions, or mere styles.[9]

Women have been assumed to mimic the masculine Ideal of Woman but also the Ideal of human/man. When women mimic men with their body or with their bodily expressions, no feminine specificity is developed since women represent embodiment and materiality in general. In this framework woman is either conceived as similar to man, and thus not as woman, or as inferior because differing from him: in both cases man is the norm for conceptualizing woman's being.

Some commentators have reduced Irigaray's conception of woman to her explication of the Ideal of "man's woman." An example is Monique Plaza's early influential materialist reading, cited to support Toril Moi's equally influential reading, which is also materialistic. Moi cites Plaza addressing Irigaray's early work: "Every mode of existence which ideology imputes to women as part of the Eternal Feminine and which for a moment Luce Irigaray seemed to be posing as the result of oppression, is from now on woman's essence, woman's being" (Moi [1985] 1995, 146–147; cit. Plaza 1978, 31–32). A more recent example of this line of critique directed to Irigaray's later work is presented by Michèle Le Dœuff. Le Dœuff (1998, xiv, 118–119) accuses Irigaray of accepting the conception of "traditional woman" defined by the "feminine" activities of nursing, childcare, and household work instead of demanding women's right to intellectual activities.

Woman, however, is not reducible to reproductive mimesis: a surplus, a disruptive excess (*excès, dérangeant*), always remains, Irigaray states (TS, 78/CS, 76). The feminine can be brought into the discourse if only woman does not give up her own "style" (TS, 78/CS, 76). This "style" can be found in "the gestural code of women's bodies," but not fully if the feminine body is only perceived and conceptualized from the male perspective.

The "Man's Woman": The Maternal-Feminine and Woman's Body

In Irigaray's work, starting with *Speculum de l'autre femme* (1974), "man's woman" means the idea of woman as it is formed and defined by and through man or the masculine norms concerning the constitution of subjectivity: "within discourse, the feminine finds itself defined as lack, deficiency, or as imitation or negative image of the subject" (TS, 78/CS, 76). In this quotation Irigaray claims that in the discourse woman forms a complement or an opposite for man. Woman also forms a reflective surface and a mirror image for the development and execution of the norm of masculinity or false neutrality. This happens in two ways. First, woman functions as a support for (masculine) identity construction and self-understanding by affirming and multiplying man's image of himself. This includes even the providence of generative characteristics, which are transformed from their perceivable and embodied forms of concrete begetting and giving birth to concrete children into giving birth to, for example, Ideas in Platonic metaphysics.[10] Second, woman and the feminine function as a reflective surface for all that which does not fit into man's ideal identity and his understanding of himself.

Also in philosophy, woman and the feminine function accordingly as the resource for the construction of the metaphysical system itself: she operates as the ground, as chaotic matter and as fluidity from which the solid form of the (philosophical) system or ontology is forged. In the metaphysical system woman and the feminine function as raw material, as support and as reflective surfaces for masculine self-understanding and self-expression; they are not given any definition independently of these supportive functions, and thus their self-directed sense lacks recognition and acknowledgment. Moreover, as the exclusion of woman as a thinking and speaking subject, also supportive functions attributed to her, and the dependency on her invisibility as thinking and speaking, are concealed as discursive operations (cf. Jones 2010, 78).

Against the background of this argument of *Speculum*, Irigaray characterizes her own practice of writing as a woman in the very last page of *Speculum* in the following manner:

> Precise references in the form of notes or punctuation indicating quotation have often been omitted. Because in relation to the working of theory, the/a woman fulfills a twofold function—as the mute outside that sustains all systematicity; as a maternal and still silent ground that nourishes all foundations—she does not have to conform to the codes theory has set up for itself. In this way, she confounds, once again, the imaginary of the "subject"—in its masculine connotations—and something that will or might be the imaginary of the female.[11]

In Irigaray's view, insofar as woman is thematized at all in philosophical discourse, as e.g., in Plato's *Symposium*, she is presented as oppositional or complementary to man, but also as inferior (cf. TA, 77/TO, 85). Woman—as she is pictured in philosophical discourse—lacks the characteristics of reason, form, clarity, activity, and spirituality but also coherence and solidity, which characterize the results and products of human activities. The features of coherence and solidity belong to man and to his products. Woman is perceived and described as unformed, fluid, sensible, passive, receptive, and emotional: embodied and exclusively being-for-the-other. Furthermore, the activities by which woman is defined imply abandonment of the clear-cut boundaries between the self and the other, e.g., bearing children, breast-feeding, and nursing.

Because women are traditionally defined by the body and its different aspects, we need to identify, explore, and transform the nature of the traditional understanding of embodiment. On the basis of Irigaray's work, I argue that feminine embodiment figures in the dominant discourse in two basic modes. Following Irigaray, I call these two figures "the maternal-feminine" and "woman's body."

By the maternal-feminine Irigaray refers to the non-differentiated materiality which serves and supports the construction of forms (SO, 81/S, 98). In the mode of the maternal-feminine, embodiment is identified with pure materiality and its functions; it functions as raw material and as a reflective surface for forms, concepts, or meanings. The feminine is identified with the maternal and both are conceived in terms of the functions of materiality, raw matter, and resource. The maternal-feminine, as the constitutive ground for all forms of being and for the Being of beings, is characterized by formlessness, passivity, and receptivity. The maternal-feminine thus forms a precondition for the formative and constructive activities of reason and spirit. Conceived as raw material or as raw matter, the maternal-feminine does not have any proper form nor is it able to generate form (cf. Jones 2010, 80).[12] Insofar as the maternal-feminine has some form, it receives this form from an exterior source: the masculine soul or spirit and its activities (Easlea 1980, 49; Witt 2003, 111). In the framework of traditional philosophy, the maternal-feminine is presupposed but is not acknowledged.

From the perspective of the phenomenology of the body, I will argue that Irigaray also gives another meaning and function to the element of the maternal-feminine, reversing it from the mere correlate of male need found in the philosophical discourse into an elemental, correlative to enjoyment, which overflows any need. She shows that as an elemental, the maternal-feminine does not have to be conceived as raw or pure matter but can be understood as already and originally structured, dynamic, and in itself meaningful. As such it would provide a meaning ground, and would be constitutive for all spiritual formations. Irigaray characterizes this function, for example, as "that which constitutes the body as living" (ESD, 98/E, 98). In my view, she refers to the basic functions of sensibility that the (masculine) body presupposes in its movements and intendings, that is, to the gestation and gesticulation provided by the real mother. The presuppositions of these maternal functions are, according to Irigaray, still unacknowledged by us and lack explication. The maternal-feminine understood in this sense is the "red blood and lymph for every body, every discourse, every creation and making of a world" (ESD, 98/E, 98).

The second mode of feminine embodiment operative in the philosophical discourse is the body of woman. This figure is usually thematized and is not just implied, and most often it appears in discussions concerning love and desire. The feminine body, exemplified by the beloved woman, can be found for example in Plato's *Symposium* and also in the phenomenological descriptions of Sartre and Levinas. Irigaray argues that in these thematizations the feminine body is understood exclusively by its functions of sexuality and reproduction. Insofar as these functions belong to women in general, they cannot individuate women and fail to represent them as singular persons (in love and desire). The general nature of the sexual and reproductive functions makes it possible to see each woman's body as a possible substitute of another woman's body. The woman-figures which Irigaray has found in the discourse also exhibit the functions of the maternal-feminine by their bodies. Irigaray thematizes the function of the maternal-feminine extensively also in *Amante marine*. For example, she assumes the position of the beloved one and writes: "And, certainly, the most arduous thing has been to seal my lips, out of love. [. . .] That your words reasoned all the better because within them a voice was captive. Amplifying your speech within an endless resonance" (ML, 3/AM, 9). And later on she distances herself from the position of the beloved one and is able to articulate the problematic nature of the maternal-feminine as a correlate for male need: "[. . .] she will only attract you by pretending and disguising the ways in which she sustains you" (ML, 33/AM, 39). This process of substitution of one feminine body with any other feminine body is possible because the position of the beloved woman is not lived, perceived, nor conceptualized as a unique person, or as a singular unity of expression and expressed.

In these ways man and woman and masculine and feminine, are conceptualized as matter and form, idea and appearance; opposites or complements. Irigaray points out that the terms of such dichotomies are exclusive, but are also situated in a hierarchical relation. The superior term of the hierarchy is the masculine and it is associated with a chain of characteristics: coherence, solidity, reason, form, clarity, activity, and spirituality. The masculine is understood and valued as the essence of humanity and is considered necessary for self-realization. In these ways, man and woman, the feminine and the masculine are clearly different and distinct. But this difference is not radical, it is not *a sexual difference* that Irigaray is trying to express. Rather, the two terms of this man-woman couple form a totality, a closed entity or couple in which one term obtains its meaning from the other.

The Variety of Man's Women and Their Expressivity

As pointed out above, I have found Irigaray to describe and examine six different woman-figures. Three of these are the hysteric, the beloved woman, and the mystic.[13] All of these positions allow certain expressions of femininity but all "measure" the sense of expression by male norms and thus femininity appears as lacking sense or even as senseless. In what follows, we will see how the "senseless" feminine expressions are accounted for in the discourse which conceptualizes woman as "man's woman." Let us first familiarize ourselves with the contexts from which Irigaray finds them.

The figure of the hysteric gains its sense dominantly from the classical psychoanalytic discourse, which is based on the conception of female sexuality based on male norm and is heavily criticized by Irigaray in *Speculum* and *Ce sexe*. The association of the womb as a cause of specifically feminine type of disorder stems already from Antiquity, and the term "hysteria" is derived from the Greek word for womb.

In Freud's view, hysteria basically results from the failure of "normal" development in the phase in which a girl's "masculine" sexuality is to be transformed into "feminine" sexuality. According to Freud, hysteric attacks result from phantasies, which are "projected and translated into motor activity and represented in pantomime" (Freud 1959, 100). Basically, Freud's idea is that some impressions have failed in finding "discharge" either in motor activity or in associative thinking because one's fear of internal conflicts or because of "modesty or social circumstances" (Freud 1959b, 30).

Irigaray's discussion of mysticism also has several reference points. In addition to the writings of the mystics themselves, Irigaray's discussion in "La Mystérique" has been detected to refer to Beauvoir's discussion on feminine mysticism in the *Second Sex* and Lacan's discussion on feminine desire in *Encore* (1972). Both Beauvoir and Lacan give a significant role to a specific mystic, Teresa of Avila (1515–1582) (Joy et al. 2002, 28; Hollywood 1994, 159, 172). Lacans's discussion has as its leading clue Lorenzo Bernini's sculpture "The Ecstasy of Saint Teresa." St. Teresa's written description of divine ecstasy has been the source of inspiration for the sculpture (Joy et al. 2002, 28; Hollywood 1994, 159, 172).

Traditionally, femininity and hysteria have been equated, basically because of the connection between the womb and the feminine body; not all women who are depicted as hysterics have hysterical attacks in Freud's sense. This idea of equation of feminine body and its inherent tendency to fall into hysteria is questioned by Irigaray. In her view, the existence of the figure of the hysteric is rather a symptom of the illness of the culture and its symbolic sphere, which is not able to provide women adequate means of self-expression and (sexual) development (see Whitford 1991, 44). After these remarks, let us explore the sense of the hysteric and the mystic as they can be found as specifications of "man woman's" femininity in Irigaray's work as "models" for women to assume in the different fields of life.

THE HYSTERIC

The figure of the hysteric shows how that imitation of the "man's woman" alienates woman from herself and her own desire. The hysteric also demonstrates that reproductive mimesis alienates women from the possibility of expressing their desire: "miming/reproducing a language that is not its own, masculine language, it caricatures and deforms that language: it 'lies,' it 'deceives,' as women have always been reputed to do" (TS, 137/CS, 134). The behavior and language of the hysteric, a pathologized woman, is covered and compromised by her tendency to respond to the more or less explicit expectations and wishes of men. These expectations can be internalized as roles or they can operate as external demands or both.

In this sense, the hysteric does not differ from the beloved one or wife, whose identities are also constituted through the expectations and wishes of the male other: father, husband, brother, or son. However, even though the hysteric's relations to herself, to the world, and to others constitute themselves through men, a non-suitable "residue" remains. This possibility is concealed by the more "successful" behaviour of the acceptable roles of the beloved woman and the wife.

The woman-figures of the discourse do not just maintain (sexual) order but also disturb it. The speech and behavior of certain woman characters, such as the hysteric presented in psychoanalytic and psychiatric discussions, and the mystic presented in religious discourse (also in the first-person mode), exemplify this possibility.

The hysteric, for example, does not fit into the norm of "man's woman." She does not form a silent resource, reflective surface or support for man's self-image. Instead, she questions the norm of "man's woman," even though non-intentionally and without acknowledging it. The hysteric does not correspond to man's ideal of desirable woman or good wife, nor can she provide status for man as a lover or as a husband. The expressions of the hysteric are uncontrollable: the hysteric may become mute, she may (or may not) cry or laugh on the occasions and moments where and when these expressions are least suitable. Yet, laughter and crying as "primitive" expressions still fit into the image of the "normal" woman as an embodied and emotional being. In the case of the hysteric, laughter and crying are excessive and/or repressed: their jerkiness distinguishes them form the feminine "style" that Irigaray characterizes as fluid and dynamic. The hysteric does not fit into the norm of "man's woman" and she also deviates from the feminine style described by Irigaray as an integral unity.

The hysteric is the first figure that Irigaray explores in her philosophical work, and it is the position which allows her to explicate the basic problem of all the other reproductively mimetic positions. All the mimetic positions share the problem that the only "ideal" which they assign to woman—apart from the masculine ideal of "man's woman" or human being as man—is disintegration: a non-ideal, a pathology. The hysteric demonstrates this by her exaggeration of the accepted feminine role. Irigaray points out that the hysteric, as a residue or leftover, has no (exchange) value for the male other. In this way she disturbs and questions the cultural practice of treating women as commodities (cf. Grosz 1989, 138).

This system, which treats women as objects of exchange rather than as subjects, is, in Irigaray's view, constitutive both for the androcentric community and its primary symbolic form, discourse. The hysteric makes visible woman's role within this system, as an object of exchange, by being the symptom of an underlying "disease." Thus she non-intentionally demonstrates the incoherence and unsustainability of "man's woman" both for men and women. Being uncontrollable and unsuitable for the masculine norm of woman, let alone the norm of human/man, the hysteric indicates the possibility that the feminine body could potentially express its own desire rather than reflect the desire of men, even if she herself is not able to express her desire nor to recognize it.

THE BELOVED WOMAN

The gestures and expressions of the hysteric resemble those of the beloved woman, a woman in her most desirable role for man. As we will see, we can find the beloved woman from the philosophical writings concerning love. I will show that in these writings we can find the beloved woman, who is desired as a body, yet, in order to be desirable, she is assumed to be spiritual in a non-individuated sense. Thus, the beloved woman is an integral feminine unity, but is as such passive, receptive, or seductive. Her expressions are restricted to a narrow variety of gestures and primitive vocal expressions. These expressions of the beloved woman are often characterized as childlike, animal-like, speaking in innuendos and laughter—"primitive" (TI, 295/TIE, 263).

The beloved woman has no articulated expression of her own, e.g., words to express herself and her desire either in love-relations or in the discourses on love. The culturally dominant figure of the beloved woman either has her own desire but is incapable of expressing it in more articulated terms, or else she, like the hysteric, is not aware of her own desire. This means that the beloved woman expresses only her lover's desire, not her own. Furthermore, only the male lover is able to speak about (her) desire in a love-relationship and in discourse. The beloved woman is a receptive and relatively harmonious gestural unity rather than undergoing disintegration, but her expressivity is limited and disconnected of the first-person lived experience in its full variety. These feminine expressions are not those kinds of expressions which could constitute discourse—or a full-fledged personhood or love relation, for that matter—but rather form an anomaly in the discursive order.

THE MYSTIC

The mystic, for her part, disturbs the religious (sexual) order. In the mystic the roles of the hysteric and the beloved woman are included. The mystic posits herself as the beloved woman, or believes that God has chosen her. The mystic deviates from the beloved woman in expressing herself actively, though she herself might think that desire does not originate in her: she is just an intermediary. Here active expressions, however, are regarded as "abnormal" in respect to the expected and approved feminine behavior. And when the mystic speaks or writes in public, her expression is often considered obscure. Even the mystic herself claims that her wisdom comes from an external source rather than from herself. Considering all these features, the mystic's expression is, at best, situated in the margins of discourse. The addressee of the beloved woman's "primitive" expression is a concrete other, a person-lover, but because of the "primitivity" of expression the communicative interaction is not actualized. The lover of the mystic is God: the ideal of man, and the relationship remains one-directional. The beloved woman serves as a reflective surface for a concrete man and the mystic serves as a reflective surface for an ideal man. In the latter case communicative interaction is impossible in principle, whereas in the first case it could become possible.

From Irigaray's *Speculum* we can find a combination of the figures of the hysteric and the mystic in "la mystérique," an idea that captures everything that is considered as cryptic from the point of view of the dominant discursive mode, and identified with woman (S, 238/SO, 191). Irigaray writes: "This [la mystérique] is the place where consciousness is no longer master, where, to its extreme confusion, it sinks into a dark night that is also fire and flames." And: "This is the only place in the history of the West in which woman speaks and acts so publicly" (SO, 191/S, 238). Woman as "la mystérique" is needed by the man who strives for his God. Woman's direct connection to perception, not alienated by higher activities of cognition and intellect, is considered to give her a capacity for revelations. Irigaray writes: "the poorest in science and the most ignorant were the most eloquent, the richest in revelations. Historically, that is, women. Or at least the ['feminine']" (SO, 192/S, 329, translation modified).

All of these three feminine figures, in their own ways, disturb and question male ideals and the discursive order. The hysteric questions the male idea and ideal of woman. The beloved woman seduces the male lover to "fall" from his higher cognitive and intellectual activities and represents by her primitive expressivity that which is left outside of the discursive order and the self-image of its subject. The mystic establishes a marginal discourse, which brings a disturbing element into the discourse. I will return to the figures of female teacher and oracle, closely related to that of the mystic, later on. In these ways Irigaray as a mimetic located the feminine figures, roles, and their expressive modes available in discourse, and put them into a new perspective by making visible their partiality. I have aimed to show how Irigaray's mimesis makes it evident that the possibility of developing the generic feminine is very restricted on the basis of these figures, roles and modes of expression alone. In addition to this knowledge concerning the constitution of the sense of woman in discourse, we still need to obtain a clear idea of Irigaray's strategy of productive mimesis as it is *operative in her writing*, but also as irreducible to any strategy, namely in *its connection to the feminine lived body*.

3

Irigaray's Activity of Productive Mimesis

*Opening of the Possibility of
Original Feminine Expressivity*

Irigaray's articulation of the (internalized) feminine roles and positions and her critical practice of problematizing and ironizing masculine discourse (productive mimesis) open up the possibility of her positive descriptions of feminine embodiment. In this way, Irigaray's writing questions the idea of discourse as a neutral frame and the idea of reality as a structure independent of the conceptual forms established by language and thought. By assuming the only available positions that allow her to enter the discourse as a woman, Irigaray, by her writing, which arises from the self-defined movement of her feminine lived body, binds the connection between feminine discursive activity and the pre-discursive feminine lived experience. This connection distinguishes Irigaray's mimesis from that of deconstructionists and defenders of strategic essentialism who do not acknowledge the role of the lived body but concentrate on the symbolic structures and develop strategies of undermining them by means of new, subversive, but merely discursive figures. The feminine lived embodiment and expression and their articulation in the discourse is a presupposition for transforming mimesis from the only activity assigned to woman into one activity constitutive for her, and basically, any bodily style.

∼

As explained, by "reproductive mimesis" Irigaray means the activity of assuming the position of woman as it is given in the masculine discourse without problematizing this position or man's authority to define it. While Irigaray argues that reproductive mimesis has to be taken into account, she does not claim that reproductive mimesis would structure woman's being or the general possibilities of existence. Instead, she develops an activity of productive mimesis that opens up the possibility of a feminine style. Irigaray's (productive) mimetic activity includes the reproductively mimetic function manifested in the feminine behavior of "man's woman," but she also distances herself from this function and opens up the possibility of developing the feminine into its full actualization and flourishment (cf. Schor 1994, 67; cf. Chisholm 1994, 268, 270, 278). Irigaray claims that the idea of productive mimesis can be found in Plato's texts, in the discussions concerning and exhibiting musical structures. This mode has, in Irigaray's view, "always to have been repressed, if only because it was constituted as an enclave within a 'dominant' discourse" (TS, 131/CS, 130; Chisholm 1994 269, 280 fn 9–10).

Productive mimesis means the activity of assuming the position of woman in the masculine discourse while being *aware* of being a woman and performing *first-person acts of expression*. Especially, the activity of writing and assuming the position of "man's woman" *in writing* instead of assuming it in behavior has become a crucial role for Irigaray. However, we cannot exclude the possibility that these roles are also, to some extent, inherent in our behavioral norms, if not as ideals then as hidden tendencies, which can be worked on with the help of the reflection surface provided by written descriptions and identifications made possible by these. Irigaray describes her methodology as follows: "[In an initial phase of obtaining access to discourse] [o]ne must assume the feminine role deliberately. Which means already to convert a form of subordination into an affirmation, and thus to begin to thwart it" (TS, 76/CS, 73–74). It is the productive mimesis "in the direction of which . . . the possibility of woman's writing may come about" (TS, 131/CS, 130). As I argue, writing is especially important as a first-person act of expression because it opens up the possibility of changing woman's position from that of resource and object to that of a self-defined subject constituted by its expressive acts. The most articulate and sophisticated modes of these expressive acts presuppose an access to discourse, which, as Irigaray sees it, can only be provided by mimesis.

Irigaray explicates her "method" of mimesis only in *Ce sexe*, an early work in which she comments on *Speculum*, and several of the mimetic positions that will draw out of her work occur in works published after *Speculum*, especially in *Éthique*, and these positions can only be found *in operation*. My overall argument is that despite the evolvement and development of Irigaray's feminine style into a self-defined style, the mimetic positions offered by the philosophical discourse can still be detected, even if their position and proportion in respect to imitation, on the one hand, and creativity, on the other, are transformed gradually so that the proportion of imitation diminishes and creativity and self-definition increase. So, I agree here with Jones, who maintains that Irigaray's original way of "weaving a countervoice throughout the text" instead of offering an alternative theory has led to exaggerated accentuation of the critical aspects of *Speculum* (Jones 2010, 81). This emphasis has, moreover, obliterated the need to inquire into the phenomenology of the feminine body which takes form already in *Speculum* simultaneously with the criticism of the masculine discourse and its impositions on women. However, it seems to me that in *Speculum* the dimensions of affectivity and spirituality are still undeveloped, or "disintegrate." A transformation in the conception of love and Irigaray's acts of writing "in love," which both are crucial for the harmonious constitution and institution of both these dimensions in the case of Irigaray's work, occurs between *Speculum* and *Éthique* (cf. Cheah and Grosz 1998, 19–20).

Irigaray Writing as a Hysteric and as a Mystic

Scholars who approach Irigaray's work from the perspectives of psychoanalytic theory and deconstruction emphasize the effect of mimetic activity on the symbolic structures of language (see Whitford 1991a, 72–73; Grosz 1989, 132–139). Accordingly, Irigaray's reading of Freud, "The Blind Spot of an Old Dream of Symmetry" in *Speculum*, is often taken as a major example of Irigaray's mimetic activity. When Irigaray's mimetic activity is described, the scholars have concentrated on the position and way of relating of the hysteric/mimetic. The "hysteric" way of approaching the position of the hysteric have been taken as the main, if not as the only, actualized mode of Irigaray's mimetic activity in the research literature (Grosz 1989, 137; Whitford 1991a, 71; Sjöholm 2001, 92; Chisholm 1994, 263–278, Xu 1995, 80–81).

The interpretation, which maintains that "hysterical" mimesis is Irigaray's principal "method," also imply that seduction is the principal mode of relating to the (male) other or his text whether we speak about the hysteric woman or Irigaray's strategy of reading and writing (see Grosz 1989, 134; 1995, 85; Ainley 1997, 28). The intimate connection between hysteria and seduction can be found in Irigaray's writings, and originally it stems from Freud's psychoanalytic writings.

In her reading of Freud, Irigaray produces the disturbing and fragmentary expressions of the hysteric. Irigaray starts with a quotation from Freud without offering us a direct reference. She then proceeds to comment on and question Freud's words on women and feminine sexuality:

> We also regard women as having . . . less capacity for sublimating their instincts than men." Which gives a more absolute power to the (counter) transference to/of the analyst—father, man, husband—and makes it doubtful whether interpretation can offer any solutions.
>
> It is assumed that woman, apart from a few exceptional individuals, has less aptitude than man for sublimation. That assumption

> is built into the very operation of sublimation, into its purpose, its conditions, its methods. And by falling back upon comparison—"less capacity"—Freud will once again have seen female sexuality as a *lesser version of male sexuality*. (SO, 123/S, 154)

In this passage Irigaray incorporates Freud sentence into her own discourse, just as a hysteric incorporates the male-expectations into her behavior, i.e., without clearly demarcating the limit of the self and the other. Elisabeth Weed characterizes this way of "quoting" the texts of others as incorporating and "inhabiting" the other's text (Weed 1994, 84). In contrast to a hysteric, Irigaray as a hysteric/mimetic does not act unaware, nor does she follow the hysteric in trying to accomplish male expectations and desires (Grosz 1989, 135–136). On the contrary, she deviates from the (male-)expectations both as woman, and as a scholar who discusses another's ideas. Irigaray does not distance herself from Freud's text by making exact references and by discussing it in a scholarly manner from an already constructed position. Instead, in addition to inhabiting and incorporating (Freud's) text, and as scholars have pointed out, Irigaray forms a distance from his discourse through irony, laughter, and re-contextualization.

In contrast to Gallop (1982, 56), who maintans that Irigaray extends to discourse fragmentary gestures and words as well as the misplaced and unanticipated reactions which remind one of the hysteric's non-style, I, however, argue that coherent interpretations of Irigaray's texts can be provided. If they are not provided by the indirect and allusive discourse of the hysteric/mimetic herself, interpretators (or analysts) can and should provide the background of the feminine condition and its relation to the hysteric/mimetic's life, experience, or work. In Irigaray's case this can occur with the help of the continuum of her own work and by returning to the other's writings, which are "inhabited" and by which she builds her discourse.

This interpretative situation could be equated with the situation of the interaction of a hysteric and a therapist knowledgeable about the hysteric's social and symbolic position. Scholars have pointed out that one source for Irigaray's mimetic activity can be found in psychoanalytic practice, the analytic forms the reflective surface for the analysis and to construct his identity. However, the social and symbolic situation of woman is not included in the fundaments of the psychoanalytic theory (or practice); and this is why the mimetic activity, in Irigaray's view, has to be extended not only to the discourse of psychoanalytic theory, but also to other discourses on which it relies, particularly that of philosophy.

In "La mystérique" Irigaray both assumes the position of a mystic and distances herself from it by speaking in the third-person but still giving us an impression that she has first-person access to the experience and discourse of the mystic. Instead of reporting her own revelations of God, Irigaray offers us her "revelations" of the social and symbolic position of the mystic and her lived experience. In this example Irigaray parodies the cryptic expressions of the mystic and reveals the motivational forces such as the desire for love behind them, but also points at the double standard of religious institutions in both appropriating the revelations of the female mystics and devaluing the feminine:

> But a "God" already draws near in these/her fainting states. What does it matter that all judge her mad if the "prince of the world" has noticed her and if henceforward he will be her companion in solitude. She awakes full of joy, only to fall back into new torments. For how, in one's unworthiness, can one keep doubt at bay? How could 'God' reveal himself in all his magnificence and waste his substance on/in so weak and wile a creature as woman? (SO, 199/S, 248)

In these ways Irigaray turns uncontrolled "feminine" behavior, which imitates "man's woman" in her text, into conscious mimicry, i.e., into a "textual strategy." "Textual strategy" in Irigaray's sense, means a goal-oriented interrogation of the idea and ideal of woman and man and their relation constituted by discourse, and also the conditions of philosophical discourse itself. As we have seen, Irigaray uses the means of irony and parody, repetition and re-contextualization to achieve these goals.

The Feminist Discussion on Irigaray's "Mimetic" Reading of Merleau-Ponty

As we have seen, Irigaray's mimetic activity of writing and thinking occurs in relation to the other's text. This means that Irigaray uses the other's text for the purpose of constructing her own identity as a woman who expresses herself in the discourse and as a philosopher, i.e., with the goal of constructing her writings or her femininity in the discourse. This way of relating to the other's text mimetically is identified as "almost parasitic" by Tina Chanter (2000, 233). Scholars identify an ethical problem here. The risk is to affirm and reiterate the hierarchy and the mode of the traditional positions of man and woman, in which man is constituted by the resource provided by the maternal-material. The risk is to repeat the gestures of silencing and excluding, but in a manner which inverts the traditional positions. A text which is extensively discussed from this point of view is Irigaray's reading of Merleau-Ponty in *Éthique*—"The Invisible of the Flesh: A Reading of Merleau-Ponty, *The Visible and the Invisible*, 'The Intertwining—The Chiasm'" (Kozel 1996, 127; Laba Cataldi 2004, 343). It is characterized as selective because it leaves out the entire middle portion of Merleau-Ponty's text and concentrates on the few pages at the beginning and end of the "The Intertwining—The Chiasm" chapter (Chanter 2000, 235 fn 15; Laba Cataldi 2004, 343; Käll 2008, 117).

Some commentators find a specific motivation for the way in which Irigaray establishes her commentary on Merleau-Ponty's text: Irigaray's text points to a fundamental problem in Merleau-Ponty's ontology of flesh by means of its structure. Suzanne Laba Cataldi, for example, argues that the omission of the middle part of Merleau-Ponty's chapter in Irigaray's essay mimes the omission of the mediations in Merleau-Ponty's ontology of "Flesh" (Laba Cataldi 2004, 343; cf. Chanter 2000, 233; cf. Käll 2008, 120, 127). The question is how can we adequately conceptualize the positions of the subject and its other on the basis of the preliminary structure of flesh from which they arise if the difference cannot be found already there? For Merleau-Ponty the flesh, that which ultimately exists, is an element "in the half-way of time and place." Referring to pre-discursive experience, it precedes the distinctions of subject and object, essence and existence. It forms a fabric or texture in which the perceiver can be exchanged with the perceivable: both are folds of the same flesh. On the basis of Laba Cataldi's reading one could suggest that Irigaray's strategy of reading is mimetic in the sense in which it has an effect on the self-other relation in its nonrecognition of difference and the mediations needed between the self and other if difference is given a space in the fundamental, elemental mode of being. It is this problem which is reflected by Irigaray's way of reading and writing about this specific text. Laba Cataldi (2004, 347) also refers to Irigaray's own characterization of composing her books as "if [she] were able to speak silently" (JLI, 101). In my view, this characterization also points at the possibility of including the mimetic strategy in the silent functioning of that which Irigaray calls the maternal-feminine, which is necessary to all expression. However, there is no necessity that the silence and support for that which comes into being should be identified as the maternal-material if a variety of modes of feminine being and expression become possible.

Laba Cataldi (2004, 344) points out that it is the unthought in Merleau-Ponty's philosophy which is indicated by the structure and argument of Irigaray's reading: Irigaray extends Merleau-Ponty to the limits of his thought. Tina Chanter identifies a similar kind of goal but maintains that Irigaray's reading of Merleau-Ponty is part of a larger project: "her work both draws on the resources of that philosophy and exposes its own blind spots, indicating where it stops short of an articulation of the feminine, and how it is unaware of doing so" (Chanter 2000, 233).

The aim of encouraging the other to extend to the limits of his or her thought is inherent in Irigaray's readings of texts. The emphasis on the imitation or duplication of the other's discourse can either be an emphasis in Irigaray's reading or an emphasis given by the interpretator of her work. In my view, however, the idea of encouraging the other to extend the limits of his or her thought could also be an element in a loving relation. This also holds whether we speak about Irigaray's readings, her work, or the reader of her work. It seems to me that in Irigaray's work the mimetic activity opens up new especially fruitful possibilities with respect to the texts which already in themselves include such openings (cf. Salamon 2010, 133). Two examples of this are her readings of Plato's *Symposium* and Levinas's "Phénoménologie de l'éros." It seems that her mimetic acts gradually, together with the articulation of the feminine first-person experience and the openings offered by the instances of the masculine discourse, leading to the possibility of a more authentic amorous mode. The amorous mode is considerably more extensive with respect to the style of a person than the seductive (and/or strategic) mode.

To return to the beginning of this section, surely, gathering bits and pieces in order to build an integral identity is an ethical problem with respect to others. This problem seems to correlate with the emphasis on mimetic behavior of women and mimetic activity in Irigaray's work. However, the carrier of the fragmentary or "primitive" identity, a woman or a writer, has no choice. In woman's case, her fragmentary or "primitive" identity and the integrity of the masculine identity are dependent on each other. The traditional position of man/neutral subject is constituted with the help of the maternal-feminine, passive, anonymous matter or the supportive functions of the feminine roles. The maternal-material assimilated into an integrity of the male identity has not been a resource for constituting *her* identity. This also holds in the case of a woman writer.

The maternal-feminine in the sense of resource, though lifted on the level of writing, does function in Irigaray's mimetic writing and is transformed into a position of speaking as a woman. For the masculine subject, the position of the speaking subject is already occupied, and this means that even if a text of a philosopher could be used as a reflective surface or raw material for constituting the feminine writing or identity, the outcome will be different because of the asymmetry of the positions.

The solution to the ethical problem identified by the scholars in the mode of dialogic and loving relationship, however, does not, and cannot, stem merely from (Irigaray's) strategically mimetic practice nor from her descriptions of feminine experience. Instead, it presupposes additional constitutive possibilities both on the part of the masculine discourse and pre-discursive feminine and masculine being. Ultimately, it is the modification and cultivation of love that can result in mimesis having a more modest and transformed role in the constitution of feminine identity. This holds both for the feminine identity and

Irigaray's way of articulating it both as a theme and by the way of her writing. The work which illuminates this process in a specific way is *Éthique de la différence sexuelle*, which is a work with a specific amorous style growing from preceding mimetic and critical acts, and a series of first-person articulations of feminine embodied, affective, and spiritual experience. Irigaray herself situates *Éthique* between the first and second phases of the threefold continuum of her work (JLI, 97).[1] As such it can be identified as *a point of transformation,* as Tina Chanter does (Chanter 2000, 221)

The Feminist Discussion on Irigaray's "La Mystérique"

Irigaray's account of female mysticism is a complex topic as feminist philosophers of religion have shown. The discussion has covered the topics of Irigaray's relationship to the female and male mystics, her relation to the others in defining what is at stake in female mysticism, and Irigaray's conception of the role of mystics in relation to the patriarchal church.

One philosopher of religion, Amy Hollywood, claims that in "La Mystérique" Irigaray "mimes" the discourse of the male mystics instead of quoting, exploring, and recognizing the self-authored writings of the female mystics (Hollywood 1994, 169, 170). Moreover, in focusing on the female mystics' bodies rather than on their writings, Hollywood claims, Irigaray fails to recognize the plurality of the mystical discourse (Hollywood 1994, 160, 161). Hollywood also criticizes Irigaray for not accounting the feminization of divine love in for example in the works of beguine mystics such as Mechthild of Magdeburg. These very same ideas are, however, demanded by Irigaray's own later work (Hollywood 1994, 172).

Rachel Jones finds another crucial male interlocutor addressed in "La Mystérique." In her view, Irigaray comments criticizes primarily Lacan's "pseudofeminine" account of Teresa's ecstasy as it is depicted and phantasized by a male sculptor. According to her, "La Mystérique" ironically comments specifically Lacan's lending of the female mystic's voice (Jones 2010, 153–154). In Jones's view, by not naming Lacan as an addressee of her discourse, Irigaray gives to Lacan the "feminine" position, which he desires and idealizes from a privileged position of a subject (Jones 2010, 144).

Morny Joy finds Irigaray appreciative of the female mystic's means and aims: "[Irigaray] finds them [female mystics] as manifesting, by means of their bodies, an eloquent protest against the strictures that have forbidden them access to education and independence." (Joy 2011, 222). Others emphasize that in Irigaray's view, the mystics fall short in challenging the patriarchal power: they accept the priests as mediators between themselves and God[2] (Joy et al. 2002,

29; cf. Hollywood 1994, 167). This criticism has also been stated to motivate Irigaray's envisions of a female divine in her own terms (Joy et al. 2002, 29). So, commentators emphasize diverse aspects of Irigaray's readings of the mystic discourse and her view on the subversivity of female mystics.

In any case, it is clear that for Irigaray, mysticism includes constitutive possibilities.[3] I would like to raise the question of whether the styles and ideas of other women writers, such as the female mystics, should be explored as *implicitly* related to Irigarays style and her ideas, though in different ways in the diverse phases of her work.[4] For example, the male-mediated way of bringing the female mystics into the discourse of *Speculum* is congruent with the respective proportions of imitative and creative elements of Irigaray's feminine style at that stage of her work. This would imply that in the later phases of her work, Irigaray's relationship to the genealogies of women and her idea of the relationships between women develops in accordance with the evolution of her existential style. We should ask, for example, whether female mystics' styles and ideas, and not only male philosopher's voices, can be found to be woven into Irigaray's writings, or even be constitutive of Irigaray's style and her ideas? This suggestion is based on Irigaray's view on the nature of the relationships between women, which will be depicted in the next part. But this suggestion is also based on Irigaray's own explicit proposal that we could find openings for perceiving the *sensible transcendental*, the ideal or divine in the perceivable, which overflows the present moment and being at hand, if only we could read the mystics, *New Testament*, and the *Song of Songs* in an appropriate way[5] (ESD, 115/E, 111). This idea of female mystics as sites of the sensible transcendental, or transcendence in immanence, has been to some extent discussed in respect to Irigaray's work (Hollywood 1994, 161; Joy 2011).

To the mystical dimension of the experiential sphere, Irigaray claims, women have traditionally opened the access for men (ESD, 115/E, 111). According to Irigaray, men have increased their power by repressing hysteria but at the same time they have lost something of their relation to their own body (CS, 136). Occasionally, as in the religious context, men can mime the hysteria of women, or "daimonic possession" continuous with it, for their own ends (S, 239/E, 115). In light of this remark, and in reference to Jones' suggestion of Lacan as an addressee of Irigaray's discourse, it seems that *Speculum* aims to make visible and challenge the practices of usurping feminine generative power in the sphere of religious experience. But this connection between the feminine and masculine also shows how the ways of relating to the transcendent in the manners traditionally associated with the feminine or with the masculine have intertwined in the sphere of religious experience. The identification and articulation of this connection could open up a space for rearticulating and living our relationship to the divine in a new manner.

Disclosing the Mechanism of Founding and Sustaining the Male-Dominance in the Philosophical Discourse and Canon

To summarize my discussion on Irigaray's mimesis until now, the two modes of lived embodiment characteristic of "man's woman" include silence, and primitive and distracted expressions. These modes include the (supportive) silence of the maternal-feminine, the fragmented expression of the hysteric and the mystic, and the seductive and "primitive" expressions of the beloved woman. These modes of feminine expression are the "dominant" ones which are repeated in discourse, and withdrawing, equivocal and ambiguous expressions have become associated with femininity. As a result, femininity lacks full expressive capacity. This is problematic for all attempts to conceive the sense of woman and for the development of feminine identity and style. This is because all of these modes of feminine (non-)expression appear "senseless" in comparison to the dominant mode of discourse and its self-understanding and offer only a male idea and ideal of woman or a pathology as directions for "development."

It is through her discursive activity as a productive mimetic that Irigaray is able to disclose the problems of the feminine figures available in discourse. For example, the pathologization of hysteric behavior seems contradictory and arbitrary when compared to the celebration of the behavior of the beloved woman. From the perspective of productive mimesis Irigaray is able to point out the underlying connections of the feminine figures.

The idea disclosed by Irigaray is that these women, who are not "obedient" or do not behave according to the male expectations—the "harmonious behavior" expected of woman—are labelled and treated as mentally ill. Moreover, their mental disorder is conceptualized as a condition which is specific to women alone. Hysteria belongs to the possibilities of each woman described by the prevailing discourse: even the most suitable "man's woman," the beloved woman, can easily slip into hysteria. Thus, Irigaray's thematizations of the figure of the hysteric makes visible the arbitrariness, partiality, and fragmentariness of the meaning of woman within discourse.

Moreover, the effects of Irigaray's productive mimesis extend further than the thematization of the meaning of woman. Irigaray acts as a hysteric, but in a strategic, selective manner and in respect to particular writings, the scope of which is framed by herself; but at the same time she operates in the most general of all discursive contexts: philosophical discourse itself. The hysteric is not only the non-ideal of woman defined by the discourse but also supports the idea of the coherence of discourse by providing a figure of its opposite, its outside, its "other." When the hysteric/mimetic speaks within the discursive order and disturbs it, she also shows the arbitrary nature of the discourse, its acts of creating, maintaining, omitting, bypassing, and neglecting. Through repetition the discursive formations become habituated and appear self-evident. As such they are taken to stand for what really exists and what possibly could exist.

In this way Irigaray's mimetic writing shows how the meaning of woman is constituted within discourse. At the same time her writing on women implies a general claim about the nature of existence as constituted discursively: that what is taken as the ultimate "truth" of being and its constituents is in fact an outcome of temporal, multilayered, and multiple processes of discursive acts and reactions. Irigaray's mimetic writing not only questions the mode of unity attributed to "man's woman" but also makes the constitutive nature of discourse visible by disclosing that the acts of creating, maintaining, omitting, bypassing, and neglecting have taken place. Consequently, she makes visible the fact that constituted meanings always, by necessity, include gaps and holes, as the deconstructive readings of her work emphasize (cf. e.g., Deutscher 2002, 18). This is because the process of constitution presupposes elements which are not included in the idea of discourse, and as such are not controllable by it.

As being is constituted in complex and multilayered discursive relations, it is not unitary or homogenous. Congruently, the neglect and exclusion of woman and the feminine is complex and multiple and not the result of one act or occurrence. Insofar as discourse is multi-levelled, also its neglect and exclusion are effectuated in a series of particular acts and silences. Thus, as Irigaray's productive mimesis shows, the exclusions of the feminine are necessarily imperfect. This is why a feminine style is imaginable and why an opportunity to bring it into the discourse is conceivable.

The hysteric is exemplary of a woman subsumed under the masculine norm. She moves according to man's intentions: on the one hand she is a "result" of man's intentions, but on the other hand she is not controlled by them. The "senseless," fragmentary and/or distracted feminine expressions of the hysteric are still first-person expressions and thus spiritual activities. As such they point to the possibility of considering the lived feminine body as a source of meaning in its own right. Despite their distracted or fragmented nature, the hysteric's expressions address the other, and as such they express a self and form a relation to the world. To make sense of this possibility of considering the feminine lived body as a source of meaning, an expressive unity, requires that we problematize and dismantle the association of woman both with objectified embodiment and mute resource-materiality.

For Irigaray, the possibility of modifying discourse depends not only on the incoherences, gaps, and holes inherent in the (illusory) unity of this discourse and its subject. The other condition of possibility is in the pre-discursive meanings not (yet) articulated in the discourse. These rudimentary meanings are indispensable for the discourse: it depends on them in its process of self-renewal. In Irigaray's view, there is in the current situation much fecundity to be found in feminine lived experience, embodiments, and expressions. This possibility of woman as a speaking and writing subject with her own origin and telos, however, has not been acknowledged by the masculine discursive order: "*the 'masculine' is not prepared to share the initiative of discourse. It prefers to experiment with speaking, writing, enjoying* 'woman' rather than leaving to that other any right to intervene, to 'act' in her own interests" (TS, 57/CS, 152–153, italics in original).

"Man's Woman"—a Mere Perspective to Woman's Being

The described feminine body is given to man *through* its functions of providing a place, care, nourishment, or offering of sexual pleasure. The bodies of the mother and the beloved woman, each in their own way, offer a dwelling place (*le lieu*) for the subject (E, 17/ESD, 10). This is expected culturally both by man and woman herself: "[W]oman cannot place herself as an object for herself. And because, unsettled by this lack of a possible 'position,' she allows herself to be placed by the other—man or mother" (ESD, 69/E, 72). This place in the mother's body is the womb, which offers shelter and a source of nourishment for the unborn child. The place offered by the beloved woman is the vagina as a source of pleasure. Both the mother and the beloved woman nourish and strengthen, in different ways, the (masculine) subject. They may fulfil his needs or privately support his activity pursuing his self-defined goals in the public sphere. In all these relations of dwelling, nourishing, reproduction, love, and desire—as they are traditionally understood—woman appears primarily as a bodily being rather than as a spiritual being.

Yet, Irigaray also thinks that woman could have a place of her own.[6] In this "occupation" of a place and interiority of one's own, Irigaray sees a possibility to open a place for woman, "by herself for herself" (*elle-même pour elle-même*). This opening of a place presupposes that woman's status as a thing and as a place is first interpreted (E, 17, 72/ESD, 10, 70).

Moreover, the feminine body when conceived as the body of "man's woman" is conceptually reduced to a small subset of its possibilities: a feminine embodied being defined merely by *the interests* of the male person and his mode of embodiment and not indicating any feminine subjectivity. Finally, in the functions of mother/wife and beloved woman/prostitute, woman's body is seen as *functional* or *useful* in respect to the needs and desires of male persons. In other words, feminine embodiment is conceptualized by ideas of instrumentality. This dominant role of usefulness in the discourse further signals a specific conception of the other's body as a mere object of use or resource, an entity to be manipulated rather than an expressive whole which indicates subjectivity and which requires a response. Thus, "man's woman"—beloved woman/prostitute and mother/wife—is "material" for man's self-representations. She is matter in the sense of indifferentiated and non-articulated manifold or she is embodied without spirituality or spiritual expressivity.

In Irigaray's view, the main problem here is that in all these roles as a resource, object of desire, and provider of offspring, feminine embodiment lacks specificity, singularity, and self-definition. As resource, it is identified with matter, and the feminine body remains non-individuated and unlimited, a worldly counterpart for the omnipotent masculine God. As an object of desire, the thematized body of woman is individuated but merely materially without spiritual uniqueness and thus appears as replaceable by any feminine body, "[the female] becomes the infinite series of one plus one plus one plus one," as Irigaray puts it (ESD, 61/E, 64). This is because the body of "man's woman" is conceptualized merely according to its sexual and reproductive functions shared equally by all feminine bodies. In this scheme the differentiation between women is difficult: from the male point of view their differences are covered by their sexual and reproductive bodies. This way of conceptualizing the feminine body independently of its specificity has a destructive effect on women's identities and their self-understanding as well as on their possibilities of developing singularity, both in relation to women themselves and to men.

The significance of embodiment in these relations, the ones in which woman's being is thematized, is discursively exaggerated and repeated to such an extent that woman has come to represent embodiment in general. Sara Heinämaa has further specified this idea: especially embodiment in the sense of involuntary movement and passive suffering—as in desire, menstruation, pregnancy, and breast-feeding—have become marked as feminine (Heinämaa 2003, 72). In all these cases the temporally evolving bodily characteristics and relations between the self and the other are conceptualized as lacking distinction or as obscure, blurred, or fluid. The implicit point of comparison is the clear-cut distinction between the subject and its object in a frontal, reflective relation.

The problem is that the masculine perspective, which has been sedimented into the discourse, presents and represents itself as the only one and thus it does not recognize its own perspectival nature. This problem of self-understanding concerns the activity of striving for truth in any domain of life. "Man's woman" and woman seeing herself as "man's woman" are both biased in being dominated by a perspective of one gender. Despite their bias and narrowness, both "man's woman" and "man's woman" internalized by woman take part in the constitution of feminine identity. Woman can become woman only if there are persons who are not women. Yet, the difference between women and men should not be understood as a relation of mutual exclusion but instead should be understood as a continuum. The external norm of "man's woman" is constituted in (linguistic) repetition, habituation, and convention, which are processes necessary for any unity. Still, repetition, habituation, and convention become obstacles for development and renewal of persons, subjects, and discourse if their maintenance becomes an end in itself.

Woman cannot become herself or be perceived as herself on the basis of the male-constituted norms. This is why an alternative norm, even if it is a norm understood as an open and dynamic *telos*, must be developed. In my view, Irigaray claims that the starting point for developing this alternative norm is woman as a unity of expression and expressed, an embodied-spiritual unity.

4

Phenomenology of the Body

The Methodological and Conceptual Framework for Irigaray's Investigations of Lived Embodiment and Expressivity

This chapter distinguishes further Irigaray's approach from that of traditional metaphysics and from the approaches of biologism, strategic essentialism, and realistic essentialism of the feminist discussion. But it also opens up a new, non-metaphysical, approach to the discussion of embodiment, affectivity, and the task of philosophizing. This occurs by introducing the phenomenological concept of the lived body and by elaborating the methodological and conceptual tools required for investigating it.

∼

In an interview given in 1987[1] Irigaray explains that already in *Speculum* she executed phenomenological inquiries into feminine embodiment from her own, singular point of view, but, connected to the aim of expressing the general sense of being woman. Irigaray writes: "*Speculum* is a critique of the exclusive right of one sex to use, exchange and represent the other. In addition, it begins to elaborate a phenomenological description by a woman—Luce Irigaray, whose name is on the book—of the self-affection and self-representation of her body" (JM 103/ JTN 73).

The disclosure of the crucial role of sexuality and reproduction in the constitution of the male-defined sense of woman ("man's woman") leads Irigaray both to problematize the traditional descriptions of sexual difference within discourse and to focus on first-person experiences of feminine embodiment and sexuality, as well as to develop the means and space for expressing these experiences. I will argue that Irigaray finds the means of rethinking sexuality in phenomenological philosophy more precisely in the phenomenology of the body (cf. Halsema 2008, 63). A fruitful account of the ontological meaning of sexuality and affectivity is provided by a French phenomenologist of the body, Maurice Merleau-Ponty, who claims that love and desire, as intense modes of affectivity, are models for thinking "how things and beings can exist in general" (POP, 154/PP, 180). This idea of affectivity and sexuality as fundamental to existence in all its modes is crucial to Irigaray's philosophy of sexual difference.

I will argue that Irigaray's descriptions of feminine sexuality, embodiment, speech, and writing are based on a phenomenological understanding of the existential styles and the holistic conception of sexuality inherent in it. Irigaray's descriptions examine and question the norm of "man's woman," but they also create, by their first-person expressive acts of writing, a new norm for sexual and embodied subjects. In this way Irigaray challenges the idea that there is one model or ideal for subjectivity. Before going deeper into Irigaray's positive descriptions of the feminine body, sexuality, and writing, I will present some basic principles of the phenomenological method and explicate the phenomenological concept of the lived body, as well as the idea of the structural similarity between writing and embodiment.

The Task and Method of a Phenomenologist

Phenomenological methodology consists of transcendental *reduction* and *eidetic variation*. This methodology allows the phenomenologist to investigate experiences by detaching them from the presuppositions of empirical sciences and everyday thinking. Ultimately, it is the existence of the object of investigation that is put into parentheses in reduction. The aim of this parenthesis is to thematize the ontic senses involved in experience and make possible their analysis and explication. To illustrate the nature of reduction, Merleau-Ponty (PP, viii/POP, viii) characterizes reduction, citing Husserl's assistant Eugen Fink, as wonder (*étonnement*) in the face of the world—as an attempt to perceive that which appears to us normally as self-evident *as if for the first time*.

These detachments from presuppositions are meant to open a new field of research: we study what comes to us in diverse intentional acts, such as perception, and *how* it comes into being. The perceived "objects," one's own body, the other's body, and worldly things become existent to us and receive their ontic senses through diverse intentional acts such as the acts of perceiving, moving, sensing, loving, desiring, hating, or thinking and judging. The act and its object are not separable but only distinguishable by analysis. A person is constituted by a network of intentional and motivational relations between acts. The phenomenological methodology investigates these intentional and motivational relations and their objective correlates. In phenomenology of the body the main focus is on the lived body; its experiential structures and its expressive potential.

Through imaginary variation (*eidetic variation*) of the objects and their acts the characterization of the general features of all acts and lived experience, as well as the experienced objectivities, become possible. It is the phenomenologist's capacity of imagination which allows her or him to disclose the invariance in the experiencing and experienced. In order to detach her- or himself from the individual—or those bound to his genre—preconceptions and habits, the phenomenologist can turn to descriptions of experiences in writings concerning historical facts or imagined possibilities of experiences as in fiction.

Phenomenological investigation, as Merleau-Ponty sees it, aims to depict the most general and universal features of perceptual experience and the experienced. As one essential feature is temporality, then essences have to be reinterpreted as dynamic stylistic unities. In other words, the aim is to describe perceptual experience and the experienced in their temporality and in the processes of their becoming and development. In order to comprehend these crucial features of the perceptual world, and perception itself, Merleau-Ponty develops a genetic conception of essence having its model in a *perceptual unity*. Essences have here a methodological role: they are not ends but means for grasping the dynamic relations between the subject and the world (PP, ix–x/POP, xv).

In Merleau-Ponty's view, the phenomenological reduction discloses the perceptual world and its subject as a field of "families of material things and of their common style, the family of things said and the world of speech as their common style, and finally the abstracted and fleshless style of something in general" (VIE, 110–111/VI, 149). Ultimately, the different styles of being, characteristic of different objectivities, constitute *the style of all styles*, i.e., the world as an ideal unity. Instead of idealization and abstraction, the aim is to put the "essences back into existence," as Merleau-Ponty formulates it (PP, i/POP, vii). Thus, phenomenological methodology discloses the world anew as open in evolving the whole of perceptual stylistic unities: persons, bodies, and artifacts. The styles of perceptual objects form a mode of significances which are *fluid* and emerge at the level of the sensible (PP, 419 fn1/POP, 365 fn1; cf. Heinämaa 2003, 50n33). This mode of fluid ideality is exemplified by Merleau-Ponty's conception of *flesh*, developed in his posthumously published *Le Visible et l'invisible* (1964).

Merleau-Ponty emphasizes that the philosopher is not a neutral, detached spectator but inherently engaged with his or her body in relation to the world, its objects, and the other persons. The task is not to cut oneself loose from these ties, which would be impossible, but to slacken them and thus to notice them: "Reflection does not withdraw from the world towards the unity of consciousness as the world's basis: it steps back to watch the forms of transcendence fly up like sparks from a fire; it slackens the intentional threads which attach us to the world, and thus brings them to our notice. It, alone, is consciousness of the world, because it reveals the world as strange and paradoxical" (POP, xiii/PP, viii).

As perceivers we have a "natal bond" (*le lien natal*) to the world perceived. Thus, our task is to comprehend it from *within*: no exterior relation is fundamental (VIE, 32/VI, 52). This is why the subject always has to include her- or himself among the topics to be investigated; and the investigation necessarily remains imperfect because of the deeply perspectival and temporal nature of the subject. This temporality and perspectivity is based on the embodiment of the subject and its sensible anchoring in its world.

The task of the philosopher, as a researcher and a writer, is to find expression for the dynamism and openness of styles of being. The philosopher tries not to "immobilize" the "things themselves" but to let them be and to "witness their continued being," thinks Merleau-Ponty (VIE, 101/VI, 136). In Merleau-Ponty's view "philosophy speaks about the world before it has become an object of speech and reducible to governable significations" (VIE, 102/VI, 136). This is possible because language is not reducible to governable significations, but opens up also toward that which it does not yet comprehend (VIE, 102/VI, 136).

This idea of the relation between the pre-discursive and the discursive is reflected by Irigaray's comment in an interview "Thinking Life as Relation" (1992): "A certain recourse, or return, to the phenomenological method seems necessary in order to make enter into the universe of the rational some natural, corporeal, sensible realities which until now had been removed from it." In this interview Irigaray tells us how her perspective into inquiring into the possibilities of feminine subjectivity demanded "faithfulness to experience and rigor in its phenomenological elaboration" (TLR 1996, 352).

Even if the philosopher is engaged in the world, he is also able to distance himself from it and perceive and describe his possible ways of reflecting the world with the aim of objectivity. However, these engagements can never be grasped once and for all or be totally comprehended because they are dynamic and change in time. Yet, as I will show, Irigaray argues that the phenomenological methodology, when combined with a one-sexed philosophical community, has not been able to avoid sexual bias and has presented as human universal structures that depend on male or masculine particularity. Irigaray's argument, however, also allows the interpretation that the methodology in problematic cases has not been phenomenological or rigorous enough, but has instead lapsed into metaphysics.

The Lived Body in Phenomenology: Own and Other

Phenomenology shows that perception is fundamental to all experience and that it is based on embodiment.[2] The distinction between one's own body and the body of another is thus crucial. This distinction was first articulated by Edmund Husserl in *Cartesian Meditations*[3] (1950). According to Husserl, my own body differs from all other bodies according to four criteria. First, my own body is experienced immediately as a field of sensations (tactile sensations, warmth and coldness, etc.). Second, my body can be ruled and governed immediately by my will. Third, my body is able to act on other spatio-temporal bodies. Fourth, my body is capable of perceiving itself as perceiving: it is reflexive in relation to itself (Husserl [1950] 1997, 97–98).

Thus, a certain impossibility for substitution is characteristic of the difference between one's own body and the body of another. My body is accessible to me in a different way from the lived body of the other subject. While my own body is in my power, the body of another is not experienced as directly accessible in a similar way: the other's body is necessarily directed by his or her intentions and motivations and not mine. I can perceive the other's body, but in a very different way than my own body. For example, I can see the other from all directions, even though not once-and-for-all but from diverse perspectives successively. But I can never directly see my own back or the movements of my whole body.

Husserl and Merleau-Ponty characterize the mobile subject-body in terms of the operative intentionality of the "I Can." Despite the characterization emphasizing capability, the lived body also displays a certain vulnerability and as such includes passivity and alterity in itself. The ultimate passivity is marked by death and mortality. However, the descriptions of Merleau-Ponty and Irigaray, but also Sartre and Levinas show that more complex and illuminative passivity can be found in the area of affective and sexual experience.

Most fundamentally, the reflexivity of the body, which is apparent in the experiencing of the so-called *double sensation*, is crucial to the conceptualization of the self-other relationship and the internal alterity of the self. The double sensation delineates an experience of perceiving one part of the body by another part, e.g., touching one hand by means of another hand or an eye with a hand (Husserl [1950] 1997, 97). The possibility of experiencing other selves depends on the possibility of perceiving one's own body.

According to Husserl, it is this reciprocity of acts that makes my experience of others (*pairing*) possible. Even if I do not have access to the other's experiences and his or her experienced body in a similar way as I have to my own, I can identify with the other's living body in its movement and expression. Husserl writes that the other's body is for me "a body in the mode There."

The other's body "brings to my mind the way my body would look 'if I were there'" (Ibid. 117). Later on, Husserl distinguishes the "heres" of the self and other by the impossibility of being in the same *place* simultaneously: "for each point of time intersubjectively grasped as identical, my 'here' and the other's 'here' are separate" (Husserl [1913] 2002, 213).

Thus, the reflexivity of my own body provides the possibility of perceiving the other's body and to recognize him or her as another "animated organism": a lived body constituted in internal relationships of motivation and intending. Another body similar to mine is distinguished from the bodies of aliens, e.g., Martians and animals, as well as from material things. The thing as a spatio-temporal unit characterized by external relations between its parts is distinguished from the lived body, which is characterized by internal connections between parts and movements of change (Husserl [1950] 1997, 114).

The body of another person is not experienced by me as unity of "I can," a body capable for operative intentionality, but is only accessible by me through expressive acts in which his or her (operative) intentionality manifests itself. Thus we perceive the other person as a unity of the expressed and expression: as a style. In other words: "it is only by means of expression that the person of the other is there at all for the experiencing subject" (Husserl [1913] 2002, 257). This is concretized by Merleau-Ponty who claims that other persons appear to me as "behaviour patterns": "each other person does exist for me as an unchallengeable style or setting of co-existence" (POP, 364/PP, 418). Gestures, postures, movements, facial expressions, intonations, and verbal expressions take part in the constitution of the existential style of a person.

From Merleau-Ponty's descriptions we can find an idea that these styles are masculine, feminine, or combinations of the two, argues Sara Heinämaa (Heinämaa 2003, 68; cf. Chanter 2000, 223). The possibility of including sexual difference in the phenomenological investigations of the lived body is also discussed by Don Welton (1998, 181): "And now we suspect that this vein [the resource provided by Husserl's and Merleau-Ponty's idea of the lived body] is not one but two, involving a structural difference between masculine and feminine embodiment."

The lived body orients itself in the space and at the same time it structures space for itself. The moving body is also directed by its intentional surroundings, by the diverse structurizations of its surroundings such as paths, gateways, or steps, the cultural codes of availability and nonavailability. These surroundings which correspond to the layer of operative intentionality already include affective meanings which are inherent in them. Moreover, these affective meanings are responded to, averted, or ignored. Thus, in phenomenology, the lived body is both a source of meanings and a receiver of meanings.[4] These meanings can arise at all levels of embodied subjectivity—sensibility, mobility, affectivity, and sexuality.

The Role of Affectivity

Heinämaa explicates the fact that Merleau-Ponty's descriptions of the body orienting itself in the world also discloses the world as attractive and repulsive (Heinämaa 2003, 63). The objects and persons, as well as the less articulated elemental "layers" of the world, can attract and repulse us due to both personal and cultural habits and dispositions of experiencing. For Merleau-Ponty, even the primary structuration of space by orientations and directedness of the lived body in respect to the other, the world, and worldly objects, occurs as fundamentally affective, characterized by passive *affective intentionality* rather than by active goal-oriented movement.

As I read Merleau-Ponty, affectivity is a principle layer of subjectivity but it is also intertwined with other "layers" of experience: no perception is neutral, i.e., without affective aspects. Affectivity is not a layer to be added to "neutral" being but belongs to all perception. So, it is always already found in the structures of subjectivity. Based on his conception of affectivity as fundamental to all experience, Merleau-Ponty develops an idea of love and desire as paradigmatic forms of affections: "If then we want to bring to light the birth of being for us, we must finally look at that area of experience which clearly has significance and reality only for us, and that is our affective life. Let us try to see how a thing or a being begins to exist for us through desire or love and we shall thereby come to understand better how things and beings can exist in general" (POP, 154/PP, 180). In Merleau-Ponty's view, inquiries into love and desire demonstrate how our relations to ourselves, to others, and to the world are always affective.

Insofar as love and desire are primordial forms of the subject's being in the world, no engagement with the world is possible without another person. Even though it is possible to love artifacts, such as books, church architecture, and sonatas, or even God, none of these forms of emotion alone is capable of *initiating* us into the experience of love, nor the meaning of existence. This is due to the specific position of the other person, another concrete embodied being. As Merleau-Ponty writes, "The very first of all cultural objects, and the one by which all the rest exist, is the body of the other person as the vehicle of a form of behaviour" (POP, 348/PP, 401).

The Holistic Conception of Sexuality

For Merleau-Ponty, sexuality belongs to the unity of existence and as such is an inherent feature of human becoming (POP, 167/PP, 197). Sexuality is not an object or a thing, neither is it localizable into any specific area of life, such as erotic life, or into any specific part of the body, such as genitalia. Rather,

Merleau-Ponty argues, sexuality must be considered an *atmosphere* (*atmosphère*), which spreads throughout the whole of human becoming (POP, 169 /PP, 196).

According to Merleau-Ponty, knowing, acting, and sexuality are in a reciprocal relation of expression and as such manifest one single structure or style. The same way of being is manifested both in sexuality as in other existential relations such as cognition and action. Thus, sexuality is not an autonomous area of experience separate from the other modes of intentionality. For Merleau-Ponty, sexuality does not explain the other dimensions of existence, as psychoanalysts contend, but it comes into being and develops in accordance with other areas of experience. Thus, sexuality should not be understood as a causal *effect* of the physiology of the body or a *consequence* of the drives and instincts but should be understood as an *expression* of existence (POP, 157–158/PP, 184–185).

Sexuality is a mode of experiencing which is not intellectual or intentional in the sense of being a pure consciousness of something. It exemplifies the mode of pre-reflective, affective intentionality: in desire the body directs itself toward another body. Merleau-Ponty characterizes sexuality as "a mute and permanent question" to the surrounding world (POP, 156/PP, 183). Furthermore, in this affective intentionality the being of a person as relational is manifested: "in sexuality is projected his manner of being towards the world, that is, towards time and other men" (POP, 158/PP, 193). In Merleau-Ponty's view the body expresses existence at every moment in the sense in which a word expresses thought (POP, 166/PP, 99). Sexuality is localized to "a primary process of signification in which the expressed does not exist apart from the expression." This "incarnate significance" in which "the existence realizes itself in the body" is, according to Merleau-Ponty, "the central phenomenon of which body and mind, sign and significance, are abstract moments" (POP, 166/PP, 193).

On the basis of Merleau-Ponty's characterizations of sexuality, his conception of sexuality can be called holistic. In this conception, sexuality, like an atmosphere, as Merleau-Ponty puts it, alternates between withdrawal and intensification. It is always present just like an atmosphere is always present, but it takes on an erotic significance only in specific occurrences. In other words, according to Merleau-Ponty, sexuality is "co-extensive with existence" (POP, 169/PP, 197).

As mentioned earlier, one's capacity to identify the lived body of another as another person is dependent on structural similarity—an expressive unity—of one's own body and the body of another. This idea of identification on the basis of structural similarity also covers the expressions of emotions: I recognize specific constellations of expressions as anger or joy. Merleau-Ponty takes anger as an example: I understand anger or cheerfulness *expressed* by the other because I am capable of expressing it myself in similar circumstances. This is made possible "through the reciprocity of my intentions and the gestures of others." Merleau-Ponty continues: "It is as if the other person's intention inhabited my body and mine his" (POP, 184/PP, 215). This possibility of capturing the sense of anger presupposes that emotion of anger is not a psychical fact behind the offensive gesture but is found in the gesture itself. Rather than being given as a thing, the gesture *is* anger (POP, 184/PP, 215). Instead of anger being given as a thing, it is constituted in the relations between of way of moving, gesticulating, the rhythm and tone of voice, and facial expressions.

Sara Heinämaa finds a new mode of isomorphism, i.e., an idea of meaning based on structural similarity, in Merleau-Ponty's account of meaning. Heinämaa gives an example of a smiling face, which "expresses the emotion of joy in the sense that it has the same structure as the other smiling faces" (Heinämaa 2003, 39; PP, 217). Here Merleau-Ponty's account of the constitution of meanings differs from the traditional idea of isomorphism between the structures of mental or ideal invisible objects and their signs or appearances, as in Platonism, but finds it in the relations between the visibles (Heinämaa 2003, 39).

According to Merleau-Ponty, communication through "understanding" gestures is primary to the more articulated modes of communication such as philosophical analysis or description. This mode of communication also holds for desiring: I recognize certain expressions as desire because I am able to desire. According to Merleau-Ponty "the blind recognition" of sexual gestures precedes the work of clarifying their intellectual significance by philosophers such as Sartre in his description of the caress (POP, 186/PP, 216). Merleau-Ponty finds a possibility of communication and dialogic interaction at the level of performing and understanding gestures: "It is through my body that I understand other people, just as it is through my body that I perceive 'things.' The meaning of a gesture thus "understood" is not behind it, it is intermingled with the structure of the world outlined by the gesture, and which I take up on my own account" (POP, 186/PP, 216–217).

As I read Irigaray with respect to Merleau-Ponty's idea of the affectivity of perception, it seems that Irigaray takes seriously the way in which feminine faces and bodies are described in masculine discourse, becoming existent to us (men) only through a specific type of act, e.g., in specific modes of love and desire. However, Merleau-Ponty contends that these dimensions are situated in a continuum with other dimensions of the subject's life and expressivity. With the help of Merleau-Ponty's broader idea of expressivity and sexuality, Irigaray is able to question the "narrowness" of the descriptions of the "object" of love and desire. For Irigaray, this questioning allows space for a more exhaustive understanding of woman's possibilities. Yet, the tendency to perceive and describe woman through specific, masculine, modes of love and desire also indicates a problem concerning the adequacy of our understanding of love in the lack of alternative descriptions issued from the feminine first-person perspective. A closely related question which engages Irigaray is: how should self-reflection, which is indispensable not only for developing one's personality but also for philosophical inquiry, be practised if the subject is constituted not only in the realm of spirituality but also in the realms of embodiment and affectivity.

Language and Significance

For Merleau-Ponty the body-subject, which orients itself in its environment and is affected by it, is a parallel to the subject operating in language. This idea can be found, for example, in this excerpt from Merleau-Ponty's *Phénoménologie de la perception*:

> I do not need to visualize external space and my own body in order to move one within the other. It is enough that they exist for me, and that they form a certain field of action spread around me. In the same way I do not need to visualize the word in order to know and pronounce it. It is enough that I possess its articulatory and acoustic style as one of the modulations, one of the possible uses of my body. I reach back for the word as my hand reaches towards the part of my body which is being pricked; the word has a certain location in my linguistic world, and is part of my equipment. I have only one means of representing it, which is uttering it [. . .]." (POP, 180/PP, 210)

Merleau-Ponty also illustrates the capacity of expression to open a world anew by saying that it is like one would be given a "new sense organ": the process of expression "brings the meaning into existence as a thing at the very heart of the text, it brings it to life in an organism of words, establishing it in the writer or the reader as a new sense organ, opening a new field or a dimension to our experience" (POP, 182/PP, 212).

The operative activities of moving presuppose a more fundamental layer in the constitution of the subject, the other, and the world. In this affective layer the goals of orientation are not yet formed and the purpose of expression is still undefined. According to Merleau-Ponty, also language "comes to be for us" primarily affective before being propositional or "used" for certain purposes. Basically, for Merleau-Ponty, the linguistic gesture corresponds to the bodily gesture: both the gesture and the word "delineate" their own meaning. Merleau-Ponty argues that the verbal form is not arbitrary but inherently connected to the emotional content of the word. The emotional content of the word forms its *gestural sense* (POP, 179/PP, 209).

Thus, according to Merleau-Ponty the origin of language lies in emotional gesticulation in which expression and what is expressed are not separated (POP, 188/PP, 219). As in movement, also in emotional gesticulation, the body and the world are simultaneously patterned. Furthermore, word and language have a "highly specific emotional essence," argues Merleau-Ponty (POP, 189/PP, 218). Merleau-Ponty states that: "what remains to me of the word once learnt is its style as constituted by its formation and sound" (POP, 180/PP, 210). According to Merleau-Ponty, affectivity is present in language in all its modes: from gestures and singing to speech and writing.

According to Merleau-Ponty, singing is an exemplary mode of expression in which the affective meaning is more easily discernible than in the articulated forms of language (POP, 187/PP, 218). Singing can be done without words. Singing is directed even to those who do not share the same language. It arises from the rhythms of the lived body. For Merleau-Ponty, another exemplary mode of expression is poetic language. Poetic language is a verbally articulated mode of language which also exemplifies the primary role of affectivity. In poetry words, vowels, and phonemes establish ways of "singing" the world. They "extract and express the emotional essence of things," writes Merleau-Ponty (POP, 187/PP, 218). By defining his conception of meaning and language according to the affective, "subjective" and "obscure" modes of language—singing and poetic language—Merleau-Ponty is able to provide us with a speaking and writing subject.

In Merleau-Ponty's view, thought and expression are closely connected: expression completes thought (POP, 178/PP, 206). Ultimately, according to Merleau-Ponty, thought can be considered as one of the expressive modes. Thought and expression, then, are simultaneously constituted: "the spoken word is a genuine gesture and it contains its meaning in the same way as gesture contains its" (POP, 183/PP, 214). As the subject of language and meaning is a speaking subject, so too is the other in communication: I communicate with "a speaking subject, with a certain style of being and with the 'world' at which he directs his aim" (POP, 183/PP, 214). For Merleau-Ponty communication is not an exchange of propositional contents but is instead a dialogical process which is operative at all dimensions of subjectivity. Communication is about "a certain lack which is asking to be made good, so my taking up of this intention [of the other] is not a process of thinking on my part, but a synchronizing change of my own existence, a transformation of my being" (POP, 183/PP, 214).

Merleau-Ponty also explains how the specific nature of writing forms the background to a conception of philosophy which understands itself as independent of expression. The "completed" thought, thought which has already obtained its expression in speech but especially in writing, gives the illusion of thought and "inner life," which existed prior to speech or writing (POP, 183/PP, 214). For the reader of the text this illusion of the "inner life" gives an impression of being directly available for the reader. The writer, for his part, is able to become a reader of his own writing and thus is able to detach himself from the process of giving expression to his thought. This apparently strict distinction of thought and its expression in speech and writing is illusory because the inner life is also inner language. Instead of silence, it is words: "thought is not internal and does not exist independently of the world and words" (POP, 183/PP, 213). In my view, Irigaray's writing shows how a reader's experience of the direct availability of the thinker's "inner life" also depends on the mode of writing and speaking, i.e., of the apparent "transparency" or "opacity" of writing, which can be produced intentionally or non-intentionally by linguistic and literary means.

Merleau-Ponty sees in language exemplified by speech and writing, alone among all other expressive processes, a specific feature which allows it "settle into a sediment": "each writer is conscious of taking as his objective the same world as has already been dealt with by other writers" (POP, 190/PP, 221). Merleau-Ponty illuminates his idea of the connection between writing and thought by comparing writing to music. Music does not provide us with anything analogous to the ideal of thought without words, instead, we are unable to imagine music without sound (POP, 183, 190/PP, 221–222).

Furthermore, language also differs from other modes of expression in that it is possible to speak about speech while one cannot paint about painting or compose about composing. For Merleau-Ponty this means that speech has specific position with respect to reason (POP, 190/PP, 221). In addition to expressing new meanings, speech and writing also consist of ready-made meanings, habitual expressions, and repetition and as such are "institutions." Speech as an "institution" of already established meanings only becomes visible with the new meanings which arise from expressions and communication (POP, 184/PP, 214). Merleau-Ponty's examples of expressions, which provide us with new meanings, i.e., transform silence into speech, are "the child uttering its first word," "the lover revealing his feelings," "the first man who spoke," or "the writer and the philosopher who reawaken primordial experience anterior to all traditions" (POP, 179n/ PP, 208n). Thus, Merleau-Ponty distinguishes between first-order expression, authentic speech which is identical with thought, and second-order expression, speech about speech which by its repetition maintains the cohesion of the open and dynamic unity of language.

Like persons and different languages, so too writings, in Merleau-Ponty's view, first come to exist for us as existential styles in which the expression and expressed are not separable. Through their affective nature, writings can invite us, leave us indifferent, or even repulse us: "[t]he spoken or written words carry a top coating of meaning which sticks to them and which presents the thought as a style, an affective value, a piece of existential mimicry, rather than as a conceptual statement. We find here, beneath the conceptual meaning of the words, an existential meaning which is not only rendered by them, but which inhabits them, and is inseparable from them" (POP, 182/PP, 212).

For Merleau-Ponty, philosophical writings also come to exist for us as existential styles. He compares the process of the comprehension of a philosophical text and the process of becoming able to communicate in a foreign culture by taking part in events and participating in communal life and writes that a piece of philosophical writing "discloses to me at least a certain 'style'—either a Spinozist, critical or phenomenological one—which is the first draft of its meaning. I begin to understand a philosophy by feeling my way into its existential manner, by reproducing the tone and accent of a philosopher" (POP, 179/PP, 209).

Irigaray's Critique of Merleau-Ponty

Irigaray discusses Merleau-Ponty's philosophy in the essay, "The Invisible of the Flesh," in *Éthique,* as we saw. Later, in *Etre deux* (1994), she returns to Merleau-Ponty's idea of sexuality as it can be found in *Phénoménologie de la perception*. In this section I will return to Irigaray's reading of Merleau-Ponty's "The Intertwining—The Chiasm" in order to connect her criticism to her phenomenological inquiry into feminine body. In "L'entrelacs—le chiasme" Merleau-Ponty continues to rethink the subject as relational and finds a chiasmatic relation between the subject and the world. This relation is exemplified by the figure of lips in Merleau-Ponty's terminology. Irigaray starts her reading of Merleau-Ponty's essay by quoting an important passage from Merleau-Ponty. In this passage the necessity of returning to the lived experience in order to redefine the adequacy of the means of reflection and intuition is pointed out. In Merleau-Ponty's view, the crucial means for both intuition and reflection, and thus the ones to be redefined, are subject and object, existence and essence (VIE, 130). After quoting the passage from Merleau-Ponty's work, Irigaray writes, referring to the nine essays issued by her in *Éthique,* which precede the penultimate essay on Merleau-Ponty, that until this moment, her approach to the history of philosophy has been in line with that of Merleau-Ponty. She emphasizes the need to "go back to a moment of pre-discursive experience, recommence everything, all the categories by which we understand things, the world, subject-object divisions, recommence everything and pause at the 'mystery, as familiar as it is unexplained, of a light which, illuminating the rest, remains at its source in obscurity'" (ESD, 151/E, 143). In distinction to Merleau-Ponty, for Irigaray the "light, which remains in obscurity" depicts the maternal-feminine, and, for her, the operations described above seem necessary to bring the maternal-feminine into language.

In Irigaray's view, Merleau-Ponty has recognized a relation between the masculine subject and the maternal-feminine (ESD, 152/E, 144). This is more than any other philosopher before him has done: "[. . .] Merleau-Ponty's seer remains in an incestuous prenatal situation with the whole. This mode of existence or of being is probably that of all men, at least in the West. Also, given the historic period when Merleau-Ponty was writing, he would have been one of the few or one of the first people to have felt this" (ESD, 173/E, 162).

Yet, in Irigaray's view, Merleau-Ponty has not been able to rethink the relationality of the masculine subject (E, 144/ESD, 152). Irigaray finds in Merleau-Ponty's ontology of flesh a blind spot, which is due to his ignorance of the sexual difference and the difference between feminine and masculine bodies. Merleau-Ponty's subject is not able to enter a world but remains in the solipsism of the quasi-uterine environment, Irigaray claims. This is due to Merleau-Ponty's ignorance of the place of the sexually other, which could provide an opening for the closed world depicted in quasi-uterine terms (ESD, 154, 181/E, 145, 168).

Irigaray argues that due to this ignorance, Merleau-Ponty's view of the relation between the perceiver and the perceivable turns in on itself. No unpredictability or unexpectedness of the other person can be accounted for in this kind of solipsistic relation. Irigaray writes: "Although a pertinent analysis of the way I form a weave of sensations with the world, it is one that excludes solitude even though its own systematization is solipsistic. This seer is never alone, he dwells unceasingly in *his* world. Eventually he finds some accomplices there, but he never meets others. His universe represents, or re-creates, a vast intertwining of umbilical cords or passages"[5] (ESD, 173).

According to Irigaray, in order to avoid solipsism we have to ask the question of the other as touching and touched, an other "whose body's ontological status differs from my own" (ESD, 157/E, 148). As there is no transcendent God in Merleau-Ponty's philosophy of immanence, this is only possible if there is "spacing or interval for the freedom of questioning between two" (ESD, 183/E, 170). In short, the basic idea of Irigaray's criticism for Merleau-Ponty is that he fails to account for the difference between the feminine and masculine bodies and their diverse relations to the maternal-feminine.

The problem of ignoring sexual difference can also be seen in the way Merleau-Ponty situates the figure of lips to depict the relation between the perceiver and the world. According to Irigaray, however, the figure of lips is not appropriate to depict the relation of the perceiver and the world. Furthermore, in Irigaray's view, Merleau-Ponty misplaces the figure: the lips belong to the morphology of the feminine body. She writes that the "singularity of the body and flesh of the feminine" is due to two facts: "the fact that the lips are doubled: those above and those below" and "from the fact that the sensible which is the feminine touches the sensible from which she/he emerges" (ESD, 166/E, 156). Irigaray further writes: "These two dimensions of which Merleau-Ponty speaks are *in* her body. And hence she experiences it as a volume in a different way." (ESD, 166/E, 156).

Sara Heinämaa argues that Irigaray's criticism of Merleau-Ponty points at a general problem with phenomenology of the body (Heinämaa 2007, 243–256).

The problem is whether intersubjectivity can be characterized in terms of seeing and, furthermore, in seeing oneself in the place of the other as Husserl claims. Heinämaa argues that Irigaray problematizes the Husserlian idea of the self-other relationship by the specific case of a pregnant woman and an unborn child. Irigaray criticizes the idea of reversibility by pointing out that the positions of the subject and the unborn child are not reversible; the mother is not able to see the child nor the child its mother. As Heinämaa points out, this problem of intrauterine life—with respect to Husserl's formulation of intersubjectivity can, in Irigaray's view, also be found in Merleau-Ponty's characterization of the visible. This specific case of the self-other relation has not been taken into account in the phenomenological investigations of intersubjectivity (Heinämaa 2007, 243–256). Instead of the reversibility of the look and the seer, Irigaray finds "a look forever organized, or disorganized around an impossibility of seeing: a locus of the irreversible" (ESD, 152–153).

5

The Feminine Lived Body

The basic ideas of the phenomenology of the body figure in Irigaray's descriptions of feminine lived experience and expressivity. The methodological shift of starting from phenomenology marks a point in which mute or senseless feminine expression can be given a new significance comparable but not reducible to that of connecting mimetic writing to the female body. The body that is now at issue is not a biological or anatomical system but consists of intentional activities and passivities and meaningful expressions, in a continuum from a very rudimentary level to a very articulate one. The phenomenological approach provides a new direction of development concerning the feminine style and in observing it in a non-partial and non-biased manner. The feminine style can be developed and cultivated toward increasing the expression and extension of oneself in accordance with the norm set by oneself, and one's peers, rather than by an external norm. This change of direction, from externally defined pathology to a self-defined attempt at developing into integrity, is made possible by the mimetic move of assuming the position of the beloved woman, but also by the conceptual and methodological resources of the phenomenology of the lived body, already inscribed into the discourse.

∼

Irigaray's descriptions of the feminine bodily experience are given from the first-person perspective. On the basis of Irigaray's descriptions of the feminine lived body, the feminine body is constituted in relations to itself, to the world, and to the others *in its own fashion*.

Irigaray starts her analysis of feminine embodiment by focusing on its elemental dimensions: movements of breathing and bathing in relation to the elements of air and water. In such relations the elements function as a mediator and as the surrounding for what appears to us. Even on this primitive level of embodiment a relationship with the maternal other is established. But this maternal other is not reducible to the function of the material-elemental. This is important to notice, since the identification of the material and the maternal in discourse has led us to ignore the possibility of individuation in respect to the maternal other. Irigaray's phenomenological explorations of the constitutive relations of subject show that no pure matter exists as another term of these relations.

Irigaray follows Sartre, Levinas, and Merleau-Ponty in developing an idea of the elemental. The idea of the elemental marks a transition from the idea of pure, formless matter to be assimilated by the subject to an idea and experience of a rudimentary *relation* to the elemental nature, which should be distinguished from the nature as a resource for production. The elemental overflows the subject's attempts to grasp it while the resource can be grasped and used for pre-determined purposes or assimilated into oneself.[1] These two modes of relating can be ways of living or conceptualizing the concrete, emotional, or spiritual situations of unacknowledged nourishment. However, traditionally, the discourse has conceptualized the subject as independent of any material conditions, whether understood as elemental or as a resource, and of the (sexually) other.

For Irigaray, the subject's relations to the nourishment, to the elemental, and to the maternal other form the starting points for articulating the fundamental layers of the constitution of the subject. Only by starting from these fundamental layers can we manage to rethink subjectivity in a way which allows a feminine style. This self-(re)formation starts already on the fundamental levels of experience in which we enjoy and bathe in the elements of water, air, and flesh. Here nourishment stems from the soil of affections and the maternal/material is identified with this soil. These relations of nourishment and enjoyment also form the basic level of woman's self-affection and self-representation. This affective directness or intentionality, the unnoticed invisible movement of the feminine body, is not constituted in terms of wilful intent, meaning or of touch (S, 286 /SO, 230). The feminine lived body reforms itself in its gestural and auto-affective unity which stems from the elemental. This unity can be cultivated into a full style, which provides an existential alternative to the fragmentation of identity exemplified by the hysteric.

Irigaray characterizes woman's movement as organic and expressive. She abandons the traditional conception of movement as locomotion, change of place, and struggles to develop new concepts for the characterization of the vital movements of the lived body. Also the temporality of woman's being, as described by Irigaray, differs from the traditional idea of time extending to eternity (ESD, 106/E, 104). Furthermore, Irigaray's idea of the temporality of feminine being is cyclical rather than linear. She writes, "The turn, or return, of genealogy is repeated indefinitely in woman, women, among women, like a ceaseless voyage" (ESD, 106/E, 104).

According to Irigaray, woman experiences her body as an innerness in a manner which does not have an expression neither in the traditional philosophy nor in the phenomenology of the body. Merleau-Ponty's descriptions of flesh and its folds offer some assistance here, even though Merleau-Ponty does not connect these terms to the feminine body. Irigaray describes feminine embodied being from the woman's first-person perspective as "her innerness for herself" (*l'intériorité avec soi*) or "herself with herself" (*elle-même avec elle-même*). The gesture, which would allow "woman to remain within herself" is, according to Irigaray, one of the most difficult ones in our culture (ESD, 68/E, 70).

Thus, I argue that the feminine body as described by Irigaray is not and should not be confused with any material or biological object or a body, which can be manipulated. It is not an object of bio-sciences, i.e., a construct of anatomical and biological properties and processes in the world. Neither should it be reduced to a material resource for production or a mere correlate of the desiring or needy masculine body. The body in Irigaray's work refers to the body-subject, which is intentionally connected to the world. The body-subject orients itself in the world and delineates the world to itself, it affects worldly things and other body-subjects and others and is affected by them. It is not a physical or material thing with causal powers described by the natural sciences. Rather, the body is in the process of becoming, determined and defined by its intentional and motivational relations of enjoyment, need, production and perception.

The feminine body-subject in this sense can be more or less conscious of its possibilities of development, depending on its own preconceptions and habits and the cultural environment. In the opening and closing of possibilities, the expressive body always appears both to itself and to concrete others, men and women, in the contexts of interaction. Moreover, it constitutes itself by imitating and reformulating others and their ways of being. The possibilities of imitation and recreation depend on the experienced and intersubjectively created space open for free movement. The lived body, the body as experiencing and expressive, cannot be circumscribed or defined by exact concepts. However, the attempt to characterize verbally the feminine lived body in its movement is necessary for the cultivation of the feminine style, and in striving for truthfulness in respect to bodily being in general. This attempt can be effectuated both in personal relationships and within discourse.

Because of the temporal, procedural, and non-closed nature of feminine style, our "object of investigation," its description must necessarily remain an infinite task. As such this task of description can remain open to new perspectives and articulations, those of other women, present and future, but also those of men. Furthermore, in my view, this describing occurs in Irigaray's work in a manner structurally analogous to Irigaray's descriptions of the *lived, organic whole* of the feminine lived body.

The Bodily Origins of Feminine Expressivity

Irigaray articulates the feminine experience of embodiment in its several modes of relating. She also accounts for the variety of these relations in her description of the feminine modes of expression but also expresses this multitude in her way of writing. The feminine subject can constitute itself and get to know itself only by expressing itself and interacting through its expression. As we have seen, Irigaray demonstrates the problems of partial feminine self-expression through the activity of productive mimesis. But she also returns to *elementary* modes of expression that preserve the fundamental affectivity of expression and the interrelation of the feminine embodiment and emotions. At this stage of her work Irigaray does not use "elemental" to refer to the primitive or the fragmented but uses it to refer to the original: that which can be found by investigating the feminine bodily experience from the first-person point of view. In this way she shifts emphasis from the fragmented and distracted feminine identity to the elementary dimensions of feminine subjectivity. It is this original existence which provides a basis for new perspectives.

Irigaray writes as a woman: "I am a woman. I write with who I am. Why wouldn't that be valid, unless out of contempt for the value of women or from a denial of a culture in which the sexual is a significant subjective and objective dimension?" (JTNT, 53/JTN, 65). In her view, it is not possible to be a woman with one part and write with another: "But how could I on the one hand be a woman, and on the other, a writer? Only those who are still in a state of verbal automatism or who mimic already existing meaning can and should maintain such a scission or split between she who is a woman and she who writes. The whole of my body is sexuate. My sexuality isn't restricted to my sex and to the sexual act (in the narrow sense)" (JTNT, 53/JTN, 65). However, elsewhere she expresses a reluctance to speaking *about* woman or constructing theories *about* woman (CS, 75/TS, 78). This can be interpreted not only as detachment of speaking about woman as an "object" of research but also about reluctance to describe her way of exploration as aiming to *construct* theoretical entities (cf. Jones 2010, 17). In the phenomenological approach, the aim is rather to evoke and describe that what is already given to us in experience and perception with the help of the phenomenological methodology.

Singing is an example of the elemental mode of expression for Irigaray (EP, 7, 128/PE, 7, 104). Its tones, rhythms, and melodies form a continuum with (poetic) language in which the expression and the expressed are not separate but mutually implied. For Irigaray, singing and poetic language form a basis for the more impersonal and neutral modes of expression, such as political and scientific language, which are more detached from their roots in speech and embodiment or claimed to be so.

Irigaray is indebted to Merleau-Ponty in her explication of the continuum between diverse modes of expression, from the "elemental" speech through poetic language to the most precise verbal formulations. Irigaray finds a possibility for woman's language in those modes of expression which Merleau-Ponty shows to be fundamental: singing and poetic speech. In the philosophical tradition, poetic language is characterized as semantically and syntactically fluid and thus as inferior to theoretical discourse and its unitary terms and solid meanings. Merleau-Ponty, however, argues that poetic language is necessary for the renewal of all language and discourse. Poetic language in Merleau-Ponty's sense forms the elemental layer of language, but it also extends to the highly sophisticated symbolic level of it.

In the models of language thematized by Merleau-Ponty, the expressed and expression are not separate objectivities and no other purpose than the goal of addressing the other is posited. We find this type of intentionality also in Irigaray's characterizations of woman's speech: "Woman, for her part, chats, tattles, gossips, weaves inventions, fables, myths. She exchanges the means of exchange without having any object. Or does she make statements without having any fixed stake in what she has stated? Forever in utterance? There is something in between 'subjects' without 'objects' other than language itself. Some sharing or some communicating of words that does not rely on the message of the communication? The message is the communication. She remains within the communication as if in-depths whose form is not always clear-cut, not univocal. She says. But what? Saying itself?" (ESD, 138/E, 131).

These non-discursive modes of feminine expression are, in Irigaray's view, exemplified in chatting, gossiping, laughing, and shouting. All these modes of expression are "almost devoid of meaning" (Ibid.). This makes Irigaray ask whether women are "the guardians of the phonetics of the language, of sounds?" and whether their expression, as it is commonly thought, is "between noise and singing" (Ibid.). Yet, even if woman's speech is traditionally thought to lack meaning, also chattering, gossiping, laughing, and shouting indicate a feminine lived body and its gestural unity.

Also the mimetic position of the hysteric includes expressive possibilities in the sense of original feminine existence. The movements of the hysteric can be transformed and developed into a feminine gestural unity. So, even the hysteric's movements indicate a potential gestural unity. Irigaray writes: "Hysteria: it *speaks* in the mode of *a paralyzed gestural faculty*, of an impossible and also a forbidden speech. . . . It speaks as symptoms of an 'it can't speak to or about itself' . . . And the drama of hysteria is that it is inserted schizotically between that gestural system, that desire paralyzed and enclosed within its body, and a language that it has learned in the family, in school, in society, which is in no way continuous with—nor certainly, a metaphor for—the 'movements' of its desire" (TS, 136/CS, 134; latter italics mine). For Irigaray *parler-femme* means an attempt to create *continuity* between the paralysis and fragmentation of feminine expression exemplified by the hysteric and the free-flowing expression of a desiring woman. In Irigaray's words: "The problem of 'speaking (as) woman' is precisely that of finding a continuum between that gestural expression or that speech of desire—which at the present can only be identified in the form of symptoms and pathology—and a language, including verbal language" (TS, 137/CS, 134–135).

The possibility for transformation and development of hysteric expressions into a feminine gestural unity can be found in the feminine love of self. Irigaray also discovers the feminine gestural unity presupposed in the descriptions of carnal love issued by male thinkers. The topic of this twofold disclosure of the feminine gestural and expressive unity given both from the first-person and from the third-person perspective will be brought up again in Parts II and III.

Irigaray follows Merleau-Ponty in arguing that the expressive modes of moving form a continuum from gesticulating and singing to speaking and writing: all arise from the experiential unity of the person. Irigaray indicates this by structural connection in her mode of writing: her written expression repeats the form of speech (ESD, 169/E, 158). The common goal of all these modes of expression, however, is a specific mode of communication: a dialogue with another concrete person. So, instead of a public speech in front of a general audience, Irigaray presents the paradigm of a dialogue between two people, me and you, between the first- and second-person positions. Such dialogic speech addresses the other but also posits questions to itself. The uniqueness of persons is shown in the manner in which Irigaray addresses her own words to her reader, "a you" who is not known but is merely invited to express her- or himself.

Despite its connection to other modes of expression, writing differs from them in important respects. While singing and speech are deeply anchored in the body of the expressive subject, writing is free from such a tie. Writing has an autonomous existence of its own, and as such it forms a structure analogous to that of a subject. It is oriented to and affected by other writings. Writing does not arise directly from the elemental expression of the body but also from the materials of language and other writings. Furthermore, writing is not mortal in the sense that a person is, but persists through time. Its autonomous existence can even lead to the forgetting of its sensible, material aspect. This idea of detaching writing from all lived bodies and attributing it instead to an absolute disembodied subjectivity has been dominant in Western philosophy. Irigaray extends this idea even to the Western practices of speaking: speaking, too, can be detached from gestures and movements (OO, 51, 53).

Irigaray's descriptions on the lived feminine body give—both by the intertwinement of structure and content—an impression of engagements which have to be taken into account and reflected by starting from the given situation. Irigaray describes both the engagements of the lived body with indistinguished materiality on the one hand, and with other women's bodies on the other. Irigaray's descriptions of the feminine lived body show the feminine body in its specific process of separation from the material-maternal. In this process a new "soil"—elemental, already structured as meaningful—replaces the mute material-maternal. In these writings the feminine expressive body is described as relational: it comes into existence not only with respect to the male reader or lover, but also with respect to other women by distinguishing itself from the identification with the maternal on the one hand, and from the position of the beloved woman on the other as we will see later.

This process of separation potentially also occurs with regard to language. Writing also arises from the materiality of language: gestures, gesture-words, phonemes, intonations, rhythms, and melodies. Furthermore, the separation of the feminine subject also concerns the expressions already available in speeches and writings. These writings are mostly male-written, which at best can have the issue of woman as their topic. As language is maintained and renewed within the confines of the expressive acts made, it can be said to have become masculine, particularly by its public, discursive forms. Irigaray's writings preserve the sense of materiality and affectivity in her writing. In this way she mimes in her act of writing both the identification of materiality, affectivity, and femininity. She also mimes the modes of expressive acts identified with woman's expression. In addressing her words to the concrete other she mimes, but also develops expressive modes which are suitable for the private relations traditionally left to woman but are also modifiable.

As the preliminary experienced and gestural unity of woman (woman's "style") is constituted in diverse relations to itself, to the world, and to others, this holds also for the spiritual-embodied unity of writing. Furthermore, as the preliminary experienced and gestural unity of woman is brought into writing, the possibility of the (feminine) style as a norm or a model in its own right, is opened up. Yet, in order for the feminine style to constitute a norm of its own, a variety and temporal extension and multilayeredness of its exemplifications is required. The writings would examine the possibilities of feminine style, invite problematizations, affirmations, and new descriptions. They also offer a point of reflection for women themselves as well as for men's conceptions of both women and of themselves seen from a woman's point of view.

Irigaray's writings reflect the idea of gestural meanings in continuum with those of intellectual meanings. Both are also constituted in the continuum of one's own expressive acts, a style in its process of developing. Irigaray compares her work as an organic whole to the organic whole of a lived body and the formation of the lived body: "I consider it as a mistake to divide my work into parts that are foreign to one another. Its becoming is more continuous and the way it develops is close to that of a living being" (P, 200). Just as Irigaray resists the tendency of seeing the body as consisting of separate parts rather than as an organic whole, she also resists this idea with regard to her own work (E, 135/ESD, 143). I take this to mean that as in the lived body, also in this open whole, the parts are related internally in a relationship of meaning from the parts, sections, chapters, passages, phrases, words, of the singular works to the works as parts of one continuum structurally identical to that of the person (Husserl [1913] 2002, 248–249). Yet, having an ideal being in Irigaray's writings, it is a (feminine) subject that is constituted in the first person acts of expression.

Irigaray's conception of a (feminine) person constituted in its relations to itself, to the other, and to the world is reflected in her way of writing. Irigaray composes her writings in such a way that they are directed toward herself and the others. Irigaray's writings address, apart from herself and her self-understanding, the sexually other, another woman, and mother, as in "Quand nos lèvres se parlent" when Irigaray writes, "I love you who is neither mother (forgive me mother, I prefer a woman) nor sister. Neither daughter nor son. I love you—and where I love you, what do I care about the lineage of our fathers or their desire for reproductions of men" (TS, 209/CS, 208). Thus Irigaray indicates the multiplicity of the relations in which she as a feminine person is constituted and indicates the separation of mother and woman. Furthermore, she also distinguishes feminine experience from the meanings given to it in masculine discourse.

Irigaray also addresses mother, other women and men as persons in all their dimensions. This addressing originates from a feminine person, in a feminine style associated both with the traditional conception of woman and the first-person experience of woman's embodiment and sexuality. In the reader, this addressing can arouse a wide variation of responses depending on the position of the reader with regard to his or her own gender and the other gender. Even the same reader can waver between diverse immediate reactions and more elaborated views.

Irigaray addresses the reader as being engaged in many ways to the world and to others. This is shown by the thickness and obscurity of Irigaray's descriptions in e.g., "Quand nos lèvres se parlent," "Ce sexe qui n'en est pas un" of *Ce sexe* and also in *Passions élémentaires*. This thickness can be traced to the sphere of embodiment, perception, and sensibility where transparency cannot be found. Still, even if the ideal of transparency gained by the detachment of ideas from the embodiment is relinquished, an intertwinement of sensible and ideal, a stylistic unity, constitutive of *fluid ideality*, can be reached. It is constituted in the internal and external relations of singular unities.

Irigaray writes about fluids, which are difficult to idealize and have a specific relation to the feminine body and the representations of the feminine, especially in "L'incountournable volume" in *Speculum* and "La 'mécanique' des fluids" in *Ce sexe*. Irigaray's idea of "another transparency"—the *mucous* (*le muqueux*)—belongs to this family of concepts depicting fluid ideality (E, 108/ ESD, 111). Irigaray explores the mucous in *Éthique*. The mucous makes possible the movement of living organisms and sense-perception: the movements of one's own body and, for example, the movement of eyes presupposed by sight. The mucous has a specific relation to the feminine body and its organic processes and to the representations of the feminine in discourse. It also makes possible the encounters between bodies in their diverse relations. Irigaray characterizes the mucous as a concept that can reverse thinking based on hierarchical dualisms. According to Irigaray, like fluids, the mucous also belongs to that which is unthought in our times (E, 107/ ESD, 110). Both fluids and the mucous have a specific relation to the feminine.

Irigaray's Holistic Conception of Sexuality

Irigaray's concept of sexuality deviates from the traditional account of sexuality which is focused on the sexual act or the biological and anatomical functions of female and male bodies. This traditional account of sexuality defines even the sexual act, first and foremost, by its potential reproductive teleology and the male perspective placed on it. This narrow conception of sexuality does not account for human (embodied) experience (E, 135–136/ESD, 142–144). Moreover, it often reduces these dimensions of existence into mere function of reproduction, a mode of reduction, which does not make justice to our temporally structured experience of being sexual; neither does it acknowledge on their own right those modes of being sexual which are not possible to structure around the function of reproduction in any traditional way.[2]

As we have seen, Merleau-Ponty articulates a holistic conception of sexuality which takes the human embodied experience into account. Thus, from Merleau-Ponty we can find a conception of sexuality which is holistic in the sense that it covers all the layers of subjectivity and the whole of its temporal continuum. According to this conception, sexuality is equally present in writing and speaking as in our everyday perception of concrete individuals as men and women. Even if Merleau-Ponty does not thematize sexual difference, he implies it in his descriptions of perceiving women and men.

I find this alternative conception of sexuality in Irigaray's descriptions of feminine embodiment and sexuality. Irigaray writes: "The whole of my body is sexuate. My sexuality isn't restricted to my sex and to the sexual act (in the narrow sense" (JTNT, 53/JTN, 65).[3] For Irigaray, Merleau-Ponty's holistic idea of sexuality offers a possibility to rethink feminine sexuality. This does not mean that her interest is restricted to feminine sexuality. Masculine sexuality should also be rethought according to this idea of sexuality. Thus, what is at issue is sexual difference.

Irigaray examines the potential of self-defined feminine sexuality by asking how the feminine body is experienced by women. On the basis of Irigaray's descriptions, it seems that we must distinguish between three different phenomena: the habitual conception of feminine sexuality based on certain modes or aspects of feminine sexuality, a feminine experience of auto-affection and an objective account of feminine sexuality.

In Irigaray's view, the experience of the own body as feminine is not provided only by the intensity of the sexual act, pregnancy, or breastfeeding, all of which are temporal and episodic occurrences, but is rather holistic (cf. Tallon Russel 2009, 240). Irigaray starts her explication from a very basic kind of bodily self-awareness, which is usually central in consciousness in everyday being but comes to the fore when intensified, e.g., in desire or by a specific kind of attitude of phenomenological exploration. According to Irigaray, the diverse modes of feminine sexuality from bodily self-awareness and affection to sexual arousal should be seen in a continuum. However, surprisingly, Irigaray maintains that feminine auto-affection is interrupted rather than intensified in the sexual act and in delivery (TS, 24/CS, 24). Irigaray points out that feminine autoeroticism differs from male autoeroticism by being minimally active and self-sufficient. A woman does not need any instrument to touch herself, she claims, and writes: "Woman 'touches herself' all the time" (TS, 24/CS, 24). Also here, Irigaray accentuates the significance of touch, which has been inarticulate in the tradition of Western philosophy and its ideas of sexual (in)difference. Irigaray's explication of feminine embodiment and sexuality does not depict the feminine body as a closed volume, such as it is for an unborn child, nor does she depict it as an envelope for the male sexual organ. Instead, the emblem of Irigaray's explication of the first-person experience of feminine sexuality is the open fold or volume of the lips, a fold of flesh. A famous essay on lips can be found in "Quand nos lévres se parlent" in *Ce sexe*, but Irigaray picks up the topic already in *Speculum*, *Amante marine*, *Passions élèmentaires* and returns to it also in *Éthique*.[4]

Irigaray writes that the lips: "strictly speaking [. . .] serve neither conception nor jouissance" (ESD, 18/E, 18). Lips are neither accountable as useful nor defined by external goals. Understood as such, the figure of lips does not allow expressive embodiment, sexuality or speech to be defined by any external demands or goals. Furthermore, lips also represent a specific type of structure. Irigaray maintains that lips form a threshold, which is always half-open and gives access to the mucous, and the lips themselves are strangers to dichotomy and oppositions (E, 18/ESD, 18). Furthermore, lips cannot be detached from the body as an organic, expressive whole. As such the figure of lips resists fragmentation and the instrumentalization of the body, but it also resists the metaphysical distinction of the soul and the body which is continuous with these tendencies.

According to Irigaray, woman's two lips stand for the unity of embodiment and expression: exchange and communication (CS, 212–213/TS, 214–215). They also stand for the relational nature of feminine embodied being (SO, 29/S, 30; CS, 23/TS, 23). Irigaray writes that lips "offer a shape of welcome but do not assimilate, reduce or swallow up" (ESD, 18/E, 18). This kind of movement has an inherent goal of maintaining openness. This goal is inherent in the feminine body, which "by the same gesture touches and touches anew becoming closer to its limits" (E, 135/ESD, 143). The same structure or morphology of sexuality can be found both in Irigaray's description of two lips and her description of feminine *jouissance:* "In some sense her jouissance is a result of indefinite touching" (ESD, 64/E, 67), and in this way Irigaray connects feminine desire to "the infinite of life . . . woman could live in love indefinitely" (ESD, 64/E, 67).

Irigaray describes how the sexual act and its temporality is experienced by a woman by using the metaphors of language and music and their structures: "A sentence without a period? A musical phrase that would never end? An expanse extending on and on forever. A horizon forever open, closed up only with difficulty, as a result of that other punctuation or rhythm" (ESD, 65/E, 68). Sensuous pleasure extends infinitely and the rhythms of movement and sensibility are dynamic. According to Irigaray, women's quest is for infinite life rather than death: infinite in expanse of jouissance here and now (ESD, 64/E, 67). For Irigaray, the infinite or the divine does not transcend sensuality but, rather, is realized in it. Further she writes: "To give itself [jouissance] in a space-time without end" is the "act of love" on the side of woman. Sometimes this "more" (*toujours plus*) of feminine desire is reduced to pathology, which, Irigaray argues, is not the case (ESD, 64/E, 67; cf. Beauvoir [1949] 1976, 181).

Irigaray's descriptions do not imply that woman is in a state of sexual excitement all the time, which is an idea characteristic of masculine fantasies articulated, e.g., in Jacques Lacan's lectures of female desire, connected to Teresa of Avila (Jones 2010, 157). Rather, they indicate a fundamental bodily self-awareness which is sexual in the holistic meaning that Merleau-Ponty explicated in *Phénoménologie de la perception*. For Irigaray, feminine *jouissance* cannot be reduced to fulfilment of needs, neither is it reducible to the male-defined feminine body. Irigaray describes woman's jouissance thus, "her jouissance is a result of indefinite *touching*. The *thresholds* [of lips] do not necessarily mark a limit, an end of an act. In the act of love, she finds herself more or less expanded, more or less deeply touched, more or less unfolded in her desire of the moment." (ESD, 64–65/E, 67–68). In Irigaray's view woman's ex-static body has "sex organs more or less everywhere" (TS, 28/S, 103fn107/CS, 28). This means that feminine *jouissance* potentially extends from bodily auto-affection to woman's writing.

The figure of lips can be seen as an alternative to the figure of the two hands in the double touch, which dominates discussions of self-affectivity and the constitution of one's own body in phenomenology. The lips cannot be analyzed according to the changing positions of the toucher and the touched, subject and object. The movement of lips is more subtle than the activity and passivity of the standard example of the double touch. Both lips are active and both are passive but neither is active in the standard sense of grasping and possessing. The lips touch each other and themselves in a way that cannot be captured by the duality of active and passive or subject and object.

By the figure of the two lips, Irigaray articulates an experience which has not been considered structured, solid, or unified enough to deserve a central place in the philosophical analysis of subjectivity. The very status of this experience as an experience has been questionable in the tradition. Rachel Jones depicts the specific figures, which are crucial in recognizing the specificity of the self-defined feminine body such as the "lips," as well as umbilical cord and placenta "characterized by intimate relations of contiguity and contact, rather than substitution or negation" (Jones 2010, 161). By showing us this kind of relations and experiences in need of articulation and recognition, Irigaray also urges us to redefine the subject of experience and its possibilities.

More specifically, it has been argued that it is the category of experience as formulated in Husserlian phenomenology that she problematizes (Heinämaa 1996, 23; 2007, 256). By neglecting such experiences and by denying their status as possible modes of experience, the tradition has constructed its general notion of experience. This notion is thus founded on unjustified omissions and prejudice. The mode of experience, denoted by the figure of the two lips cannot be accounted for in terms of intentionality of conscious acts nor in terms of the operative intentionality of governing movement (the "I can"). It belongs to the relations of enjoyment and affective perception.

Moreover, the figure of the two lips also marks a precondition of articulated speech and singing and thus it also concerns the higher layers of subjectivity. It governs feminine existence at all levels without leaving behind the affectivity and sensibility from which it arises. As Canters and Jantzen (2005, 110) have pointed out, this structure is also exemplified by the figure of the flower, which is not part of the feminine lived body but has a structure of intimacy and separation similar to the feminine lived body and its two lips. The figure of a flower is explicitly discussed by Irigaray in *Passions élémentaires* (1982): "The flower opened: the flower offered in its appearing. Without its dark becoming, without the pulse of its unfolding/folding. Without the movement of its opening/closing: the spreading apart of petals through another's affection and their touching each other again to safeguard the self-other" (PE, 34, cf. 94–95/EP, 31, cf. 29, 78).

The figure of the flower, or the rose, also works as an emblem for the structure of her layered writing and her works which are composed of separate texts in close intimacy and contact and also connects to the mystical discourse (EP, 78–79/PE, 94–95; OA, 8). I will later return to this structure of unity, multilayeredness, and distinction, with respect to writing.

Thus, Irigaray's description of the two lips is not only a result of phenomenological investigations concerning feminine experience and feminine sexuality. In her view, our philosophical traditions and its concepts of identity and wholeness are based on a male imaginary and male bodily experience. The lips are not simply bodily or spiritual but an intertwinement of both. The identity of the lips is not fixed or solid but is fluid and dynamic. It is an essentially invisible and almost non-perceptible cyclical movement—even if it is not the kind of movement traditionally studied and presented as the paradigm of moving. Even though the lips are not in themselves enough to constitute a feminine identity or subjectivity, they offer a structural model for this kind of identity as dynamic, relational, and open.

Ultimately, through questioning the dominant notion of unity and wholeness, Irigaray's idea is to question and rethink ontology more generally. To this end, language has to be renewed. This demand is presented, for example, in Irigaray's characterization of feminine syntax, which is in accordance with her characterization of the feminine "style" in a passage quoted earlier in this book. Irigaray writes: "what a feminine syntax might be is not simple or easy to state, because in that 'syntax' there would no longer be either subject or object, 'oneness' would no longer be privileged, there would no longer be proper meanings, proper names, 'proper' attributes. . . . Instead, that syntax would involve nearness, proximity, but in such an extreme form that it would preclude any distinction of identitities, any establishment of ownership, thus any form of appropriation" (TS, 134–135/CS, 132).

This description of feminine syntax with its emphasis on nearness and proximity corresponds to Irigaray's characterization of the auto-affection of woman as constantly touching herself without any mediation. The figure of two lips functions as an emblem for both this form of affection and its possible expressions in speech and writing. Thus, Irigaray's concept of feminine captures the openness and dynamism of the feminine body and its expressions; its specific mode of relationality.

The Feminine Embodied Soul and the Divine

In Irigaray's understanding, woman's mode of embodiment and sexuality is better described by metaphors of fold and threshold than by the metaphors of layers or by the distinction of matter and form. The feminine soul is constituted and captured in experience and perception in which the sensible and the ideal are intertwined and not in a soul which is detached or separated from bodies and from embodiment:

> The whole is not the same for me as it is for you. For me, it can never be one. Can never be completed, always in-finite. When you talk about Infinity, it seems to me that you are speaking of a closed totality: a solid, empty, membrane which would gather and contain all possibilities. The absolute of self-identity—in which you were, will be, could be.
>
> For me? A fluid expansion, never closed once and for all. Not even by projects or projections. (EP, 89/PE, 109)

In Irigaray's view, "man's woman" has functioned and served as a passage or medium for God and the Ideal defined by and in relation to men. For this reason women do not have a divine and a divine soul of their own, neither do they "*possess* a soul." More precisely, as we will see in the descriptions of carnal love, women are characterized and defined as lacking spirituality and ensoulment as they are defined and conceptualized in masculine discourse. However, the lack of male-defined spirituality also means a certain liberty: a creative opportunity arises from woman's respective "poverty." Woman is thought not to *possess* a soul nor higher spirituality—and yet she is capable of reading, speaking, and writing and she herself knows that in addition to being embodied, she is also spiritual.

Moreover, she is also implicitly recognized as spiritual and ensouled by the sexually other. This paradox motivates a reconsideration of the soul-body unity, a reconsideration which, as we saw earlier, has been initiated by Merleau-Ponty. A new conception of the soul can be developed and cultivated on the basis of the feminine world of experience but also on the basis of the feminine as it is conceptualized by the masculine discourse which has detached itself from its roots in embodiment. Irigaray suggests that the reason for woman's lack of soul could be tracked down to the fact that women experience themselves and live their lives as "passages" to the ideal rather than as its "proprietors." Women experience and live themselves as "passages" in several ways: their bodies and emotions function as means of (spiritual) birth and development for the child and for the male. Also the nourishment, care and education of the children is a "passage" to ideality formed by women in a shared dwelling taking place during certain periods of time. Woman also serves as the passage from "nature" or from the sphere of mere experience to the discourse and to the divine by constituting a "primitive" expressive unity. This function is served by the mother and by the beloved woman but also by the mystic, the teacher, the wife, the oracle, and the sorcerer. I will later further describe and analyze these positions and the account of women as "passages" as Irigaray finds them especially in the philosophical discourse.

Yet, Irigaray argues that if women want to retain the passage that they also constitute and offer for themselves, then they must create and recreate language. In addition to providing material and primitive forms for man's language and its ideal disembodiment, women must start speaking a language of their own. Insofar as women do not share language between themselves, they will face difficulties in their attempts to "be for themselves" and "be in themselves." This difficulty is crucial, since it compromises the opportunities of building a feminine world for women. The ambiguity of women's world reigns: the world of women has never been realized and it is still repressed, latent, or merely potential.

Women have served in the creation of the world of man and in the mediation of his relation to his own body and his world, but they have not been able to cultivate their own bodies, their worlds, and their expressions. Woman's lack of language and discourse has contributed to her assimilation into a male order. This assimilation has also allowed the differences among women to be reduced to the similarity of the "man's woman."

In *Éthique* Irigaray argues that the mucous is always experienced from inside and that in this respect it corresponds to the idea of the soul as an inner realm. This and the simultaneity of the forgetfulness of both woman's soul and the mucous are the reasons why Irigaray asks whether the mucous could be the place for woman's soul (E, 107/ESD, 109). The connection between the bypassed mucous and the forgotten soul of woman is the basis for Irigaray's idea of another kind of unity than the traditional idea of unity as substance or solidity. Irigaray's suggestion of woman's soul or style is "a texture of duration" ("le 'tissu' de la déploiement de la durée") (Ibid.). In this scheme the mucous serves woman herself rather than the "erection" of the male subject.

In another scheme, where the mucous and the feminine serve the masculine being, their functions look different. In Irigaray's view the mucous is a necessary for the expansion of time insofar as the masculine erects itself on it, and does not have a temporality of its own. However, in her view, despite its dependence on the mucous as its "ground," the masculine understands itself as having a solid ground which obscures the need for thinking of the mucous. This is possible because neither mucous nor fluids apply to the dominant idea of being understood according to the model of solid entities.

Irigaray further describes the properties of mucous in the following way. Mucous, discovered in the pre-discursive unity of the feminine, "loves itself only in the act," "without positing," as "half-open" (E, 108/ESD, 111). It serves for breath, singing, and love, which all relate differently to men and women. In Irigaray's view, the rejection of mucous is visible in the lack of its gestures: only "broken" and "jerky" gestures are compatible with a conception of sexuality, which Irigaray calls mechanical (*le corps machinique*) (ESD, 111, 142/E, 108, 135). This conception of sexuality divides the body into separate parts in accordance to the model of machine rather than a living organism. Furthermore, the technocratic conception of sexuality understands eroticism, distinguished from love, by quantitative measurements and external standards. In Irigaray's view, however, the gestures of mucous could harmonize love into a "progressive and durational enterprise" (ESD, 111/E, 108). Mucous characterizes the relations and movements in between the parts of one's own body, but also between the bodies of woman/woman, woman/man, man/man. According to Irigaray the feminine relates to mucous and/or the fluids in its own way. In my view, this is for two reasons. The first one is the genealogy of the experiences and meanings of the feminine as presupposition, negation, opposite, or complementary to the masculine "solidity" stemming from the idea of the male body and sexuality as "organized around the single, visible sex organ, in ways that reflect and reinforce the model of self-identical unity," as Rachel Jones puts it (2010,163). The second one is the morphology of the lived feminine body in its multiple sites of pleasure.

Woman for Herself: Writing and Phenomenological Exploration

When conceived as a stylistic unity, in the existential sense, femininity is constituted essentially in diverse relations. The subject relates to itself, to others, and to the world and has a capacity to perceive and reflect on itself in its relations. Yet, the possible sense of woman's being does not seem to be fully actualized in all these relations. Rather, it seems that only one aspect of femininity and woman's becoming is actualized: woman-for-the-other, and this only partially as woman-for-the-male-other. Yet, in lack of woman's first-person experiences and ideas of femininity and woman formed in and by them, the male third-person perspective has come to mean the "whole truth" of woman. Fortunately, (philosophical) discourse is not unitary in representing this "truth" of woman, but contains unavoidable discordances, breaks, gaps, and holes as Irigaray's activity of productive mimesis, which aims at disclosing discourse as constituted and heterogeneous, shows.

Irigaray's acts of mimicking "man's woman" and also her acts of describing, investigating, and writing the feminine first-person experience take part in the constitution of a singular feminine subject with a style in her own right. Yet, as this subject is constituted in writing, it questions the already existing meanings of woman. Moreover, in order for the feminine style to be cultivated and to flourish, no singular style is sufficient: expressions of singular women in their temporal continuity as well as relations between the expressions of singular women have to be established within the discourse.

A multiplicity and plurality of articulations of women's first-person experiences, but also their submission to the (ideal) community (of women) and its critical potentiality is necessary for the constitution of the feminine generic style. In addition to offering a possibility for woman's self-knowledge both as a singular person and as a general existence, the written articulations of feminine experience express the world as lived and modified from a new point view: the point of view of the feminine subject. As Irigaray notes in articulating the effects of Simone de Beauvoir's work,

> She gave an account of her own life while backing it up scientifically. She never stopped recounting it, bravely, at every stage. In so doing she helped many women—and men?—to be more free sexually, especially by offering them a sociocultural role model, acceptable at that time, of a woman's life, a teacher's life, a writer's life, and the life of a couple. I think she also helped them to situate themselves more objectively in relation to different moments of life. (JTNT, 9/JTN, 9)

In order not to fix the possibilities of singular woman but also women as a gender, constant rethinking and revaluing is necessary. Moreover, new habits and conventions, both when it comes to our ways of living and our ways of thinking and writing, have to be formed.

Thus, I argue that for Irigaray, phenomenological investigations of embodiment provide means for bringing the feminine as a subject and as a stylistic unity into discourse and in so doing develop it into a full-fledged style. This is effected by two passages. First, on a thematic level, Irigaray describes a specific way of experiencing and living embodiment and spirituality. Second, the lived, expressive, and self-defining feminine body is also indicated by Irigaray's own *writing*. In describing and writing she addresses the other person in his or her concreteness, but she also relates to herself as an embodied subject and as a writer constituting and constituted in time. Furthermore, by studying and criticizing the descriptions of the feminine body available in masculine discourse, and by thus disclosing the masculinity of the only perspective available in discourse, Irigaray demonstrates the embodiment of the masculine subject.

Thus, in addition to indicating the openness and relationality of the body, the pursuit of objectivity is an additional motivation for Irigaray to leave space for descriptions by others, e.g., by unanswered questions and non-concluded ends (cf. Joy 2006, 5). The ultimate aim is to constitute an open, temporally evolving written whole which is sensitive to changes in the relations with oneself, the other, and the world, but is also ideal in being, at least in principle, available for any reader independently of time and place. From the point of view of

Husserlian phenomenology, the intersubjective is constituted by diverse descriptions and articulations of experience. As in phenomenology, the intersubjective means the objective in the sense of shared meanings; the variety and extension of diverse written descriptions and articulations is crucial in striving for truth. In addition to the self-experience of the phenomenologist, the descriptions and articulations of experience issued by other writers, especially novelists and historians, form the material for investigating the general features of experience.

If the goal is not only to strive for objectivity concerning femininity and woman's becoming but also for the objectivity of bodily experience and experience in general, then it is necessary to develop expressions for feminine experience. To this end investigations and descriptions based on first-person feminine experience is needed. Moreover, in order to avoid falling back on the discourse of "man's woman," investigation into first-person experience and its temporal genesis is necessary (cf. Heinämaa 2009, 25). Also a dialogue among feminine and masculine persons as well as between feminine and masculine persons and subjects is indispensable. This community of speaking and writing subjects that criticize, comment, and complement each other's descriptions of experience and generalizations based on them should include the greatest possible variation of styles if the aim is objectivity. However, objectivity cannot be *achieved*, and the pursuit of objectivity requires dialogue and interaction with others. This is due to the temporal, perspectival, and dynamic nature of both the subject of phenomenological research and its "objects."

The relation, which most obviously includes both the perspective of woman and that of man as embodied, is the relation of love. Furthermore, love and desire disclose the process through which anything comes into being for us, as Merleau-Ponty argued. When Irigaray's view of woman as the object of desire and (carnal) love, is read against the background of Merleau-Ponty's idea of the methodological status of love and desire, we can disclose a new perspective in discussion on the sense of being as dual and its disclosure. The discourse on carnal or erotic love also exemplifies the non-unitary nature of philosophical discourse, now in a fruitful and productive manner.

Conclusions to Part I

This part has explored the sedimentation and relatively fixed structures of the feminine style and non-style as they are represented by masculine discourse. The possibility of renewal, of masculine discourse, its conceptualization of embodiment, and of woman herself, all depend partly on the first-person embodied experience of women and its expressions. However, this possibility requires that already existing conceptualizations have to be challenged, and a new specific way of inquiring into experience has to be found. For Irigaray, I suggested, this is provided by the phenomenological methodology. Phenomenological methodology and its conceptual resources facilitated these pursuits for two important ends: it was able both to question the established notions of embodiment, spirituality, and essence/existence and to open up new perspectives on woman's (and man's) first-person experience and to understand this experience in terms of embodied spirituality.

Part II

Desire

In this part I will focus on the mimetic positions of the beloved woman and female teacher. As we already saw, the relation of love is involved, in one way or another, in all the mimetic positions of woman presented by Irigaray. Accordingly, I will argue that for Irigaray carnal love is crucial for the constitution of the sense of woman and femininity.

In what follows, we will see that the position of the beloved woman includes a transformative potential of a new type when compared to the other mimetic positions: if there is a change in the relation of love then the positions of the hysteric, the mystic, and the wife also change. Love includes the mimetic position of the beloved woman and its possibilities of transformation, but love is also an emotion and a way of relating that can be cultivated and that is closely associated, even identified, with women and femininity.

In the philosophical conceptualizations of carnal love even a radical mode of sexual difference can be found. The identification of the feminine and eros, as well as the intransitivity of the positions of the beloved woman and the lover, is thematized already by Emmanuel Levinas. Levinas's articulation means that sexual difference is not a topic which is motivated from the lived experience of woman, but can arise from the perspective of a male lover or philosopher. In philosophy, carnal love is the topic which forms the grounds for Irigaray's mimesis, marks a shift in the evolvement of the mimetic positions from hysteric and mystic to the beloved one and the female teacher with her own, non-intimate, type of generativity, and also, as an intersubjective experience, opens the (philosophical) discourse for Irigaray as a woman lover in a new way.

I will show how Irigaray, by occupying mimetically the position of the beloved woman and female teacher and by modifying the discourse of carnal love from these positions, gradually transforms the meaning of woman as an object of carnal love or a resource of man's self-erection into a subject of love. Feminine expression in love and about love offers a new perspective on love, but also on its traditional male subject, who, from the point of view of a woman lover is not only spiritual but also embodied.

The figure of the beloved woman can be found in certain philosophical writings in which the body is thematized, at least implicitly, as sexually specific. As already indicated, these writings on love and desire include Plato's *Symposium* and Socrates' speech in it, and Sartre's and Levinas's phenomenological investigations of erotic relationships. Even if the philosophical discourse is quite unitary in representing "man's woman" from a distance, and as perceived in a seemingly disinterested and realistic attitude, the discourse still includes necessary discordances, breaks, gaps, and holes which can be used to problematize the conviction of the objectivity of the dominant male perspective. The heterogeneous and non-unitary discourse is disclosed by the mimetic acts that imitate the speech of the beloved woman and by the self-defined expressive acts of the woman lover.

Irigaray calls "love of the same" the "primitive" or preliminary mode of relating to the maternal-feminine or to the elemental as a resource. This mode of love, which can be more or less aware of itself, is constitutive for our self-love and has its specific role in the constitution of the subject, be it masculine or feminine. Yet, between adult persons love is essentially a relationship between two subjects as Irigaray sees it. It has, however, been (mis)represented and (mis)understood as love of the same or as a relation of the masculine subject to its feminine object in the interests of specularization and mirroring.

Still, love also includes a potentiality for transformation through interaction and dialogue. When carnal love originates from concrete interaction between two subjects instead of the one-directional relation between the subject and his illusion of woman, a new possibility of creating and transforming discourse arises. When this idea is combined with Irigaray's ethics of sexual difference, not only woman and man, masculinity and femininity, but also carnal love and love for wisdom can be understood in a new way.

The possibility of seeing both the beloved woman and love at their most potential, however, presupposes that we articulate and recognize the problems of our habitual ways of understanding, conceptualizing, and experiencing love, and that we distance ourselves from these habits. This must be accomplished in several dimensions: in relation to ourselves as persons, as well as in relation to others, and ultimately, in relation to the world. Irigaray discovers the possibilities of love as it is described in discourse through her mimetic acts, but she also develops these possibilities through her caressing style of writing which strives at the mutual fecundity of the lovers.

6

Irigaray's Account of the Beloved Woman as a "Man's Woman"

Irigaray demonstrates that despite its androcentric function and its seeming conformity with male standards, the figure and position of the beloved woman has a great transformative potentiality. The beloved woman represents a feminine gestural unity rather than disintegration and as such is connected to the first-person feminine expressivity associated with women, and thematized by Irigaray in her descriptions of singing, crying, and senseless speech. By highlighting the expressive potentiality, Irigaray further enriches the potentiality of the feminine embodied subject in its relation to itself and to other women.

∼

If we keep in mind the holistic conception of sexuality presented by Merleau-Ponty, then male desire, constitutive of the sense of mimetic woman-figures, should not be conceived only as sexual desire in the sense of the traditional narrow notion of sexuality. Indeed, the position of the beloved woman can be occupied merely for a short time. The temporal character of this position is necessarily episodic, since the position is formed primarily in the process of falling in love or in an act of making love in a narrow sense rather than in a free, unrestricted companionship between whole persons, which, of course, also can include the intensification of desire and love in the act of making love. The beloved woman is suitable for the masculine desire both in terms of sexual needs and the needs in the broader sense of (maternal) care and (emotional) nourishment: she offers support for the masculine love of self (*l'amour de soi*) by maintaining the self-image of the male person/subject as lovable (cf. Firestone 1979, 122–123, 131).

Furthermore, in Irigaray's view, woman, both as a potential mother and as a beloved woman in the sexual act, represents the place for man from which to desire and to which to desire. The beloved woman forms such a place for man both concretely and symbolically. Woman's functioning as a supporting ground and as a reflective surface to man's self-posited goals is essentially one-directional: the positions of the lover and the beloved woman are not interchangeable in these relations.

The mimetic positions of the hysteric, the wife, and the mystic are constituted also in their own desire for the male desire. To submit to the male norm of desirability becomes the aim and ideal for feminine being (cf. Beauvoir [1949] 1976, 540; Firestone 1979, 127, 129). This can occur to the extent that woman's own advantage is seriously compromised, as in hysteria. Margaret Whitford (1991a, 71), for example, formulates the connection of the hysteric and love in the following manner: "In hysteria, the subject of enunciation whose discourse is always directed towards the 'you' for validation is willing to produce symptoms, if that will obtain the desired result (love)."

In order to be desired or loved, woman has to submit herself to norms given by man. The norms of desirability are culturally coded, but as Irigaray's work shows, the male perspective is dominant in most cultures. The male norms of desirability can be found for example in literature but also in philosophical writings, which define what woman essentially is or is not, and what she should be. In addition to how she is documented in writings and images of various kinds, the norm of woman's lovability is mediated by the practices and aims of education, both in the family and in public institutions, but it is also transmitted through everyday interaction and communication (cf. Heinämaa 2009, 18).

As many feminists and feminists philosophers in addition to Irigaray have noted, being desirable in man's eyes tends to function as the only ideal for woman's success. The male ideal of a desirable woman directs the ideas of woman's good life, feminine aesthetic, and moral beauty. Lacking other aims and ideals, women easily internalize the "man's woman" and its ideals of desirability, and mistake it as her own identity and self-posited aim. This bias inherent in feminine identity has an effect on woman's self-relation as well as on her relations with other women and with men. In all such relations love, in the sense that Irigaray understands it, can be either actualized or not.

In this framework man's love for himself and love between men are both possible because the woman functions as a necessary object of exchange and as a supporting ground and resource. In Irigaray's view the constitution of masculine commonality "represents the love of a production by assimilation and mediation of the female or the females" (ESD, 100/E, 100).

Irigaray's point is that the beloved woman does not love herself as a woman, as a daughter, and as a mother. In her view, "love of the self in its feminine mode" (*l'amour de soi sur le versant féminine*) has, historically, been, and still is, complex and difficult to establish because "a whole history separates her [woman] from the love of herself" (ESD, 65/E, 68). This is because, "the female has been used in the constitution of man's love of self" (ESD, 62/E, 65). The feminine other is lovable insofar as she or he is suitable for the needs and desires of the male lover, e.g., insofar as she supports the idea of the male lover as a disincarnate self. It is even questionable whether the beloved woman is able to love man: "How can woman love man without loving herself?" Irigaray asks (ESD, 66/E, 68). In fact, in Irigaray's view, she cannot. Neither is man's self-love actualized in its whole potentiality.

The Narrow Notion of Sexuality: Masculine Sexuality and its Counterpart

The mode of embodiment that characterizes "man's woman" as constituted by male desire implies a narrow, instrumental, notion of sexuality. The narrow notion of sexuality is focused on the sexual act or intercourse and it understands this act according to a model which is based on the morphology of the male body. Irigaray calls this model the relaxation-discharge model (*détente-décharge, tension-décharge*) defined by the primacy of the orgasm of the male body (E, 135, 65/ESD, 143, 61; PE, 123). According to this model, the sexual encounter has an external aim in the generation of (male) offspring, and in the orgasm it satisfies the fulfilment of pleasure. The concept of movement characteristic to this notion of sexuality is movement as orientation toward a pre-posited external goal (ESD, 101/E, 100; ED, 136 cf. BN, 501/EN, 425). In this mode of love the external goal or product is posited at the cost of immediacy and presence, the "here" and "now" of the self-other relation (EP, 92/PE, 113).

In the narrow, instrumental understanding of sexuality, the body is conceived as an instrument that serves in striving for the pre-posited, external goal of reproduction and orgasm rather than having inherent aims or directionality of its own, which in the sexual encounter could intend towards another body, another person, or another desire. Irigaray points out that when the body and sexuality are understood instrumentally they are modelled by a machine rather than by an organism. According to Irigaray, the dominant focus on genital sexuality is a form of disincarnation, even if it focuses on the body and disregards spirituality (E, 135/ESD, 143; PE 96). The model of the machine separates sexuality from the sensuality of embodiment and its inherent possibilities, and thus also from the possibility of cultivating the relation between two sensual subjects.

Irigaray argues that man's sexual morphology has had a fundamental effect on the general idea of sexuality (ESD, 64/E, 67). In her description, the male sexual organ is experienced as an external tool-like entity and masculine desire is directed teleologically toward a goal which is external to the activity of caressing and loving. Moreover, man's self-love can be realized in loving only one part of the self, which, according to Irigaray, conforms "principally to the dominant sexual model" (ESD, 61/E, 64). Irigaray also claims that a structural difference of feminine and masculine auto-affection, and a structural difference in relating to the other person in the sexual act (narrowly defined), can be found in feminine and masculine bodies. In her view, the auto-affection of the feminine body is interrupted, not mimicked, by the male organ, while the auto-affection of masculine body is mimicked in sexual intercourse.

By these explications Irigaray argues that the dominant mode of sexuality in discourse is masculine and that this conceptual bias has remained unrecognized throughout the centuries. Thus one could think that the masculine mode of embodiment forms a less problematic basis for the instrumentalization and fragmentation of the body. Yet, the masculine body is also a lived body, which is not reducible to these instrumental concepts and norms, and it too might suffer from alienation when submitted to them.

The masculine wish to maintain a virile self-image shapes man's expectations and projections toward woman, not only toward the beloved woman (who might cease to be one in the case of sexual disappointment) but also toward the woman who has fulfilled her task of testifying man's virility by becoming the mother of his son. Thus, woman is valued only as a potential mother who serves in the reproduction of children (ESD, 63, 98–100/E, 66). Irigaray characterizes this aspect of the erotic relation between man and woman by saying that the problems that man has in the establishment of self-love through other means than through his sexual virility produce "social and intellectual pretension," "a show of overconfidence," and "exaggeration of the importance of erection in seduction" (ESD, 62–63/E, 66).

The overemphasis on the importance of an erection compensates for the lack of sexual *love*, and male fecundity is shown by the reproduction of the child, which is a proof of a man's virility. In its current form man's self-love is based on a combination of a restricted mode of temporality and affection. Work, home, wife, and children understood and loved as extensions of man are also required for man to love himself (E, 65/ESD, 62).

The figure of the mother also has another important function. According to Irigaray, the male version of self-love is realized through woman and through the search for the "first home" (ESD, 60/E, 64). The lost primary female other, the (M)other, is sought in other women. These others form an endless series of women who are substitutes for each other: none of them can provide that return to the first relation, which was initially sought by the male subject (ESD, 61/E, 64). Only God can give a similar illusion of the fulfillment of all needs. Thus, the figure of the (M)other is confused or associated with that of God but in an inarticulate way (ESD, 61/E, 64).

The idea of an other, who is perfect for my purposes, God or (M)other is constructed within the subject's sphere of ownness and similarity. This sphere, however, is not recognized as such. In this way God/the Ideal, functions as the guarantee for symbolic systems, language, and signs. It is posited as external to the world but conceived of as a creator that guarantees the cohesion of the world by giving it an ultimate meaning (ESD, 139/E, 131–132). The ultimate ends of the undifferentiated love of the same and love of God are structurally the same.

The structure of subjectivity thus constituted—the complete transcendence of the Other with regard to the Subject—is thus questioned by Irigaray. In her view the beloved woman is loved as a replica which reminds one of the omnipotent but undistinguished (M)other, but she is able to become merely a mother, and thus she suffers the cost of this setting in being compared and submitted to the perfection of God. For Irigaray, the relation of love which uses woman as a resource or object and love of God both support the masculine subject's illusionary idea of itself and of love. Woman as the "raw material" for the constitution of the masculine subject is, however, "raw" or "pure" only in the projections of the masculine imaginary. In reality the feminine has its own original structure and unity of meaning; it is already constituted as meaningful—a pre-discursive gesticulation and gestation of the feminine lived body as we earlier saw. Thus, what is indispensable for the masculine subject in carnal love, is the feminine as lack of a fully developed style rather than the feminine as raw material.

The Act of the Beloved Woman: Seduction

In Irigaray's view, because "man's woman" is constituted in relation to male desire, woman does not have a space or means to develop her own desire. This also holds for the beloved woman. Irigaray argues that when woman has internalized the ideal of "man's woman" she does not experience herself as a dwelling place from which to desire and to which to return. She does not have any place of attraction and support for herself. Thus, "woman tends *toward* without any return to herself as the place where something positive can be elaborated" (ESD, 9/E, 16). According to Irigaray, the (internal) space which could function as a locus of woman's self-love is dedicated to man, child, and household[1] (E, 72/ESD, 70).

Instead of desiring, expressing her desire, and loving herself, woman suffers, ultimately from disintegration and paralysis with regard to herself. So these problems of disintegration and paralysis hinder the cultivation of feminine embodied subjectivity, but paradoxically, do not prevent woman from being a beloved woman. For the male-lover the beloved woman's muteness or "primitive" expression is not a problem. Rather, inexpressivity and lack of meaningful expression are crucial for the lovability of the beloved woman: the beloved woman is desirable exactly *because* she expresses male desire rather than her own.

This idea of lovability can be found in traditional descriptions of love which do not allow for the possibility that the beloved woman would have her own independent meanings and expressions of love. The figure of the beloved woman as capricious, incoherent, irresponsible, animal-like, and childlike is an incarnation of the male idea and ideal of the erotic. The beloved woman is unable to express her desire in loving relations, let alone to include her expressions into the discourse on love. Being alienated from herself she does not know herself and she cannot be anticipated or relied on either by herself or by men. Or, she is considered inconstant and capricious, one to whom thought and interior life remain strange, but who is asked by man to bring him out of himself through her games of seduction (ED, 106/TBT, 58; cf. Grosz 1989, 139). Yet, the perspective of the productive mimetic could show that woman's unreliable, capricious, and non-anticipated behavior is motivated by the contradiction of her condition: being the celebrated and desirable beloved woman on the one hand, and experiencing herself as inferior to her lover on the other.

The activity related to the figure of "man's woman," especially the beloved woman, is seduction. Seduction can be focused on sexuality but it can also extend to any dimension of subjectivity. In both cases, the crucial feature of seduction is that it only acknowledges that some aspects of a person are manifested while the person as a whole remains unrecognized: the seduced person is reduced to that what is expected and wished from her, i.e., that which is considered as seductive by the lover. In the case of seduction the uniqueness and wholeness of the seduced person's style of being is disregarded.

This partial and selective perception of another person is very different from the recognition of the other as a source of original meanings which overflows any meanings given by the perceiving subject in her or his temporality and freedom. But it can also extend to a person's perception of herself and be the *only* affect of "a mechanical doll for lovemaking" (ESD, 146/E, 138), as Irigaray's puts it. Irigaray further writes: "The seductiveness that woman or women exert over people is rarely a *for herself or themselves*. It serves rather to uproot the female from her condition of *in self* [. . .] by transforming her into a *for the other* [. . .]" (ESD, 146/E, 138).

The attitude of the lover is crucial here but so also is the attitude of the beloved woman. The lover's attitude can "disclose" and address the beloved woman as a resource, as an object, as material, as a projective surface, or else his attitude can "disclose" and address her as another lover. The interested perception of another person is to be distinguished from such perception in which the other person overflows the interests of the perceiving subject. In this kind of affective perception the other person is perceived in his or her temporality and freedom.

The Effects of Irigaray's Writing as a Beloved Woman

These varieties of possibilities in the phenomenological discourse of carnal love are, however, disclosed almost only by Irigaray's mimetic acts of expression created while occupying the position of the beloved woman in relation to the texts of Sartre and Levinas. Yet, as we will see, also Merleau-Ponty's writings offer some material for elaborating such possibilities. The expected and anticipated (feminine) behavior of the seduced is described in Sartre's account of desire and the caress in *L'être et le néant* and in Levinas's phenomenology of eros in *Totalité et infini*. Before Irigaray's readings of Sartre's and Levinas's accounts of carnal love, Irigaray also mimetically takes the position of the beloved woman. From *Ce sexe*, *Amante marine* and *Passions élémentaires* we can find Irigaray as a beloved woman in an amorous relation.

The beloved woman of these works, however, is not yet developed into a position from which to form a dialogue with a male lover. Rather, she expresses her despair and discontent but without a particular interlocutor apart from herself and the reader. In *Ce sexe*, for example, Irigaray addresses herself and the reader:

> What has become of me? 'I love' lies in wait for the other. Has he swallowed me up? Spat me out? Taken me? Left me? Locked me up? Thrown me out? What's he like now? No longer (like) me? When he tells me 'I love you' is he giving me back? Or is he giving himself in that form? His? Mine? The same? Another? But then where am I, what have I become? (TS, 206/CS, 206)

In this passage the beloved woman, thanks to the shifts in meaning already established by other mimetic exercises, has already begun to doubt herself and the motivations of her seducer. She has also started to suspect whether seduction exhausts all the possibilities of loving. Yet, the emphasis is still on the relation to oneself rather than on the relationship between self and other.

Passions élémentaires continues this questioning of a disillusioned beloved woman. Here, as in *Ce sexe*, Irigaray takes the position of a beloved woman and speaks mimetically in a way which makes her engagements evident: she is always already within an erotic relation rather than speaking from an external position about it. Yet, in order to modify and cultivate love, the position of the beloved woman has to be changed *from inside*, since the beloved woman has no opportunity to break out from the closed couple. As the quotations above show, the beloved woman is neither capable nor is she expected or encouraged to express herself within the confines of the closed couple.

In *Passions élémentaires* Irigaray as a beloved woman explains that she has sung, cried, and spoken, but has not been heard let alone understood: "And

I was speaking, but you did not hear"; "Et je parlais mais tu n'entendais pas" (PE, 9/EP, 9). The feminine lover sings and cries because her speech is not heard and her writing is not read, despite all her attempts. In crying and singing, the feminine lover expresses herself in a manner that can be interpreted as simply hysterical. But when Irigaray, acting as a productive mimetic, expresses these feelings of desperation and anguish in the public discourse of philosophy rather than in the privacy of the kitchen or the bedroom, the interpretation proves problematic. Her first-personal "elemental" expressions give an alternative source and standard for the hysteric's disintegration: the unity of feminine expression. Rather than acting "childish" or being "out of her senses," she tries to be heard as a woman, as herself, in a situation that makes this almost impossible, but not quite.

Paradoxically, Irigaray creates the possibility for woman to be heard as herself, and to become herself, by articulating this impossibility within the confines of discourse. Both the beloved woman/hysteric and Irigaray as a beloved woman/mimetic show their dissatisfaction with living a love relation as it is established. This dissatisfaction already gives clues of feminine desire and its expressions. In this way, Irigaray shows against expectations that woman crying and singing can have and does have sense. Irigaray as the productive mimetic opens a perspective from which a woman can realize that she occupies or easily falls into the position of the beloved woman. Through this distancing the position of the beloved woman is disclosed as one possibility among several: the ideal of "man's woman" and the aim to be desirable for man are put into a new, critical perspective.

In addition to expressing feminine desire in carnal love, Irigaray, as a productive mimetic, also shows a possibility for a concrete interrelation. Being heard as a woman and becoming a woman, opens a possibility of a dialogue between the two: "[s]peaking (as) woman would, among other things, permit women to speak *to* men . . ." (TS, 136/CS, 134).[2] I will argue that the possibility of interrelation is also included in masculine discourse in its descriptions of erotic love, which thematize the feminine body. This opening offers a possibility of rethinking erotic love within discourse and to question love as a relationship of reflection, mirroring or "usurpation" of the resources offered by the other.

7

Opening up the Possibility of Woman's Self-Love and Love among Women

*The male-defined figure of the beloved woman (*aimé*) affects women's relations to themselves and to each other, argues Irigaray. The articulation of these effects to feminine love of self and to love among women opens up a possibility of rethinking and reliving relations between women. It does this by offering the means to distance oneself from this specific and celebrated role of the beloved woman as it may have been internalized by us. But the articulation also opens up the possibility of redefining ourselves and encourages us to experience love as the self-defined subjects of our affective lives. This possibility already presupposes the recognition and acknowledgment of the full potentiality of the feminine lived body, its sexuality and expressivity. Irigaray's criticism of the actualized modes of feminine love of self and love among women, and her articulations of their potentiality, contribute to the development of feminine style and self-definition by offering means for greater differentiation and self-knowledge for individual women in our relations to ourselves and other women.*

∽

Irigaray argues that for woman to be able to love herself and other women, she has, initially, to distance herself from what she has become: from being a mere body or a resource for the (male) other. The cultivation of the feminine expressivity is necessary if women are to be separated from each other and emerge as independent subjects, i.e., in order to develop feminine style. This means that the critical task is not just directed at the masculine perspective for woman, but also at women's self-images. Moreover, explorations on the relationship between woman's self-images and conceptions, on the one hand, and feminine auto-affectivity, i.e., the first-person sense of one's bodily and affective being, on the other, are necessary.

The first task is to focus attention to feminine embodiment in its relations to other feminine bodies. According to Irigaray, women, who identify themselves as "man's women" should become aware of themselves as daughters and potential mothers, and should also realize their relations to other daughters and to potential mothers. Woman's self-love can only be cultivated within these relations. For the realization of this task Irigaray creates a new vocabulary, which is based on the feminine embodiment and affectivity as it is experienced by woman herself. For example, in Irigaray's view, each woman should be able to love herself and thus be capable of providing an "envelope" to a child, and also able to love herself as someone who has been nourished by such an "envelope" offered by her own mother (ESD, 105).

Furthermore, Irigaray argues that "an openness which allows access to difference" should be brought into the mother-daughter relationship (ESD, 69, 112/E, 71, 109). She warns that without an opening, the "envelope" easily becomes a trap which locks the mother and the daughter into one unit (ESD, 105/E, 103). The differentiation can be supported by cultural models and by new ideals of mother-daughter relation, but it also requires a modification of the woman-man relation.

The second task is connected to the first: woman is to be distinguished from male ideals or projections. Moreover, it is also necessary that woman's singular body is distinguished from the anonymous embodiment of the maternal-feminine. Irigaray discovers in the pre-Socratic Greece of Homer an affirmation of the body and its connection with the masculine, but she states that this sense of being a body as a source of individuation, and the affirmation of embodiment as such has been forgotten (E, 99/ESD, 99; see also Jones 2010, 70). For Irigaray the problem is that the body is not affirmed and respected as a particular body but is merely acknowledged as anonymous materiality, which functions as a "ground for erecting space-time." According to Irigaray this interest in anonymous materiality is transformed into "the architecture of the world or world(s), into a system of symbolic and mercantile exchanges"; it is transformed into "fabrication and creation of tools and products" (ESD, 100/E, 99). This means that "[g]ermination, birth and growth according to natural economy" is substituted by the artificial instrument and product and their modes of unity (ESD, 100/E, 99). The elemental embodiment conceptualized as pure matter is associated with the maternal.

In fact, it seems to me, that for Irigaray, there is some truth in this identification: we, as women and men arise from the silent and supportive gesticulation and gestation of a maternal body, its flesh and blood (ESD, 97/E, 97). The elemental maternal functions of nourishing, life-giving, and caring on which we are dependent as embodied subjects are not recognized in the scheme of traditional idea of subjectivity. By perceiving and affirming the body, and especially the maternal body, so that it no longer represents the inferior side of any hierarchy but is acknowledged as a generative force, the problematic traditional identification between woman and body can be dismantled, but also reconsidered. This necessity for giving the generative powers of especially the maternal body the place that it deserves in our accounts of ourselves as human beings is emphasized by Rachel Jones in her study on Irigaray's critique of the tradition of Western philosophy in *Speculum* (Jones 2010, 136–148).

I will later argue that Irigaray's critical discussion on Sartre's philosophy of intersubjective relations supports the interpretation that Irigaray does not presuppose maternal-material as a non-meaningful ground, but on the contrary questions the idea of pure matter as a fundamental conception of Western metaphysics (see also Jones 2010). It is the misidentification of the maternal-feminine as "pure matter" that produces the problem of the nonrecognition and unacknowledgment of the silent support of the mother's gestation and gesticulation. Within the discourse of love of the same, the maternal-material functions as the passage and mediation between matter and form as well as appearance and idea, but it also serves as a ground for these hierarchical distinctions. It is both "the waters," the element that fills the empty spaces between solid things, and also "the firmament" needed for the solidity to "erect" itself (ESD, 98/E, 98). In Irigaray's words "love of the same is love of that which will not know itself as differentiated (unless we rethink the whole of the history of philosophy)" (ESD, 97/E, 97). The nonrecognition of the function of the maternal-feminine and its nature leaves in obscurity the diverse relations that women and men have to embodiment. The consequences of this nonrecognition and unacknowledgment, such as undifferentiated "symbiotic" or fusional relations, are different for man and woman. Yet, in all cases, they are equally destructive for love relations between the two.

The realization of the distinction between the feminine and the maternal presupposes feminine expression. Expression, for its part, is dependent on the lived body. Ultimately it is the feminine lived and expressive body, the preliminary feminine unity, which can by its cultivation show that the bodies and expressions of man and woman are distinct even if there is no explicit awareness of their difference and separation: "Scarcely does she know herself, scarcely does she begin to glimpse nostalgia for herself—her *odyssey*. To be able to tell her tears from those of Ulysses. *Not because they were weeping the same tears* but because she took part in his quest for love for himself" (ESD, 71/E, 73, latter italics mine). It is woman's participation in man's search for himself and the resulting illusionary view of both sexes that obscures the possibility of a feminine style. But it is exactly the original unity of feminine gestures that resists the reduction of the feminine to anonymous materiality and to the needs and desires of the male body. In order to transform the relation of the sexes, the original unity has to be brought into discourse and this is possible by first-person acts of expression: the beloved woman needs to become a woman lover.

Irigaray emphasizes that our modes of loving ourselves should be rethought: "who loves who" is different in woman's case and in man's case. Irigaray even questions the adequacy of the formulation "love of self" in her descriptions of woman's self-love. She writes:

> *Love of self* creates a particular movement, a kind of play between active and passive, in which, between me and me, there takes place this double relationship, neither active nor truly passive. I do not set a completely inchoate material into motion. The material is, in some measure, already given. Neither the subject nor the self is fixed in its position or its given, otherwise the two would be separated without any possibility of love. A liaison takes place which corresponds to no other coded or codable operation: neither active nor passive nor middle-passive, even if this operation is the closest. (ESD, 59/E, 63)

This is because woman cannot relate to herself as an object. Moreover, she does not *see* her sex or herself as desiring. Irigaray explains: who loves who in woman's case is different: she cannot love herself as an object, but perhaps as an innerness, a place or passage, and its movement (ESD, 69–70/E, 72), and further: "Woman is loved/loves herself through the children she *gives birth to*, that she *brings out*" (ESD, 63/E, 66).

Irigaray's descriptions of the experience of feminine love of self are missing from the confines of the dominant discourse. They become possible only by the problematization of woman's position and the prevalent notions of the bodily experience of love and the self-love presupposed in them, phenomenological descriptions of embodiment and amorous relations included. According to Irigaray, the possibility of feminine love of self "is left in the shadow of a *pre-object*, and in the suffering and abandonment of the fusional state which fails to emerge as a subject" (ESD, 70/E, 72, italics in the original). This is because other goals than woman in-herself and for-herself are valued both by men and women themselves. This fusional state can only be developed and cultivated into feminine self-love and love between women if woman is "no longer [to] depend on man's return for her self-love. Or at least not absolutely" (ESD, 65/E, 68). Irigaray also characterizes this mode of self-love, in accordance with her characterization of the feminine "style," as nonthetic ("l'amour de soi non thétique") (ESD, 112/E, 109).

Irigaray emphasizes that it is difficult to establish love among women. What is particularly problematic in the woman's situation is that the daughter has to abandon her love for the mother in order to be able to love her father or a man, as Freud's theory of sexuality argues (ESD, 101/E, 100). This leads to a relation of substitution between the mother by the daughter and to rivalry and hate between them. The position of the mother is unique, and (in the current order) becoming a mother means that this place has to be taken without any support between mother and the daughter (as a mother) (ESD, 102/E, 101).

The rivalry between the mother and the daughter results from man's problematic relation to the maternal, on the one hand, and from the lack of full-fledged feminine identity on the other. In order to be desired by man, woman has to take the position of his mother and abandon both herself as a woman and also abandon her own mother. Thus the mother and daughter figure as rivals with respect to men, yet also as accomplices in their own abandonment. This situation paralyses the love between women already in its initial stage and establishes and supports instead the privilege of love between mother and son. The situation reduces the maternal function to the service of the generation of a son rather than a daughter or woman's own renewal.

The abandonment contributes to the constitution of the male commonality by exchange of women. Creation of feminine commonality, i.e., love between women, can correct the biased situation which is founded on the dominance of the male perspective in the constitution of the sense of woman. The conditions of love between women can only be established by acknowledging symbolically the fact that women support life with their bodies, by their gestation and gesticulation, and by marking it symbolically. In Irigaray's view, what women give does not have the symbolic form of a product and thus, lacking other modes of comprehending what giving could mean, remains a resource for free use (ESD, 103/E, 102).

Also an interval of "exchange" between women is required for love between women to actualize itself. This can be established by speeches and nonverbal gestures, by a symbolism which corresponds to the feminine body (E, 103/ESD, 105). This symbolism helps women to distance and separate themselves from the relations of rivalry with the real mother, from the position of (M)other and from the desire of man, father, son, or brother. Thus, Irigaray argues that language and the discourse must be modified so that they become capable of expressing feminine embodied and affective experience. This is necessary so that women can be many, so that women could form a community and have access to society and culture. In my view, this requirement is necessary because the feminine and embodiment form the most marginalized and "excluded" dimensions of discourse. When these two elements are combined with the aim of questioning the basic structures of discursivity, as Irigaray does, they would provide great subversive potential.

For Irigaray, not only mothers and daughters, but also women should love one another "both as mothers with maternal love and as daughters with filial love. Both of them; and in a female whole that, furthermore, is not closed off. Constituting, perhaps, both of them in one female whole that, furthermore, is not closed up, the sign of infinity? Achieving, through their relations with each other, a path into infinity that is always open, in-finite" (ESD, 105, 111–112/E, 103). Thus, Irigaray argues that the woman lover must be aware not only of the infinite nature of the sexually other, but also of the infinite nature of herself and the other of the same gender. This also holds true for the erotic relationships between women, but it is not restricted to them; and what is at stake is holistic, rather than the narrow notion of sexuality (see Lehtinen 2001). In my view, this is possible only if the feminine gender, and not just the individuals constituting it, is understood as an open and infinite whole. This demand is met if woman's being is understood as a stylistic unity, constituted by individual styles.

I argue here that Irigaray's conception of woman is not unitary and closed but is constituted of differences and connections between women. The feminine style of individual expressions only becomes perceivable when expressions are numerous and diverse enough. Relations to other women and to the mother are necessary for woman's self-knowledge. These are constituted in and by language. Only by acknowledging the perspectives of other women and by incorporating them into herself can a woman perceive her own life realistically as a woman and examine and widen the range of her possibilities. A realistic perception of oneself is assisted by knowledge of the habitual position and stereotyped notion of one's gender with regard to male desire provided by feminist articulations and analysis of the feminine condition. For these reasons Irigaray writes that nowadays "[w]omen want to find themselves, discover themselves and their own identity. Which is why they are seeking each other out, loving each other, associating with each other. At least until the world changes. As the historical moment indispensable for women, as the period necessary to achieve love?" (ESD, 66/E, 69).

8

Male Phenomenologists' Promise of the Uniqueness of Woman in Carnal Love

The fact that women as gestural, expressive unities can be found in the masculine discourse provides a specific constitutive possibility. The idea and experience of a feminine gestural unity is necessary for the development of the feminine as an independent style and form in its own right.

For Irigaray, the specificity of women as a gender in carnal love provides a possibility for formulating a philosophical conception of carnal love in which a woman would be considered a unique person, a particular woman. I find such a conception in Irigaray's work, but the idea of the uniqueness of the feminine other figures already in the early work of Emmanuel Levinas. Levinas characterizes the positions of the subject and his (feminine) other of the erotic relation in *Temps et l'autre* (1947) as follows:

> Does a situation exist where the alterity of the other appears in its purity? Does a situation exist where the other would not have alterity only as a reverse side of its identity, would not comply only with the Platonic law of participation where every term contains a sameness and through this sameness contains the Other? Is there not a situation where alterity would be borne by a being in a positive sense, as essence? What is the alterity that does not purely or simply enter into the opposition of two species of the same genus? I think the absolutely contrary contrary [*le contraire absolument contraire*], whose contrariety is in no way affected by the

relationship that can be established between it and its correlative, the contrariety that permits its terms to remain absolutely other, is the *feminine*. (TO, 85/TA, 77)

The connection between Irigaray's and Levinas's thinking is pointed out by Irigaray herself, through her readings of Levinas's works, but it is also emphasized by many Irigaray scholars and other feminist philosophers. Against this background, it seems that Irigaray's critique of Levinas is internal in its approach and appreciates Levinas's insightful articulation of sexual difference and eros. If this holds, then we can say that Irigaray criticizes the solutions that Levinas offers but does not interrogate his questions or his goals (Sandford 2000, 5; cf. Chanter 1995, 202, 208–209; Heinämaa 2003, 90; Chanter 1995, 202, 208–209 cf. Joy 2006, 56, 57, 64).

As we will see in what follows: even if the beloved woman is not seen as a self-defined expressive unity, a subject, in erotic relations, she is not just desired as a "body." This means that the possibility of a certain unique existence is implicitly attributed to the beloved woman. The philosophical descriptions of love that Irigaray discusses correspond to the perception of woman as lacking full-fledged stylistic integrity. Yet, in these descriptions woman does not appear as fragmented or incoherent as she does in the figure of the hysteric; instead, she is able to express herself in a relatively unified, primitive rather than (only in) a fragmented manner.

It seems to me that in contrast to the descriptions of hysteria, philosophical descriptions of carnal love allow woman a certain coherence in her own terms: a primitive and pre-discursive expressive unity of embodiment and affectivity is attributed to her in those descriptions. This primitive unity of meaning is necessary for woman to be desirable at all. Merleau-Ponty explicates this idea by pointing out that one does not fall in love with a madwoman; one can love a madwoman only if one has fallen in love with her before her falling into madness (PP, 195/POP, 167).

Moreover, even the paralyzed and fragmented gestures of the hysteric whose "illness" Irigaray questions can be harmonized by love found in the self or received from the other person into a gestural unity. This support offered by love to the fragmented unities of words and gestures also structures Irigaray's work. Her own position as the beloved woman differs from that of the hysteric in its primitive unity. This unity is constituted by modes of expression, which remind one of the rhythms and intonations of singing and crying and stem from the first-person expressive body instead of stemming from (internalized) an other person's or culture's expectations.

In addition to Merleau-Ponty, Sartre also emphasizes that we only can love embodied consciousness. According to Sartre, the love relation requires that the other is taken and intended as a consciousness, a freedom capable of choosing me and not someone else. Even the aims and goals of the lover reflect this freedom: the lover does not simply wish to possess the beloved woman physically, but, in Sartre's view, he also wants to "capture a consciousness"[1] (EN, 406/BN, 478). Sartre distinguishes between "merely" sexual relationship and an erotic relationship of love without sexual acts as well as the combination of the two. He makes clear that when the beloved woman is intended as an object of merely sexual desire she is only desired as a body that can be substituted by any other body. Yet, both relationships include the other as desirable, lovable, or both and thus presuppose that she has her own unity of embodied-spiritual experiences. Monika Langer explains in the following way Sartre's idea of sexual desire: "In desire, incarnate consciousness projects itself toward a concrete human individual, rather than toward a lifeless thing. Thus, reciprocal incarnation [expressed according to Sartre by the caress] presupposes an awareness of the humanness and the otherness of the object of desire" (Langer 1998, 110; cf.109).

Carnal love implicitly presupposes that the object of love, the provider of offspring, and the one who is taken to guarantee their nourishment, care, and education is a unity of spiritual-embodied life. Levinas emphasizes this by arguing that while the beloved woman loses her face and the unity of her expression in the erotic encounter, the erotic relation still requires that she has been a face and will be a face.

As a bodily-spiritual unity the other is a concrete other; potentially graspable or caressable by look, touch, or both. Love and desire are established in the sphere of intersubjective relations by the gesture of the caress. In caress, the other can be touched and respected in his or her temporality and openness but can never be totally grasped or comprehended: he or she cannot be totalized. Affective intentionality refers to a fundamental layer of experience: before positing objects of consciousness or goals of orientation in movement, we are withdrawn or attracted by lived bodies and things depending on their subjective and intersubjective meanings. This means that the caress can be understood as a manifestation of fundamental affective intentionality, which takes place between two lived bodies united in desire. Goal-oriented operative intentionality, which is characteristic of the situational body, is suspended in desire. Thus, the caress, as it is described by the phenomenologists, opens the possibility of a concrete interaction in the nonteleological practice of love, but it also offers a discursive possibility.

Irigaray develops her concept of the caress on the basis of her inquiries of the feminine lived body and its expressive possibilities, but she also uses the descriptions of the caress provided by Sartre and Levinas. In Irigaray's writings, the criticism of other accounts of the caress and her own positive account are intertwined. I, however, will first present her positive account of the caress. Then I will proceed to study Sartre's and Levinas's accounts of carnal love and the critique that Irigaray launches against them. Irigaray's approach to Sartre's and Levinas's accounts of desire and the caress deviates from the basic mode of approaching the philosophers' texts precisely in its positivity and in the attempt to form a dialogue rather than a scholarly investigation. Irigaray's attempt to be fertilized by the other text without losing oneself is also here exemplary for her idea of the intersubjectivity of the couple.

9

The Continuum of Caressing Gestures in Accordance with the Holistic Conception of Sexuality

Also a possibility of developing new modes of relating to male others both in prediscursive experience and in the discourse are opened: as "primitively" expressive, the figure of the beloved woman offers a possibility for a concrete interaction—instead of a specular relation—with the sexually other through the gesture of the caress.

∾

In Irigaray's work, the theme of the caress is taken up in discussions of Levinas, Sartre, and Merleau-Ponty in *Éthique*, "Questions à Emmanuel Lévinas sur la divinité de l'amour" and *Être deux*. The caress is connected to Irigaray's own idea and figure of the lips, which is emblematic of feminine sexuality, embodiment, and expression, and the critique implied in it to the phenomenological notion of experience. The position given to the caress by Irigaray implies a critique of the central position of the phenomenon of the double touch—a touch of oneself by oneself—in the phenomenology of the body. Even though a person can caress him- or herself, the caress obtains its sense primarily from the caress which occurs between two persons and thus the caress forms a concrete possibility for building intersubjectivity between woman and man.

For Irigaray, the caress is not restricted to the relation of voluptuosity between two persons, but refers back to the primary relation with the mother: the mother is the first person whose touch we experience (ESD, 186/E, 174). This touch can be effectuated by a hand, as when a mother takes care of her baby. For Irigaray the caressing touch, however, also refers to the touch by which the whole body of woman by its surrounding, even overwhelming, presence and rhythms of movement caresses the unborn child. The caressing touch also refers to the elemental dimension of nature, experienced as enjoyment, but deviates from the attitude constitutive of operations in the world of instruments. The two latter modes of the (maternal) caress are implied in the caress which occurs between woman and man. Their different relations to embodiment, sexuality, and to the mother is reflected in the ways of caressing but also, Irigaray claims, in conceptualizing the caress.

In later sections I will show how Sartre's and Levinas's ideas exemplify Irigaray's point on the idea and gesture of the caress having its origin in the male body. Before that, however, let us explore how Irigaray herself describes the caress in accordance with her desire or will as a woman, as being "more careful about intersubjectivity," as she puts it (ED, 50/TBT, 24).

Irigaray argues that the caress is potentially constituted at all levels of subjectivity and language. As we will see, Irigaray's caressing attitude and the caress as its gesture can in principle structure any dimension of life and subjectivity. Thus, the concept of the subject at issue is a broad one: it covers all dimensions of subjectivity from movement and affectivity to thought, from pre-discursive gestures to verbal expressions in speech and writing.

The caress is necessary in the process in which the subject is constituted and it is crucial to the movements in which the possibility of a feminine subject is opened up. The intentionality of the caress makes possible pre-discursive experience, which occurs between two separate persons but in which the subject-object distinction is dissolved. This is why, according to Irigaray, in voluptuousness we are able to renew the relation to ourselves but also to the other: to open up the possibility of sexual difference. In Irigaray's view, voluptuousness or sensual pleasure can "reopen and reverse this conception and construction of the world. It can return to the evanescence of subject and object. To the lifting of all schemas by which the other is defined. Made graspable by this definition. *Eros* can arrive at that innocence which has never taken place with the other as other" (ESD, 185–186/E, 173). The gesture of the caress gives us flesh and spirit, the actual and potential at the same time: "searching for what has not yet come into being for himself, he invites me to become what I have not yet become," Irigaray formulates (ESD, 187/E, 175).

Thus, for Irigaray, the caressing mode of relating does not remain only within the voluptuous but can also make possible a new type of intersubjectivity without abandoning voluptuousness. Voluptuousness as well as its feminine modification in the caress reopens the space-time of fecundity. For Irigaray, fecundity means "generosity without calculations" (ESD, 25/E, 32). Fecundity of the soul and the body, created in the caress, is a possibility which has "never been understood," according to Irigaray (ESD, 25/E, 32).

For Irigaray, the caress is "a gesture between us," which is "neither active nor passive" (TBT, 25/ED, 53). The caress is "an awakening of gestures, of perceptions that are at the same time acts, intentions and emotions" (TBT, 25/ED, 53). Described in this way, the caress refers to the lived body as thoroughly intentional and capable of opening toward the other. For Irigaray, the caress represents an "intersubjectivity of I-me and I-you," a relation between two subjects capable of saying "I" and "you" (TBT, 27–28/ED, 54–55). The caress is an address and an invitation to the other and as such it invokes our common history as persons, and as women and men. The caress is an invitation to the other but also an invitation to return to oneself and cultivate one's own integrity (TBT, 27/ ED, 52).

Irigaray characterizes the caress as a gesture-word (*geste-parole*), which silently or in speech or writing asks: "Who are you?" (ED, 40, 51/TBT, 26). By the address, the caress is able to transcend the immediacy and the interestedness of the self and its sphere of ownness. As a *geste-parole* the caress belongs to the sphere of intimacy but it also transcends this sphere and belongs to the intersubjective, that which opens toward others in communication and dialogue (ED, 51/TBT, 26). As an intersubjective gesture the caress requires the consent of both partners (ED, 52/TBT, 26). It fails if the other or the self loses itself or subjects itself passively to the other's intentions. As such, Irigaray's caress presupposes the integrity of both lovers, but it also cultivates this integrity. In the caress, both lovers can exist as concrete and whole instead of being fantasized, neutralized, or fabricated (ED, 52/TBT, 26).

Rather than being motivated by economic goals, considerations of use, or sexual desire narrowly understood, Irigaray's gesture of caress is contemplative and inherently motivated by the fecundity of intersubjective relations. The caress as Irigaray sees it presupposes a particular kind of generous attitude both in respect to our personal tendencies to reduce the other and use him or her as a resource, and in respect to the reductive tendencies of our philosophical discourse.

10

The Philosophical Discourses of Carnal Love

Obstacles and Openings for the Becoming of a Woman Lover

Irigaray's detailed critiques of the three philosophies of carnal love demonstrate how in each case the beloved woman is understood and addressed as a mute or "primitively" expressive subject. In this way, her criticism points at the inadequacy of the classical phenomenological articulation of eros, which fails to take into account the potentiality of the self-defined feminine embodied, sexual, and spiritual experience.

But the inclusion of the feminine beloved in the discourses established by Sartre, Levinas and Plato (Socrates) is the reason which allows a woman—Irigaray—to express discursively, as a woman and not as a neuter, her lack of satisfaction with the classical descriptions of woman. Moreover, another interesting constitutive possibility arises in the following tension: woman is denied full expressivity but the idea of an erotic relation implies that she has her own spirituality.

~

As Irigaray's analysis of "man's woman" shows, even in carnal love, woman and the feminine are often presented as resources or objects. This representation of woman and the feminine can be found, for example, in the philosophical works of Sartre and Levinas, as well as in Plato's presentation of Socrates' philosophy in *Symposium*. Yet, in Irigaray's interpretation, these works also indicate another possibility based on the promise of woman's uniqueness in carnal love. As we will see, in carnal love, woman cannot be substituted by a man. Instead, woman is expected to be feminine according to the standards of the male ideal of woman. Thus, in carnal love, woman is intended as "man's woman": she is expected to differ from man but not to deviate from his ideals. My argument is that the specificity of the feminine gender is integral and crucial to carnal love, and that this is exactly the reason why Irigaray focuses her critique on the philosophies of carnal love.

Carnal love as a theme and a topic provides Irigaray access to discourse as a woman rather than as a neuter. As such, carnal love provides an ideal opportunity for Irigaray's productive mimesis. Yet, carnal love as a theme and practice is not exhausted by Irigaray's productive mimesis. This is because the feminine expressive body is already implicated in the above-mentioned philosophical descriptions and discourses of carnal love, and thus the task posited by Irigaray for productive mimesis—to indicate the feminine lived and expressive body—is fulfilled by masculine discourse itself. By implicating the expressive feminine body, masculine discourse on love offers a possibility to create concrete interaction and dialogue between man and woman. Thus, even if the feminine expressive body is inadequately or misleadingly presented, since it is only primitively expressive and definitely not a body of a woman writer, a female teacher, or a woman philosopher, the philosophical discussion of erotic love provides a possibility to develop a feminine style on the basis of feminine gestural unity.

Irigaray picks up this possibility of woman as an embodied-spiritual unity offered by the (philosophical) discourse in her descriptions on woman and love, and also in her acts of describing. We have already seen a glimpse of this in Irigaray's idea of the continuum of the caressing gestures. In this chapter I will present the accounts of carnal love issued by Sartre and Levinas, as well as Socrates' discourse on eros in Plato's *Symposium* and Irigaray's criticism launched against them.

Before addressing Sartre's and Levinas's discussions on carnal love and Irigaray's critique of them, a methodological remark must be made. Irigaray's critique focuses on the thematic results of Sartre's and Levinas's descriptions and analyses but it also problematizes their terminological and conceptual choices which are constitutive for their ways of writing. My methodology reflects this duality. The aim is to study and illuminate the unity and the breaks of Irigaray's own discourse and to contrast it to the homogeneity of the discourses of Sartre and Levinas. In contrast to Penelope Deutscher (2002, 149, 151), who argues that the homogeneity of Sartre's and Levinas's discourses in Irigaray's work results from Irigaray's totalizing way of reading their works, I argue that the homogeneity results from the similarities in their ideas of carnal love. As I see it, these similarities originate from their unquestioned assumptions inherited from Platonic metaphysics.[1]

Sartre's Conception of Carnal Love as an Impasse

Sartre's conceptions of desire and love in *L'être et le néant* (1943) are based on his distinction between the subject, consciousness (for-itself), and the object, facticity, or body (in-itself). Sartre investigates the "primitive" relations between the self and the other in terms of (1) love, language and masochism and (2) indifference, desire, hate, and sadism. For Sartre, these attitudes can both be mixed and included in one another. Sartre's discussion of these topics contributes to the general aim of describing the existential subject in all its essential dimensions.

All of these attitudes are based on an initial conflict which cannot be solved: the positions of the subject and the object can be occupied in various ways and they move constantly but they cannot be undone. The subject may, for example, want to be captured by the other or may want to capture the other depending on his "chosen attitude." In Sartre's account, the crucial means for gaining freedom and making the other lose it is the gaze. When acting in these relations, the subject does not aim at maintaining the tension between him- or herself and the Other, but tries to dissolve it and to conflate the duality of freedoms into a single transcendence (*une même transcendance*). Sartre points out that it is inherently paradoxical to try to become a single transcendence, since the Other's capacity to justify the subject's existence would be cancelled or undone along with his otherness (BN, 477/EN, 406). Despite this impossibility, the singular transcendence is a regulative principle of interpersonal relations in Sartre's account. In his description, the attitude of love includes this illusionary aim in its most intensified form.

Seduction and Substitution

According to Sartre, the positions of the subject or lover and the object or beloved woman are interchangeable: they can be occupied by both partners and thus the constellations change constantly. Seducing is mutual. For Sartre "the body is the totality of meaningful relations to the world" (BN, 452; cf. Langer 1998, 105). Accordingly, sexuality is discovered as "a 'skeleton' upon which all human relations are constructed," as Monika Langer (1998, 107,109; BN, 527) formulates it. Despite its dualistic structures, Sartre's understanding of sexuality does not contain any distinction between man or woman or the masculine and the feminine. Sartre does not give any explicit consideration to the question of sexual specificity, he just states that the sexual organization of the body is contingent (BN, 515–516). In Sartre's view, "woman and man *equally exist*" (BN, 498/EN, 423, italics mine).

For Sartre, in love both the lover and the beloved woman want to be objects for one another. In love the other's freedom is the main objective of the lover. This is why the subjectivity of the Other must remain intact: otherwise there would not be anyone who could give the value of the self as the origin of the world ("l'objet-fond sur quoi le monde se détache"), as an end in itself (*la valeur absolue*), rather than as an instrument for achieving an end (*l'ustensilité*). Sartre emphasizes that only thing-objects can be fully grasped by consciousness and be used as tools for its purposes. The other as a beloved woman cannot be fully grasped or instrumentalized, since she as an Other can make the I into an object by her gaze and can (at least temporarily) overflow the I's power to make her into an object.

Sartre notes that it is in love that this ontological capacity of the Other is best revealed and, according to his examples, this is both for better and for worse: there is no inherent morality in Sartre's conception of carnal love. Sartre presents an example of a woman who is in love (*l'amant*), and demands that the man that she loves (*l'aimé*) sacrifice traditional moral values for her sake, even if this means that the lover would destroy himself. She is anxious to know if the man would betray his friends for her, if he would steal for her and even kill for her in order to affirm her as the value of all values (*le fondement objectif de toutes les valeurs*) (EN, 409–410/BN, 481–482).

Sartre argues that the objective of love is the reciprocal wish to be loved. To love is to establish the beloved woman as the foundation and the center of one's existence and to expect the beloved woman to do the same. At the same time, the beloved woman cannot will to love the lover, or vice versa, since if she forms the foundation for the lover, and the lover becomes an object to her, the lover cannot provide a foundation to her subjectivity. This basic conflict is the reason why seduction (*séduction*) is the activity and language of love for Sartre (EN, 411/BN, 484).

Other's Expressivity

The idea of seduction as the proper activity of love depends on the essential freedom of the consciousness of the Other. Seduction is needed because of the conflictual aims of the beloved woman and the lover. Through seduction I try to avoid showing the subjectivity of the other to him or her, and I can also try to be constituted as an object for the Other by not looking at him or her. In seduction I aim at appropriating the Other by taking on the status of the object or thing, and thus I try to bring the Other's consciousness and my consciousness into one single consciousness. The "primitive" expression of the seducer differs from the more articulated forms of language: it is capable of bringing about experience and not just knowing (BN, 484–486/EN, 411–413). In order to clarify Sartre's conception of language, let us study his description in *L'être et le néant*. All expression exposes the I to the Other and to the Other's aims of possessing me. To wit, the I is language in the sense that whatever it's acts are, and transcends the possibilities of these acts by obtaining external meanings from the Other. These meanings escape the I's power and are experienced as possession effectuated by the Other (vrt BN sivut EN 414/BN). For Sartre, the Other's freedom of interpreting my expression is primary, rather than my freedom of expressing myself: the Other has a position of dominance. According to Sartre, "language reveals the freedom of the one who listens in silence" (BN, 486/EN, 414). For Sartre there is no path which departs from my object-state that can lead to the other to my transcendence. He writes: "Attitudes, expressions and words can only indicate to him other attitudes, other expressions and other words" (BN, 487/ EN, 414). All expressions, words, and gestures are implicit references to the Other's alienating existence, in other words to the interpretations and meanings that the Other provides for my expressions. Rather than serving as a means of contact or communication, language makes visible the radical alterity of the Other: no contact is ultimately possible.

Thus, instead of considering language as a means of communication, Sartre argues that language fundamentally exposes the separating line between the I and the Other. This conception leads Sartre to talk about the unpredictable meanings provided by the Other in the negative sense and to characterize language as theft of thought (*un vol de pensée*) (BN, 487/EN, 414). The meanings of language are provided by the Other and thus I need the Other to manifest my thoughts. Yet, the Self does not address the Other or speak to him or her, let alone discuss with him or her while in desiring nor while describing desire. Free consciousness holds the secrets of its intended meanings, expressed in words and gestures, and the Other lends his own intentions to his gestures and words of consciousness. Although the Other is claimed to escape the meanings provided by me by his transcendence, Sartre considers this primarily as a failure of my project of grasping him.

The ungraspability of the other's consciousness manifests itself also in my attempts to seduce the other: it can only succeed through interaction. The free consciousness of the Other makes me "blind," since I cannot know what my expressions mean to the other (BN, 511/EN, 434). I cannot hear my own words and I cannot see myself smiling; I am incapable of seeing my body or hearing my own speech in the way that the other sees and hears it (BN, 487/EN, 414). So, Sartre argues that "the problem of language is parallel to the problem of bodies, and the description which is valid in one case is valid in the other" (BN, 487/EN, 414).

The Desired Body as Inert Flesh

For Sartre, desire is a specific mode of subjectivity: the relation between consciousness and facticity in desire is very different from the relation that characterizes the subject that chooses itself as metaphysical, i.e., as indifferent and unchanging. In desire, the consciousness loses its transparency and becomes opaque (cf. Joy 2006, 13). Thus it can be compared to troubled water which is blurred by something that cannot be perceived or distinguished from the water. Sartre differentiates desire from the "clear and distinct appetites" of hunger and thirst (BN, 503/EN, 427). In other words, a new mode of existing as consciousness and embodiment is constituted in desire. Expressions such as "overtaken" (*il vous prend*), "overwhelmed" (*il vous submerge*) and "paralyzed" (*il vous transit*) designate the existential function of desire: in desire consciousness "chooses to exist its facticity on a different plane" (BN, 504–505/EN, 428). Rather than transcending its facticity and the contingency of the body, or trying to escape from them, the desiring for-itself attempts to exist in its own facticity and contingency in order to apprehend the body of the other insofar as it is flesh, pure facticity. Monika Langer explains that for Sartre "[t]he pre-reflective bodily cogito, usually overlooked, is here [in desire] experienced. The body alone 'knows' how to reach the other in his flesh" (Langer 1998, 109). The object of desire is another human being, a body in a situation, an organic totality including a consciousness but also a body in the world among other bodies (EN, 434/BN, 511–512).

More specifically, Sartre claims that his account of desire is able to account for why "we" desire a "particular woman" (*une femme*), a transcendent object (*l'objet transcendant*), and "not simply our sexual satisfaction" (*notre assouvissement*) (BN, 500/EN, 425). As desired the body differs from its usual mode of lived embodiment in being pure facticity, flesh. Normally it belongs to a situation, and as an instrument or a point of view it transcends toward its possibilities and toward the object. Whether an instrument, a point of view, or a correlate of desire, the other's body is an experienced whole which must be distinguished from the physiological, objectified body of the sciences but also from the anonymous materiality presupposed by metaphysics.

Sartre argues that desire is nonreflective (*irréfléchi*) and as such cannot "posit itself as an object to be overcome" (BN, 500/EN, 425). Sartre explains that in desire the subject attempts to strip his own body and the body of the other from spontaneous movements and to make both exist as pure flesh. Thus, in desire, consciousness makes itself flesh (*chair*) in order to incarnate the Other's consciousness (BN, 507/EN, 430). Thus it tries to enclose the Other's consciousness within the limits of a thing, to "ensnare" it into a body, touched and possessed as such (BN, 508, 510/EN, 431, 434). This goal, however, can only be obtained as an illusionary result of a fleeting moment. In this sense, desire turns out to be impossible in Sartre's conception. The freedom of the Other is manifested in his capacity to escape these attempts to "seize" and "take hold" of him or her. These attempts imply the possibility that the other makes me an object.

Caress as Possession of the Other's Freedom

For Sartre, the caress is a concretization of the attempt to "appropriate" the Other's body and to "possess" her freedom (BN, 506/EN, 429). The caress attempts to incarnate the Other and to "ensnare" the Other into his or her flesh. My caressing hand, like all desire, tries to make my own body mere flesh in order to touch the other's body in its own passivity and pleasure; by caressing itself with the other's body rather than by caressing her (BN, 509/EN, 432). For Sartre, flesh means nakedness: the body is stripped of its spontaneous movements. The "clothing" of the movement makes the naked dancer appear covered. The caressing gesture is not restricted to the sense of touch; a look can be caressing, if it "claims to fulfill desire."

In its initial phase, the caress does not aim at taking hold but rather aims at "placing one's own body against the Other's body" (*porter son proper corps contre le corps de l'autre*). Sartre further specifies: "Not so much to push or to touch in the active sense but to place against" (BN, 507–508/EN, 431). Sartre writes that "I place it [my hand] against the flank of the desired woman" (BN, 508/EN). Whereas a look and a stroke remain focused on the surface of the body, the caress shapes the body and gives it a new mode of being. The caress does not just shape the Other's body, it also modifies one's own body. So the caress reveals both the self and the other as carnal, and moreover, it reveals both as flesh. The caress is a double reciprocal incarnation (*double incarnation réciproque*) (BN, 508/EN, 431).

In distinction from the gaze and language, the caress in this initial phase opens a possibility of concrete interaction by problematizing the habitual positions of the subject and object. Sartre does not explicate this possibility but Glen Mazis, in revising Sartre's conception of the caress, does: "it is not the case that through the caress one is reduced to a fascinating object for the other as subject, but rather one is affirmed and affirming through this reciprocity as a separate coexistence. Rather than the caress being a reduction of the living possibilities from the flesh—a 'stripping away' to make it 'pure being-there' as Sartre said—it is an attempt to touch in both an emotional and literal way these possibilities as affirmed through the body" (Mazis 1998, 150). The caress also provides a temporary transformation of our relation to the surrounding world. Whereas the active, manipulating body in its operative intentionality reveals the world of instruments, the caress reveals the world as flesh. Langer explains, "[f]lesh is neither pure spontaneity nor inert 'matter' " (Langer 1998, 107; BN, 506). The "fleshy body" revealed in the caress gives us an immediately sensible elemental world: "a breath of the wind, rays of sunshine posited upon me without distance and revealing my flesh with their flesh" (BN, 509/EN, 432). This revelation of the immediately sensible in desire leads Sartre to think that desire is not only a blockage of consciousness, but is also an "ensnarement" of the body by the world (*l'engluement d'un corps par le monde*) (BN, 509/ EN, 432; cf. SP, 69, 70). All the attempts of the consciousness to exist itself in facticity and contingency are effectuated in order to "to possess the Other's transcendence as pure transcendence and at the same time as a body."

For Sartre, the caress is a temporally episodic occurrence also when it belongs and contributes to a specific intimate encounter: the caress can always turn into a grasp and the caressed hand can subsequently be grasped. This is why desire, mediated by the gesture of caress, refers to its possible failure in nausea and sadism. Sartre writes: "desire continues naturally not by caresses but by acts of taking and penetrating" (BN, 516/EN, 438). However, taking hold, seizing, and entering the other's body also transforms one's own body into a synthetic instrument, to be apprehended as a body in situation, no longer as flesh (BN, 516/EN, 438). Ultimately, the possibilities disclosed by Sartre's analysis of the caress are (1) the body as an instrument, (2) the body as a point of view, and (3) the body as passive and immanent flesh (BN, 505/EN, 429).

Irigaray's Challenge: The Inauthenticity of Sartre's Descriptions

Irigaray challenges the seeming neutrality of Sartre's dialectics. By assuming the position of the beloved woman in her address to and inquiry into Sartre's descriptions of erotic relations, Irigaray argues and shows that Sartre writes about carnal relations as if the Other were a feminine Other (ED, 37).[2] This occurs in an unacknowledged manner: in Sartre's examples woman constantly occupies the position of the object of man's desire, even though she is an object whose freedom is at stake. In addition to Sartre's specification that the transcendent object of desire is a woman, he also implicates the femininity of the beloved woman in his examples and formulations. As we saw, Sartre indicates by textual means that the subject of the description as well as the reader is a man, similar to himself. Woman cannot occupy these positions despite the seeming neutrality of the description. In order to do so, she would have to question not just the philosophical content of Sartre's work but also the textual means of delivering this content.

Sartre's Distinction: The Body and the Soul

While Sartre thematizes the body in a way which implicates sexual difference, his conceptual and terminological choices do not provide means for developing these possibilities. Irigaray argues that Sartre's dualistic ontology and the idea of the radical non-attainability of the Other produce the play of seduction as the activity of love and desire. For her, the idea of the Other as radically transcendent is a problem, and she shows that this idea is motivated by a specific strain of the philosophical tradition: the Platonic doctrine of ideas. According to Irigaray, Sartre exemplifies Western philosophers in thinking that consciousness completely transcends the body and in assuming that the Other is beyond all perception[3] (TBT, 17/ED, 37).

For Sartre, Irigaray writes, "the other is facticity, a present objective reality that stands beside me. As such, the other can be both touched and seen. Yet, the other is also consciousness, and, as such, the other transcends his/her body" (TBT, 17/ED, 36). Further she emphasizes that the idea of a dualism between body and consciousness is very strange and inadequate when studying desire, and she writes: "This male philosopher represents the impossible ideal of desire in the following way: the transcendence of the other is to be possessed as pure transcendence inaccessible to sensible experience, but nevertheless as body" (TBT, 18/ED, 37). This makes Irigaray wonder how a carnal relationship is possible at all (TBT, 18/ED, 36). Sartre's answer is that the other's consciousness must be manifested in her body and thus becomes touchable, and this manifestation is accomplished by my own acts (TBT, 18/ED, 36–37) On the basis of this, Irigaray claims that Sartre's *L'être et le néant* offers us only "enchantement"—seduction—as a starting point for finding a possibility of relationship: in desire the self tries to enchant the other in order to make him desire. It is through seduction that the consciousness of the other is made manifest by its descending to the body and can be possessed (TBT, 18/ED, 37).

The Problematic Goal of Desire

For Irigaray, the main problem of Sartre's account of desire is his idea of "taking" or possessing" the Other's free subjectivity as the aim of desire. According to Irigaray, the "chase for the other's freedom loses the mystery of the other" (ED, 37/TBT, 18). As such desire can only be directed at oneself, at the own and the similar, at the same (ED, 38/TBT, 18). The identification of the subject with its other only leaves one possibility: the aim to dominate the other, who is perceived primarily as a threat.

An alternative account in Sartre of the significance of the conflict underlying all intersubjective relations, including carnal love and the caress, is presented by Monika Langer. She claims that Sartre's aim is to accentuate the distinctness and uniqueness of the self and the other, and no hostility is necessarily included (Langer 1998, 111). Langer's reading, however, does not explain why Sartre's terminology, which is devoid of positive characterizations, leads to reading his account in the mode suggested by Irigaray.

From Irigaray's point of view it is evident that when carnal love is taken to aim at the possession of the other in his freedom, then all realization of sensibility is lost and nausea takes its place (ED, 54 /TBT, 28). Furthermore, Irigaray argues that the aim of grasping the other, whether through the mediation of the touch, the gaze, or comprehension, is not a gesture that would allow for or guarantee the other's freedom: there is no caress in such grasping or possessing as Irigaray understands it (ED, 40/TBT, 20). Debra Bergoffen (1997, 26) argues that it is due to the lack of reciprocity that the caress in Sartre's work is "either relegated to the role of foreplay or sacrificed to the erotics of sadism or masochism." Another possibility would be to perceive and affirm the other in her difference, which opens up the possibility of the ethics of love[4] (Bergoffen 1997, 217).

On the basis of my analysis of Irigaray's critique, it seems that Sartre's remarks on language connected to love and desire can be questioned in two fundamental respects. The first problem concerns the mode of (non-)interaction and non-reciprocity between the subject and the object. Because Sartre does not understand language as communication in desire and love, he is led to exaggerate the transcendence and non-attainability of the other. How is the experience of the otherness of the Other possible if his consciousness radically transcends both his body and his speech? What else does the self have except images and meanings created by him- or herself, if the other cannot accurately speak for her- or himself when addressed? Further, if the Other is not an other, but rather a not-me, then nothing seems to prevent endless substitution of one object of desire by another. This structure of substitution is articulated by Sartre's account of a collective, anonymous intersubjectivity, as Irigaray points out: as a worker or as a citizen I am equal and can be substituted by any other (ED, 70–71; EN, 475–476).

Femininity and Neutrality

The second problem in Sartre's account is the position of the feminine other in the general structure of intersubjective relations. In Sartre's self-understanding his descriptions of love and desire are sexually neutral. Yet, the feminine other figures in his illustrations and examples without her being included in the discussion of other modes of being subject. This also holds for language insofar as it corresponds to the "being-for-the-others," as Sartre understands it: while language is explained to mean "being-for-the-others," only a "primitive" language of seduction is attributed to the feminine other.

It is seduction that effectuates the collapse of the general structure of intersubjectivity and subjectivity and establishes a different form of relating. Seduction, practiced in relation to the feminine other furthers the collapse of subjectivity and intersubjectivity, which amounts to a loss of subjectivity. If this analysis holds, then the feminine person is not an Other in the proper sense of the word but intermediates between some kind of ambiguous and ambivalent alterity of the other and alterity of the matter or "being-in-itself" in Sartre's terms. This ambiguity is not explicit in Sartre's scheme, but is exposed by Irigaray's close reading.

Irigaray says that Sartre's conception of the Other, as a consciousness transcending its own body, does not correspond to incarnate speech; and incarnate speech, for its part, is indispensable for the couple to avoid fusion and to remain two.

Moreover, the more articulated forms of language are also unable to serve and promote the encounter with the Other. Lacking expression except the "primitive" mode of expression characteristic of seduction, the Other can be substituted by any other and by the idols of the subject himself. For Sartre carnal love does not include an Other capable of challenging the subject and his aims, and this is why it can only be characterized as an intensification of sensibility, understood as negativity and quantitativity. It is understood as a collapse of subjectivity rather than as a mode of subjectivity.

According to Irigaray, the seeds of the failure to think existence as an intertwinement of embodiment and spirituality are already to be found in Sartre's idea of consciousness as pure transcendence and pure freedom, and in his corresponding idea of the body as pure facticity. These starting points lead Sartre to understand the soul-body dualism in terms of possession. According to Irigaray, Sartre's ontology leads us to an idea of sensations (TBT, 23/ED, 47), in which sensibility is connected to quantity, death, and negativity; and the elements are seen as modes of materiality that trap or ensnare the body in the world rather than as nourishing and sustaining it. The idea of possession as the goal of carnal love also motivates the conflict as one of the modifications of love. For Sartre, the ontological impossibility or failure of desire depends on the conflictual nature of the self-other relation. But as Irigaray argues, it is not that he finds a conflictual ontology through his analysis of concrete relations, rather it seems that he ignores those features of concrete relations that would lead to another direction.

In Irigaray's view, conflict as the structure of the self-other relation is not necessary or fundamental as Sartre believes. The conflict can be resolved by questioning the aim of appropriating the other's liberty. The objectifying gaze is not the primary gesture of the intersubjective encounter (TBT, 19/ED, 31). Rather, Irigaray argues, we should realize that the conflictual ontology and its culmination in an objectifying gaze presuppose another type of gaze: the affectionate gaze of the mother, which makes space for subjective becoming and also affirms this becoming. The maternal fundament is ignored by Sartre, as it has been ignored by his predecessors (TBT, 31/ED, 59; cf. Deutscher 2002, 149).

The omission of the maternal fundament points to a more fundamental problem: the facticity and passivity of the body (TBT, 32, 37/ED, 62, 69). Irigaray attacks Sartre's understanding of the lived body. According to her, the intentionality of the body in the mother-child relation is reciprocal: affective bodily intentionality is operative in the consciousness of the mother, in her loving gaze that is directed at the child, and it is also operative in the attention of the child directed at the mother (ED, 59, 61). On the basis of this, Irigaray claims that parental intentions are inscribed in our bodies. They are reawakened in the later relations of love and desire, and if we want to understand these emotions we must take the genealogy of the affections into account. Only by articulating and cultivating the parental intentions inscribed in our affective systems can we distance ourselves from the assumption that they are simply given or nonexistent. If these intentions and their genealogies are not taken into account and rethought, they never develop into intentions toward other selves. Instead, they remain infantile intentions directed at the (M)other and aim at symbiosis or fusion, repeating indefinitely the settings of the first love relation into infinity.

Ultimately, I argue, Irigaray questions the conceptual scheme of Sartre's whole enterprise through her critique of his analysis of carnal love (cf. Chanter 1995, 129; Deutscher 2002, 155). She also questions Sartre's methodology. According to Irigaray, Sartre's neglect of the lived experience of sexuality (*veçu sexuel*) leads to the problematic conception of consciousness as one and homogeneous. Sartre fails to understand the alterity of the other as well as the potentiality of the love relation in its potentiality precisely because he makes ontological assumptions and carries them into his descriptions of the phenomena. He ignores the lived sexual experience of both woman and man (ED, 38; cf. Bergoffen 1997, 27). Glen Mazis formulates a similar critique, but without any reference to sexual difference: "Sartre's descriptions of sexual intimacy are misguided [. . .] by a set of assumptions that underlie Sartre's philosophy as a whole and which he imposes on the phenomenon of sexual intimacy, rather than allowing what is distinctive about this phenomenon to reveal itself" (Mazis 1998, 144).

Levinas on Love and Eros: Need and Desire

Emmanuel Levinas gives new emphasis to the phenomenological discussion of the subject by giving the self-other relation a fundamental role in it. Levinas develops further the implications of the subject's embodiment and finitude and explicates them in terms of vulnerability and responsibility in the face of the Other. He discloses the primordial layers of subjectivity by studying the relations of "enjoying in the elemental," "dwelling in the hospitality of the feminine," and "needing nourishment." He argues that the subject is able to reach transcendence through "labor" and "possession," and thus establish a relation to discourse and truth, which both presuppose the Other. Levinas calls "metaphysical desire" the movement in which the subject is constituted as free. Metaphysical desire is fundamentally distinct from need and lack: it cannot be fulfilled, not even in principle. Desire only grows richer and stronger in desiring and does not fade away. The face of the Other is the correlate of metaphysical desire: in metaphysical desire a person is approached as an Other and not as an object of need. In Levinas's view, the face of the Other is meaningful in a manner that differs from all other expressions. Levinas characterizes the meaning of the expressive face as follows: "To signify is not equivalent to presenting oneself as a sign, but to expressing oneself, that is, in presenting oneself in person. [. . .]. In the face the existent par excellence presents itself. And the whole body—a hand or a curve of the shoulder—can express as the face" (TIE, 262/ TI, 293). In Levinas's account we listen to the Other, his "call," in order to reveal his face. The face is not seen but is heard. In my view, the emphasis on listening is meant to convey that the face cannot be understood as revealed once and for all. Speech, as the presence of the face of the Other, unfolds in time and escapes from the meanings, which are given to it at any one point in time. The Other is characterized by the spatial terms of "asymmetry" and "height": for Levinas the Other is primary and the self is responsible to it.

In addition to Levinas's description of metaphysical desire, the relationship with the Other is best described as disinterested love. Examples of the persons that we can love in this way include "the stranger, the widow, the orphan" (TIE, 251/TI, 281). In such relations, I am responsible to the Other, who is needy. The figures of the stranger, the widow and the orphan differ from the "neighbor," who is a partner in reciprocal exchange in need. According to Levinas, the structure of reciprocity also characterizes the relation with the beloved woman (TIE, 254/TI, 285).

Levinas argues that love is essentially ambiguous. This is because love requires a balance between the opposites of object of need vs. an absolute outside, sensibility vs. transcendence, modesty vs. immodesty. When characterizing love he emphasizes that it is structured by the Platonic division between carnal and spiritual love, which is maintained and affirmed by the Christian tradition (TIE, 255/TI, 285). In Levinas's view love can be placed between need and metaphysical desire. He motivates this claim by the notion that the self knows beforehand what it seeks in love (TIE, 254/TI, 285). The intention of the self is predetermined and the other is already known insofar as he or she is assumed to respond and to fulfil the need of the lover. Edith Wyschogrod (2000, 126) interestingly points out that love and knowledge are similar in one crucial respect: both "seek to be reunited with an object to which we have already been bound." In my view, this similarity of structure stems from the idea of Platonic eros and from its basis in the idea of knowledge as recollection (TIE, 254, 270/TI 285, 302; cf. TIE, 63/TI 57–58).

Metaphysical desire and disinterested love transcend the sphere of the self and the similar (*the same, le même*), but need cannot do this. Because eros wavers between metaphysical desire and need, love is not purely a relation to the absolute Other. Love is an in-between state to the extent that ambiguity of need and desire itself has become erotic (TI, 284–285/TIE, 254–255). The ambiguity of love explains why, in Levinas's view, both spiritual love and carnal love do not and cannot concern the origin of significance—the absolute Other, the face of the Other which only manifests itself in ethical relation and disinterested love. Interested love, in contrast to disinterested love, is needy whether its object is spiritual or material. Thus, Levinas claims that the structure of ambiguity characterizes both modes of erotic love: spiritual and carnal. Their similarity becomes evident when they are compared to disinterested, non-erotic, love (TIE, 251, 255/TI, 281, 285).

Eros and the Feminine

The face as the correlate of metaphysical desire is presupposed in eros, but is also dissolved. The presupposition of the Other as a face distinguishes need, which belongs to eros, from non-erotic need in the sense of hunger and thirst. As love presupposes a face it also presupposes discourse, but it "falls short of it" (TIE, 254/TI, 284). Insofar as eros transcends the sphere of the self toward the other, it presupposes transcendent other who is not reducible to an object of need. Levinas's eros is "love for the love of the other," and not an act of loving the other, and as such it reminds one of Sartre's idea of the objective of love. Eros requires self-love, and thus means a return to the self; in this sense eros is a "dual egoism" (*egoïsm à deux*), closed to itself (TIE, 266/TI, 298). This is because eros is confined by voluptuousness, and this makes it essentially an intimate relationship. Intimacy can only be established between two lovers. Voluptuousness "excludes the third party, it remains in intimacy, dual solitude, closed society, the supremely non-public" (TIE, 265/TI, 297; cf. Chanter 1995, 206). Levinas claims that no intersubjectivity is possible in this relation. Intersubjectivity for Levinas should be understood in the sense of opening toward the language, discourse, and truth through which the Other can be addressed as Other instead of similar to me or as reducible to my needs. Distancing himself from Sartre, Levinas argues that the contact established in eros does not aim at unification, but at the engendering of a child, a son (TIE, 266, 267–268/ TI, 298–299, 301). Intending a son, the couple opens itself to fecundity and the future. Fecundity is a relationship to the future understood as that which cannot be anticipated or controlled, as that which does not have its origin in the self but in the son (TIE, 267/TI, 299).

In Levinas's philosophy, the feminine represents primitive layers of subjectivity, which are presupposed in full subjectivity and personhood and which are disclosed in the dissolution of personhood in eros (cf. Perpich 2001, 35). According to Levinas, the feminine becoming of the subject transcends the idea of the subject in the self (TI, 253/TIE, 284). The dissolution of the face and of personhood in eros is an opposite development to the constitution of the face-to-face relation in discourse. Eros presupposes the face even though it does not allow the other person to reveal himself as a face because of lack of expression (TIE, 253/TI, 284). Face is respected in the ethical relation, but disrespected in eros (TIE, 262/TI, 294). In other words, the feminine, as it is described in Levinas's *Totalité et infini*, indicates the face of the Other, the face as the origin of all meaning, but is not approached as the face.

Levinas defines the beloved woman as the beloved woman or the feminine beloved one, *aimée*. The grammatical form accentuates the femininity of the beloved woman: she is "*aimé qui est aimée*" (TIE 256/TI 286). The beloved woman is "the other in her frailty" (*faiblesse*) (TIE, 256/TI, 286). Levinas characterizes the feminine in the following way: "The simultaneity or the equivocation of this fragility and this weight of non-signifyingness [. . .], heavier than the weight of the formless real, we shall term *femininity*" (TIE, 257/TI, 287). The beloved one in the feminine is not an intentional object but rather she is "[t]he secret [which] appears without appearing, not because it would appear half-way, or with reservations or in confusion" (TIE, 257). The feminine as the correlate of eros is withdrawal, not an essence nor an object to be known. The feminine is not the correlate for the intellect or expressed by "the language of seeing," which discloses its objects once and for all in their essence (TI, 257/TI, 287). Instead, the feminine is "not a this or a that; clandestinity exhausts the essence of this non-essence" (TIE, 257/TI, 287). On the basis of these descriptions, it seems that the feminine cannot be seen or heard but rather must be touched in caress, which, as a movement toward the invisible, transcends the sensible. Interestingly, here Irigarays and Levinas's ideas of the specific relation of the feminine to the tactile dimension of subjectivity connect.

The Beloved Woman as the Correlate of Caress

Levinas explains that in caress the body of the beloved woman does not manifest itself as an existent (TIE, 258/TI, 289). In eros even the body has dissolved into a non-entity in two senses: It cannot be characterized either as an object body or as a lived body. The beloved woman as a correlate of caress is not to be identified as the inert physiological body, the lived body [*corps propre*] of the operative intentionality of the "I can," nor with the body understood as expression, or face (TIE, 258/TI, 289). Instead of these, Levinas, following Sartre's idea of nudity as a body without goal-oriented movement, speaks about "erotic nudity" (TIE, 258/TI, 289). Erotic nudity exemplifies the original meanings of immodesty and profanation that are fundamental to eros and caress as its manifestation (TIE, 257/TI, 287). The ambiguity of need and desire attributed to love, the equivocal of eros, also characterizes the beloved woman in traditional terms: "The Beloved, at once graspable but intact in her nudity, beyond object and face and thus beyond the existent, abides in virginity" (TIE, 258/TI, 289).

For Levinas the activity and virility of the subject is transformed and it turns to passivity in eros through voluptuousness. When changed in this way, the subject "owes his identity not to his initiative of power, but to the passivity of love received" (TIE. 270/TI, 302). In voluptuousness the subject is "passion and trouble, constant *initiation* into a mystery rather than *initiative*" (TIE, 270/TI, 302–303). Levinas's description suggests that the subject loses its basic characteristics in voluptuosity because of the feminine other: "The relationship with the carnal and the tender precisely makes this self arise incessantly: the subject's trouble is not assumed by his mastery as a subject, but in his being moved [*attendrissement*], his effemination, which with the heroic and virile I will remember as one of those things that stand apart from 'serious things'" (TIE, 270/TI, 303).

The voluptuousness of eros is concretized in the caress. Levinas writes: "The movement of the lover before this frailty of femininity, neither pure compassion nor impassiveness, indulges in compassion, is absorbed in the complacence of the caress" (TIE, 257). The caress is an opening between a subject, which operates in a state of dissolution, and the feminine other, which brings about the dissolution.

For Levinas, the caress searches that what *is not yet*, but it is also a temporal openness to the future (TIE, 258, 264/TI 288, 296). In contrast to Sartre, Levinas argues that the caress should not be conceived as an embodied consciousness in the state of lost freedom but must be understood as a special mode of intentionality that refers to that which cannot be predicted or anticipated (TIE, 258). Yet, the openness of the caress is limited, since the caress also turns inward: "[. . .] *the common action of the sentient and the sensed* which voluptuosity accomplishes, closes, encloses, seals the society of the couple" (TIE, 265/TI, 297). In the voluptuousness of the caress "the other is not only a sensed, but in the sensed affirmed as sentient, as though one same sentiment were substantially common to me and the other" (TIE, 265/TI, 297).

Levinas's account of the caress differs from Sartre's in other respects. For Levinas the caress forms an ambivalent couple: "It is inward but intersubjectively structured, not simplifying itself into a consciousness that is one. In voluptuosity the other is me and separated from me" (TIE, 265/TI, 297). Moreover, the partners of the couple should not be characterized as compromised by freedom (TIE, 265/TI, 297). In voluptuosity the other or his freedom is not objectified nor is his freedom subordinated to the will of the lover. Instead, it is freedom that is desired and encouraged (TIE, 265/TI, 298). In contrast to Sartre, for Levinas's voluptuousness and the aim to possess are to be kept distinct from one another (TIE, 265/TI, 298).

Feminine Expressivity

According to Levinas, the feminine face in eros is connected to the beauty of art, not to the beauty of truth. It is about "false signification," "a word that bespeaks not a meaning but exhibition" (TIE, 263). Levinas writes: "The face of the beloved woman does not express the secret that eros profanes; it ceases to express, or, if one prefers, it expresses only this refusal to express, this end of discourse and of decency [. . .]" (TIE, 260/TI, 291). He characterizes the "primitive" nature of erotic expression by saying that it is due to the equivocation of the voluptuous: "In the feminine face the purity of expression is already troubled by the equivocation of the voluptuous" (TIE, 260/TI, 291). In eros "[e]xpression is inverted into indecency, already close on to the equivocal which says less than nothing, already laughter and raillery" (TIE, 260/TI, 291). Edith Wyschogrod explains the role of expression in Levinas's account of eros as follows: "The equivocacy of pleasure hovers between speech and its abandonment. What is expressed in the face of the feminine is the refusal to express. Expression is transformed into immodesty" (Wyschogrod 2000, 130).

Despite his distance from Sartre, Levinas is unable to include genuine intersubjectivity in his account of carnal love even if he recognizes the structure of intersubjectivity to be inherent in voluptuousness (cf. ED, 54). This is because genuine intersubjectivity is necessarily connected to language and communication and the regulative ideals of truth or objectivity but the erotic relationship is detached from them. Levinas writes:

> The beloved is opposed to me not as a will struggling with my own or subject to my own, but on the contrary as an irresponsible animality which does not bespeak true words. The beloved, returned to the stage of infancy without responsibility—this coquettish head, this youth, this pure life "a bit silly"—has quit her status as a person. The face fades, and in its impersonal and inexpressive neutrality is prolonged, in ambiguity, into animality. The relations with the Other are enacted in play; one plays with the Other as with a young animal. (TIE, 263/TI, 295)

It seems that Levinas accepts Sartre's notion of seduction as the primary language and activity of love. He describes the muteness of eros as follows: "The face, all straightforwardness and frankness, in its feminine epiphany dissimulates allusions, innuendos" (TIE, 264/TI, 296). Thus, eros is not manifest in expressions or discourse, but in allusions and innuendos, and is by definition ambiguous and equivocal. The language that Levinas attributes to the erotic relation has no relation to truth. It is distinguished from discourse, which is constituted by expressive acts. Ultimately, the feminine other is "the other refractory to society, member of a dual society, an intimate society, a society without language" (TIE, 265/TI, 297). To conclude, Levinas's account of eros attributes an preliminarily "intersubjective structuration" to muteness or senseless expressivity in voluptuousness but does not account for intersubjectivity extending from erotic relation to the more articulated and, in his account, potentially ethical modes of relating to the other.

Irigaray's Challenge: Levinas' Eros as a Lapse in the Dichotomous Hierarchy of the Masculine and the Feminine

Irigaray argues that there is a methodological tension in Levinas's thinking and that this tension produces the problems of his articulation of the caress and the erotic relation. Irigaray claims that Levinas's methodology is a mixture of two diverse discursive approaches. On the one hand, there is the descriptive-phenomenological method. On the other, there is a metaphysical or onto-theological conviction of the Other, which situates itself within the paternal genealogy of the father and son (QEL, 183). The genealogical aspects of his account make the supposedly neutral face of the Other appear as masculine and exclude the possibility of a feminine face (QEL, 183; cf. Sandford 2000, 39, 42). Irigaray refers to Levinas's earlier work and argues that the feminine face and the masculine face cannot substitute for one another (QEL, 179, 181, 183). The feminine other is not perceived as someone to be heard without special effort and the call of the beloved woman is not responded to; her face is not seen before it is detached from the habitual (ESD, 192, 208/E, 178–179, 191).

Irigaray claims that Levinas's account makes the erotic relation between the self and the feminine other appear as a relation of substitution but in another way than in Sartre's account. For Levinas, the lovers become parents, mother and father, instead of being transformed as woman and man. This is because a son operates as the guarantee of the fecundity of eros in Levinas's account. Irigaray interprets this by saying that that Levinas's eros remains sterile in cases where the lovers do not take the roles of the parents. These "lovers" do not form a couple regulated by the aims of remaining two and fertilizing each other. However, it is not only the lover who needs to assume his position as an ethical subject; the beloved woman also acts complicitly in this process insofar as she forgets to follow her duty to become lover instead of beloved woman (ESD, 198/E, 184).

According to Irigaray, animality, perversity, and infancy are all "appearances presupposing the feminine." They are mistakenly thought to disclose the feminine as such, but they are only capable of disclosing the feminine insofar as it is within the limits self-posited by the masculine subject (E, 192/ESD, 209). Thus, Irigaray's critique is ultimately that Levinas's discourse does not respect the feminine other, she is not respected in her identity and freedom, i.e., as another person or a subject. Woman does not have either a face or her own form of temporality. Rather, the beloved woman serves as a constituent for the temporality of the other: she conditions the future of the lover (QEL, 179). This implies the abandonment of that which is most prominent in the loving gesture: to open to the other here and now.

Irigaray claims that in Levinas's "desire-seduction," the beloved woman is a part of the lover's world or his field of activity, and lacks her own desire and expressive activity. Without language, the beloved woman remains without a "path" that would lead to herself and back to her own origin (ESD, 196/E, 182). Eros is dissociated from discourse, and thus, the beloved woman lacks language, identity, and face, which are all provided only by discourse. In my view, Irigaray's emphasis on language, which is not that of the lover's, refers to possible articulations of feminine lived experience and to a nonexistent language and discourse which would allow its expression. Lacking her own language, the beloved woman is circumscribed by a language which emerges from internal contradictions of the lover (ESD, 195–196/E, 181–182). Irigaray points out that in Levinas's account, God, but not woman, has access to discourse.

The Beloved and the Mother as Substitutable

Levinas's neglect of the expressivity of the beloved woman creates the illusion that the beloved woman can be substituted by any other woman and by a mother. Moreover, Levinas also ignores the difference and separation of the genealogies of the beloved woman and the male lover as well as their different relations to the maternal. The feminine can enter only one type of relation, i.e., the erotic, and it cannot connect the other modes of relationality and subjectivity with it. Irigaray claims that this narrow idea of the feminine other is motivated by the masculine wish that the feminine would form the site for masculine needs and expectations or provide a surface for projections. Thus, the beloved woman forms an imaginary volume that also represents an abyss, a bad infinity, and as such forms the opposite to the Transcendent God, the good infinity. This opposition can be discovered in Levinas's vocabulary, e.g., in his characterization of the caress as a "profanation." Irigaray sees this as a nostalgic notion and claims that it manifests the desire to make visible "the first dwelling place" (ESD, 188/ E, 175–176).

The confusion of the positions of the mother and the woman also arises, according to Irigaray, from the perspective of the son, with whom the lover/father identifies. Simply by his existence, the son demonstrates that the womb (of the beloved woman) is no longer accessible to the lover, as it is to the son. This realization creates the nostalgia of the lover, but he does not recognize it as such (ESD, 189/E, 177). Despite Levinas's attempt to describe the (masculine) subject as orienting toward the future, in Irigaray's view the eros of this subject is bound to nostalgia for the past. Irigaray argues that the masculine is identified with neutrality and is associated with the activity of world-constructing. As such the masculine appears as a proprietor who is oblivious of that which serves as the foundation of all constructions—the maternal-feminine (E, 190/ESD, 206–207).

An important structural feature distinguishes Levinas's account of eros from the ethical relationship: whereas the ethical relation is openness to the infinity of Other, the erotic relation is identified with the couple as a closed totality.[5] However, Irigaray argues that this closure comes from the orientation towards an external goal, a son, and from the failure of relating eros to the discourse and is not essential to carnal love as such. Moreover, she points out that the couple, as Levinas describes it, is not symmetrical. The beloved woman (*aimée*) remains in the anonymity of love, but the lover (*amant*) is able to enter into an ethical relation through eros (E, 175/ESD, 187). Thus, Irigaray claims that despite his good intentions Levinas repeats the traditional idea of the hierarchy of sexual positions.

Edith Wyschogrod provides a more positive interpretation of Levinas's phenomenology of eros and woman's position in it. She argues that "[w]oman can be 'interlocutor' and teacher; but in her feminine role she is disingenuous, elusive, seductive, and dangerous. The failure is not hers but belongs to the infraethical status of the erotic itself" (Wyschogrod 2000, 131). Wyschogrod's interpretation is challenging, but she does not take into account the asymmetry of woman and man with regard to the carnal: in other words, she disregards the fact that in the masculine discourse woman is associated with body and materiality. Correspondingly, she also neglects the identification of neutrality and humanity with masculinity.

Irigaray argues that if metaphysics could be surpassed, then carnal love could provide woman with a face. She claims that the surpassing of metaphysics would create a possibility for woman to discover her face and to maintain it (E, 184). I take this to mean that a descriptive-phenomenological approach could be fruitful if it could be purified of all metaphysical factors: if all onto-theological assumptions could be put aside, then a feminine person could appear as herself. It seems that Irigaray conceives of love as an attitude which, by the activity of abstaining from habitual notions of the self and the other, lets the other become her- or himself. A radical reinterpretation of the established conceptions and practices of carnal love could also lead to "the other, to the feminine, god, or a new stage of spirituality or rationality" (QEL, 183).

Eros and Caress: A Possibility of Renewal?

Irigaray follows Levinas in arguing that the possibility of renewal is to be found in eros and the caress, and in their structure of being in-between. This emphasis can also be found from Diane Perpich (2001, 42), who describes Levinas's caress "as an incessant recommencement of the movement toward the other."[6] But, Perpich notes, if the caress does not reach the feminine other in its incessant movement, the ego is left to its solitude. Levinas characterizes eros by saying that it lingers between immanence and transcendence and between need and desire. He calls eros ambiguous and equivocal but does not conceive of eros as an intermediary, which addresses the other *person* as an end in itself, as Irigaray does. Furthermore, Levinas claims that the tension between the lover and the beloved woman is surpassed in eros by fecundity, which produces a result external to the erotic relation itself, namely the son. Irigaray claims that this removal of the tension and distance between the partners, and the related emphasis on paternal genealogy, is due to the neglect of the possibility of the feminine subject in its own terms. Irigaray writes: "The feminine would remain in search of its cause and sought out as a cause, but never thought through as such. Always relegated to another kind of causality. At best, defined qualitatively. Women the adjectives or ornaments of a verb whose subject they can never be" (ESD, 209/E, 192).

Irigaray puts forward a critical question and asks if Levinas's model for the Other is God. Further, she asks if this implies that the beloved woman is abandoned for the desire for God, who cannot be touched (E, 196/ESD, 214). Sexual difference, which could prevent the substitution of woman by the mother or another woman, is sacrificed for the ethical, which concerns the man-man relationship, the relation between father and son (QEL, 182).

Irigaray's critique of Levinas's concept of eros touches upon an idea fundamental to Levinas's ethics.[7] This fundament is the abstract Other, which is understood according to the model of God or a neutral stranger substituted by any other. Irigaray calls Levinas's Other "indefinable" and she argues that the "indefinability" of the other leads to a discourse of "more" or "less" other; other and otherness being equated with childhood, sickness or poverty or strangeness. Or alternatively, the indefinite other can "represent my/the absolute perfection or grandeur as the Other, Master or Logos" (JAT, 104). Irigaray criticizes Levinas for not defining the other: "Who is the other if the other of sexual difference is not recognized or known?" (QEL, 181). These examples of alterity cannot include sexual difference, which cannot be conceptualized in quantitative terms. Stella Sandford's interpretation of Levinas agrees with that of Irigaray in judging that Levinas's Other does not permit any "relative designation," and as the feminine other is already qualified by femininity, it cannot be part of the ethical relation (Sandford 2000, 45).

Irigaray's critique of Levinas is accepted by several feminist commentators (Vasseleu 1998, 106, 108; Chanter 1995, 207, 218; Joy 2006, 70; cf. Poleshchuk 2009, 224, 251, 254). Moreover, Sandford even claims that the erotic relation of Levinas's later work is "*opposed* to ethics and, correlatively, the feminine becomes opposed to the Other strictly understood" (Sandford 2000, 33, italics mine). In my view, Sandford's conclusion is mistaken, and Irigaray's critique is more to the point: Levinas does not oppose the ethical and the non-ethical, but uses the erotic as a *preparatory step* for ascending to the ethical for the masculine subject (Chanter 1995, 218). Levinas's framework is unable to explain how to live the relationship with the sexually other who, in Irigaray's view, is the most remote and distant despite her closeness. The role of expression is crucial here: the sexually other cannot be approached as her- or himself without communication and dialogue.

Tina Chanter argues that Irigaray follows Levinas in his attempt to surpass the dualism of the sensible and the ideal (Chanter 1995, 205). Ultimately, however, Irigaray claims that Levinas's concept of eros, despite its promising openness to sensibility in the caress, is essentially idealistic: it separates the sensible and the ideal instead of disclosing the ideal in the sensible itself. Stella Sandford argues that Levinas accepts the idealistic concept of transcendence as striving for the Ideal, first explicated in Plato's *Symposium*, as well as the androcentric notion that this movement of striving means the overcoming of the feminine (Sandford 2000, 109). In this respect Levinas follows the Platonic tradition of the Western philosophy.

Platonic Tendencies in the Phenomenologies of Carnal Love

Irigaray's comments and critique are meant to support and encourage us, as philosophers, to fully separate ourselves from the metaphysical tradition of Platonism and from the religious discourse which is based upon it. To this end Irigaray examines Socrates' discourse on love in Plato's *Symposium*. As we will see, her idea is that the Socratic-Platonic conception of love operates as the background and comparison point for Sartre's and Levinas's conception of carnal love (cf. Sandford 2000, 92–109).

Irigaray's critique explicates certain crucial connections between the phenomenological accounts of love and the classical conception of eros first spelled out in Socrates' discourse on love. The most important connection is the division of love into two terms: Socrates argues that the male lover of carnal love is very different from the male lover of wisdom, and his later successors agree. In Socrates' case the division is based on a metaphysical theory, which Sartre and Levinas cannot accept on account of their phenomenological approaches. Despite this clear difference, the three accounts of eros still agree in their dualism and androcentric assumptions. For Irigaray, phenomenology of love still suffers from Platonic remnants.

In order to present a general argument about all the three conceptions of carnal love, I will first explicate Socrates' discourse on eros in the *Symposium*. I will focus here on Socrates' discourse on eros, and its dualistic approach, which considers carnal love to be hierarchically inferior to spiritual love. I will later return to the *Symposium* and study it from two additional perspectives.

Socrates on Carnal Love

Plato's *Symposium* consists of several speeches, which are all given in praise of eros. The speeches are delivered at a party, which was organized by the tragedian poet Agathon to celebrate his first victory in a drama competition. Most commentators on Plato's *Symposium* pay special attention to Socrates' speech. Irigaray also focuses on this section in her rereading "L'amour sorcier. Lecture de Platon. *Le Banquet*, 'Discours de Diotime' " in *Éthique*. Some scholars have questioned the legitimacy of this focus by arguing that Plato's idea of love and wisdom is essentially dialogic and is expressed in the dialogical structure of his text (see e.g., Nussbaum 1979, 133; Corrigan 2004, 2).

Irigaray, on her part, intentionally repeats the standard approach to the *Symposium* by focusing on Socrates' speech. Her reading of the *Symposium* critically modifies the traditional account which submits the plurality of different perspectives on eros to the idea of eros that is attributed to Socrates, and neglects the dialogical structure of the text for an explication of a unitary "content." The tradition also celebrates Socrates as The Philosopher, who is defined by the ability to detach himself from all that is carnal and temporal and to approach the absolute and the eternal.

The basic idea of the canonical account of Socrates' speech on eros is that the different modes of love form a "ladder," which ascends toward the essence of beauty. It is claimed, however, that not all persons are equally well-positioned to approach the truth and instead are limited by illusionary appearances localized in the world of embodiment. According to Socrates, some men are "teeming in body" and choose women as their beloveds (*Symposium*, 208e–209a). These men strive for immortality by begetting children rather than striving for the Ideal (208e–209a).

Other men are pregnant in their souls and choose other men as their beloved women. These men are potentially able to produce spiritual works, i.e., "beautiful learning," together with or for their beloveds (211c–211d). Some of these men are capable of transcending the beauty embodied by singular men: by loving one beautiful body they learn to see the beauty of the soul and begin to "ensue beauty in form," i.e., the beauty going through all beautiful bodies as one and the same (211c–211d). Yet, the ideal as it is manifested in the perceivable, i.e., beauty shared by all individual bodies, is not sufficient for the philosopher, the lover of wisdom, as the interpretative tradition sees him.

So the philosopher must abandon his love for one embodied person as well as the ideal as it is manifested in the perceivable.[8] Both must be surpassed in order to grasp the essence of beauty in contemplation: the beautiful exists "ever in singularity of form independent by itself, while all the multitude of beautiful things partake of it in such wise that, though all of them are coming to be and perishing, it grows neither greater nor less, and is affected by nothing" (211b–211c). Ultimately, the philosopher's aim is to become one with the Ideal: "the very essence of beauty" detached from all appearances in embodiment and perception (211d–211e).

The pure Ideal correlates with the best part of humanity: the divine soul which is able to come to itself through the process of disembodiment. When one is able to "look" upon "essential beauty," nothing distinguishes the lover of wisdom from the Ideal, the unity of the ideal essences, which is the source of all true knowledge. Socrates tells us that he was persuaded by these words of his teacher, the Mantinean priestess Diotima:

> 'But tell me what would happen if one of you had the fortune to look upon essential beauty entire, pure and unalloyed; not infected with the flesh and color of humanity, and ever so much more of mortal trash? What if he could behold the divine beauty itself, in its unique form? Do you call it a pitiful life for a man to lead—looking that way, observing that vision by the proper means, and having it ever with him? Do but consider,' she said, 'that there only will it befall him, as he sees the beautiful through that which makes it visible, to breed not illusions but true examples of virtue, since his contact is not with illusions but with truth. So when he has begotten a true virtue and has reared it up he is destined to win the friendship of Heaven; he, above all men, is immortal.' (211e–212b)

Thus, this kind of lover transcends all embodiment and all the differences, both internal and external, with respect to the other and to the world. The lover of wisdom, the ideal lover, transcends his own embodiment and the perceivable world correlative to it. In Irigaray's terminology, this kind of love can be called "love of the same," and it means loving that which is familiar or similar to oneself. It is love which, in Levinas's words, seeks "that what it already knows," and in which the new and the unexpected are submitted to the familiar and recognizable.[9]

Vigdis Songe-Møller argues that for Plato in the *Symposium* "ideal love could be represented by the attraction one might feel on seeing a beautified version of one's own reflection. The attraction is that of what resembles oneself, or more accurately, of what resembles one's own ideal. For Plato, ideal love is the attraction between elements that are masculine, good and unifying" (Songe-Møller 2002, 96, 104). The conception of love distinguishes carnal from spiritual love and sets them into a hierarchy: carnal love is lower in all senses of the word. Women are identified with their bodies and assumed to be incapable of giving birth to spiritual "children" and insignificant in the practice of loving wisdom. Embodied women are also assumed to have a negative impact on their masculine partners: men attracted to women are claimed to be unable to beget spiritual children.

According to the canonical reading, the lover's soul fuses with the disembodied Ideal. Heaven is the ultimate goal of spiritual love. The body seems to guarantee the separation of singular souls: without body, no difference remains. This is because of the metaphysical assumption that the Ideal, which is the most human part of a human being, is, in principle, the same for humanity. As the most human form of existence can only be achieved by male persons, the role left for women is to "mimic" the idea of the human in their masculine lovers by reproducing children.

However, the canonical dichotomy of the soul and the body can be undermined by a closer reading of Socrates' speech on eros. According to Socrates' discourse carnal love is a necessary precondition for spiritual love. It is only by falling in love with a beautiful body that eros can be initiated and the Ideal reached. Thus, embodiment and carnal love connected to it, can be seen as a necessary precondition, as a preparatory step, for the "higher" forms of love. The human body is also indispensable in the production of the works of love, whether children or beautiful speeches. Moreover, as Irigaray points out, the body refers to another body, a maternal one. The maternal body, for its part, demonstrates that the self has a carnal and non-autonomous origin. When read in this way, Socrates' speech shows that the origin of the masculine subject is heterogeneous: on the one hand it is in the non-Ideal, the mother and the body, and on the other hand it is in the Ideal, father and the soul. However, the canon teaches that the origin of the philosophical subject can only be in the Ideal, at least when it comes to his self-image of the philosophical subject, and his understanding of the nature and aim of his philosophical method.

11

The Male Lover, the Feminine Beloved One

A Specific Way of Understanding (Carnal) Love

In the philosophical descriptions of carnal love given by Plato (Socrates), Sartre, and Levinas, the apparent neutrality and absoluteness of the (masculine) subject is temporarily suspended on account of the possibility of "falling" into sensibility, which would constitute masculine embodiment. Here too Irigaray's work shows yet another constitutive possibility: carnal love demonstrates that the masculine subject has a specific, expressive style of its own, and a specific perspective on love and that this subject does not provide an absolute truth about love. The perspectival nature of these truths, however, is not acknowledged by the philosophers themselves. This can be seen in the fact that the philosophizing subjects that issue the descriptions, separate and distinguish themselves strictly from the masculine lovers that they describe and analyse in their texts. Yet, Irigaray's alternative discourse shows that the classical descriptions of carnal love are dependent for their sense on the describer's possibility of identifying with the masculine-embodied lover.

∽

What is common in the descriptions of Sartre and Levinas, on the one hand, and Socrates's discourse in Plato's *Symposium*, on the other, is the idea that carnal love is a failure of subjectivity. The intense experience of embodiment and neediness is constitutive of carnal love and it makes this form of love a temporary failure of subjectivity or a failure of ideal humanity (cf. ED, 47). Insofar as carnal love is characterized as a degradation or collapse of the normal state of the subject, it is understood as episodic and temporary in the life of the subject. In the accounts of Sartre and Levinas and in the dialogue of Plato, the subject of carnal love loses the determinate factor of his subjectivity: personhood, face, clarity of consciousness or spirituality.

For Sartre and Levinas, the feminine gender is crucial to descriptions of erotic, embodied existence and the discussions about carnal love. In more spiritual and less embodied forms of experience the subject appears as sexually neutral. The implicit idea is that sexual difference is significant only in the most animal and least spiritual interrelations between human beings. In my view, the narrow, instrumental and reproductive notion of sexuality lies behind their inability to relate the beloved woman in carnal love to the highest forms of subjectivity and to guarantee her a temporality and infinity in her own right.

In order to distance herself from this tradition Irigaray first has to explicate the meaning of woman as a deviation from the ideal but also occasionally identified with it. For example, in Sartre's and Levinas's accounts, carnal love divests or deprives woman of her ideal human form: the beloved woman is more attainable and less respected than the radically transcendent Other, God, or the subject whose ideal God is, but she resembles the radically Other by being beyond communication. Irigaray's aim is not to affirm or support these meanings but to invert them. In Irigaray's view this task must be taken both in concretely lived relations of love and in the philosophical practice of articulating the meaning of love. Ultimately, this leads to an attempt to reconceptualize the relation between the sensible and the ideal, as we will see.

In my view, the relation of carnal love, as Levinas and Sartre understand it, and as it was described in Socrates's discourse, includes the desired woman as a non-person or as a living being at the limit of personhood. Because she lacks her own expression, the essential constituent of personhood, she has no possible exit from the status of object or non-person in these descriptions. In all these accounts of love the feminine body is disconnected from other feminine bodies in their expressive functions and from feminine spirituality. Insofar as the feminine body is provided with any expression, the expression is claimed to be "primitive." As the feminine cannot occupy the position of speaking and writing in this framework, the layers of feminine subjectivity cannot be used for woman's own becoming. This leads to the gratuitous utilization of the feminine in the constitution of the masculine subject and his identity and self-understanding.

In all the accounts of love, beloved women cannot be distinguished from each other because they lack expression and personal identity. This is for two related reasons: first, woman lacks expression in love, and second, her erotic role is defined functionally in two ways, either through the capacity of giving pleasure or of providing offspring. Woman's reproductive capacity is conceived as a constituent of fecundity that gives the man a form of immortality and a future in the son, a future that eros as such cannot provide.

Lacking actualized expression woman cannot become a subject and cannot distinguish herself from other women and the general functions of the feminine. As such she is not perceived or loved on her own terms. She can be substituted by any other woman capable of giving pleasure and providing offspring. The functional definition of the beloved woman belongs to the teleological idea of eros which subjects love to certain goals of life and subjectivity. Both the subject and the object of such a relation is understood as an episodic or temporary moment of intentional life which in its entirety extends to all dimensions of spirituality. Thus, fragments of persons are put in positions that should be occupied by whole persons.

As we have seen, the masculine lover and the beloved woman occupy very different positions in the descriptions of carnal love issued by Sartre and Levinas and Plato. The masculine lover has a subjectivity from which he degrades and to which he is able to return, but the beloved woman has no subjectivity or merely a "primitive" one. This is because the genealogies of the two partners are conceived differently by the tradition, already in Socrates' speech in Plato's *Symposium*. The asymmetry is furthered by the view that the erotic relation has a different place in a woman's life than it has in a man's.

In these accounts of carnal love the male subject does not recognize its dual nature as both embodied and spiritual, but projects his embodiment and his momentary degradation from his proper subjectivity to the feminine other (Irigaray ESD, 213/E, 196; cf. Joy 2006, 69). Irigaray emphasizes that a concrete other is necessary for carnal love, but the possibility of "falling" into embodiment in carnal love is also inherent in the subject itself. Morny Joy articulates this mode of projection with respect to Levinas's philosophy in the following way: "In so far as eros becomes uncontrolled, given the gendered nature of Levinas's graphic descriptions of the passive beloved woman, would it not be 'masculine' passion that is responsible?" (Joy 2006, 69). So it is doubly self-deceptive to attribute the condition of man's animality and carnality to the (feminine) other. First, the idea of degradation constitutive of carnal love compromises the aim of maintaining one's own way of being and one's self-responsibility while living the carnal love relation. Second, the attribution of the degradation to the external source is simply false because the possibility and condition of erotic transformation is found in the subject itself.

The collapse of proper subjectivity and the abandonment of discourse and truth are characteristic of carnal love in this framework. Despite the alleged muteness of carnal love, philosophers try to articulate and describe this condition within the discourse, to bring it into discourse and to repeat expressive acts, which shape the discourse according to the interests of the masculine subject. As I will argue, the task of discussing carnal love is motivated by the idea of philosophy as love for wisdom first articulated by Socrates in the *Symposium*.

The Male Lover and the Male Philosopher

But who then is this male subject that speaks about carnal love but does not speak as a lover? It is the apparently neutral male subject who is disembodied in either of two alternative ways: either he lacks all sensuous bodily motivations but regains such motivations, or he lacks sexual motivations. Thus, in his own view, the subject of the discourse of love is both capable of identifying with the lover but also capable of detaching himself from the degradation that characterizes the lovers. Both Sartre and Levinas justify this detachment by their aims of striving for wisdom in the description of experience and the experienced. The masculine subject of carnal love is not understood as a stylistic whole of intentional life with a specific perspective on the world but is conceived as a collapse of a neutral and self-sufficient subjectivity.

Irigaray argues that it is exactly in this detachment from oneself as a lover of another person and as a lover of wisdom that the subject lacks self-knowledge, especially knowledge of his own masculinity. The (masculine) subject should allow and acknowledge for himself the possibilities of striving for his own ideal and of collapsing from this ideal. The acceptance of the dialectics of striving for the masculine subject would provide a more objective view of himself and his own possibilities without any need of projecting the "less than the Ideal" onto the feminine other. If he could recognize his own dual nature, then he could investigate his engagements, even affective ones, and the other as she is intended in these relations.

The idea of a collapse or degradation from what is considered the highest dimensions in subjectivity is fundamentally problematic to the aim of bringing the feminine style into discourse. The core of the problem lies in the fragmentation of the subject of carnal love. To put it simply: within the traditional framework, the subject cannot enter a sensual love relationship without compromising his (or her) subjectivity (cf. Bergoffen 1997, 29).

An additional and related problem is that the fragmentation or degradation of the masculine subject is claimed to result from the encounter with the feminine other. It is the feminine other that degrades the subject from his proper being. Thus it seems that a hierarchical distinction between erotic experiences and the feminine, on the one hand, and the higher spiritual and intellectual dimensions of subjectivity, on the other hand, leads to an idealistic notion of subjectivity.

The main problem for any attempt to promote the development of the feminine style of being is that the unity of the feminine gestures does not reach and cover the more articulated and valued spheres of subjective life, such as religious, political, and theoretical discourse in respect to the human ideal. In other words, the cultivation of the feminine style requires forms of expression which can reach all dimensions of subjectivity. Despite the restrictions imposed on feminine subjectivity in carnal love, the feminine can escape the grasp of the subject, and as such is free with a potentiality of full subjectivity.

We have seen that Levinas's and Sartre's discourse on carnal love implies the freedom and subjectivity of the feminine other, but we have also seen that they do not explicate this precondition or study its consequences for human intersubjectivity. This is most acute in their inability to address a feminine interlocutor and to invite her to speak and write about love. The neglect is most obvious in their inability to acknowledge a perspective which could deviate from their own. At the best, we can find some discursive space for fragments of feminine expressions and feminine style of expression, but we cannot find any open space for a feminine style which would reach all the dimensions of subjectivity.

Insofar as carnal love is conceived as a collapse from the ideal, it seems that carnal love lacks all internal goals and ideals. Only external goals, such as the intensification of excitement, pleasure, or procreation, seem to characterize carnal love. This problem extends to spiritual love insofar as its products are emphasized at the cost of the activity itself. Ultimately, it is the hierarchical distinction between carnal and spiritual love that obscures all possibilities of love. The sense of woman's being as well as the sense of love is fragmented and divided and both in a similar manner: one single perspective, the masculine, dominates the constitution of both senses. Only the speech of the beloved woman, her first-person acts of expression, can and does question this situation. Only she can question the reduction of woman to a "primitively" expressive love-object of carnal love and the congruent idea of love. This speech is actually what Irigaray's works offer to us, as I will argue in the next chapter. By assuming the mimetic positions of the beloved woman and the female teacher, she is able to produce an opening for a new discourse on love, which includes the feminine subject both as a topic and as an interlocutor.

However, both feminine expressivity and carnal love are described in the masculine discourse. The idea of "nakedness'" or "poverty" is described in terms of ascent and degradation by Plato as well as by Sartre and Levinas, and also includes an opportunity of erotic renewal whether we speak about pre-discursive experience or about discourse.[1] Moreover, the inherent 'poverty' of Eros is due to its feminine genealogy, as Irigaray emphasizes: according to the myth presented by Socrates/Diotima in *Symposium*, Eros was wanted by her mother. The "poverty" of Eros[2] originates from its genealogy and date of conception, the day when Aphrodite was celebrated (E, 30/ESD, 24; *Symposium*, 203–204a). The mother of Eros is, according to the myth, a semi-god Penia, poverty, who conceived with another semi-god Poros, wealth. As the offspring of these two semi-gods, Eros is neither rich nor poor but moves between these two opposites. The character of Eros always in search of beautiful things is often forgotten: he is taken to be rich already (E, 31; *Symposium*, 203–204a). This forgetfulness is related to the idea of the Eros-philosopher as the beloved woman master, the one who already possesses beauty and happiness.

12

Irigaray Writing, Speaking, and Acting as a Woman Lover

In her dialogue with Sartre, Levinas, and Plato (Socrates), Irigaray takes the mimetic position of the beloved one, but she also distances herself from this position by striving for radical self-definition as a woman lover. This is possible thanks to her previous acts concerning the figure of the beloved one, its role and position in the philosophical discourse, by her mimetic writing, on the one hand, and by her articulations of the feminine first-person lived experience and expressivity, on the other. Also the redefinitions of the relationship between carnal and spiritual, personal and public, made possible by an alternative account of Diotima's eros, contribute to this process.

～

Irigaray questions the established conceptions of carnal and spiritual love and transforms them into a new account of love. This occurs on the basis of the discursive and experiential opening offered by the figure of the beloved woman, on the one hand, and by the half-actualized possibilities opened in the accounts that the three male philosophers, on the other. These entail the uniqueness of the beloved one and the "poverty" and dynamism of desire itself. The realization of this possibility requires a critical analysis of the masculine discourse on love. It also requires a specific mimetic position of a *female teacher*, who presents, acknowledges, and accepts the woman as an expert in love and procreation. This figure, represented by wise woman Diotima, can be found in Plato's *Symposium*. However, despite its potentiality, this mimetic woman-figure is also problematic in Irigaray's analysis. She shows that despite the fact that Diotima is presented as a female teacher of love, her expertise is not fully rooted in the feminine body and its expressions because her teachings are delivered by a sequence of male philosophers.

The occupation of the various mimetic positions, the descriptions of the feminine embodied and affective experience, and the criticism of masculine discourse are indispensable for challenging the established philosophical conceptions of the carnal love which takes place between woman and man. Irigaray does this by developing, as a woman lover, her own account of carnal-spiritual love between persons. This account, I argue, is indebted both to Diotima's speech in the *Symposium* and to Merleau-Ponty's phenomenology of sexual relations, but it transcends their aims and solves the problems of sexual difference that Irigaray diagnoses in them and in the philosophical discourse more generally. These problems inhibit the potentiality of love from actualizing.

Moreover, Irigaray's discourse on personal love contributes both to the thematic explication of the feminine style and to its concrete development. Through Irigaray's activity of writing, the muteness or "primitive" expressions of the beloved woman and the fragments from the speeches of a woman teacher are transformed into a discourse of a woman lover (*amante*)—and in two related senses: as a lover of another person and as a lover of wisdom exemplified by Irigaray herself.

My inquiry into Irigaray's philosophy shows that in order to question the neutrality of philosophy and the disembodiment of the philosophical subject, it is not enough to demonstrate that the subject of personal love has been conceived as masculine by traditional philosophers. This is because of the crucial philosophical gesture of separating and distinguishing between the subject as an agent and patient of carnal love, on the one hand, and the subject as the self that philosophizes, analyzes, and conceptualizes the relation of carnal love, on the other. Thus, in order to institute a self-defined feminine subject, it is not enough to assume the position of a woman lover in personal relations. Nor is it enough to act as a feminine interlocutor in discussions concerning the topic of love.

The phenomenologists of the body do not address a feminine interlocutor nor do they recognize any feminine authority to have an influence on their views on love.[1] Yet, such interlocutors are available and have been operative in the tradition. The very beginning of the philosophical discourse on love refers to a feminine authority on love, and to a female teacher. This woman character that Irigaray wants to mimic, is Diotima, a Mantinean priestess, whose teachings are introduced and defended by Socrates in Plato's *Symposium*. This mimetic position cannot be reduced to the position of the beloved woman locked in the privacy of the closed couple. Irigaray develops and cultivates it to question the presuppositions of Plato (Socrates), Sartre, and Levinas, but also to create a concept of love appropriate to the becoming of feminine subjectivity. The dialogical position of Diotima as presented in Plato's *Symposium* provides Irigaray with the possibility of gaining access into the discourse on love. This position depends on the idea of the feminine genealogy, which recognizes the feminine authority of love at least in some spheres of life.

However, Irigaray emphasizes that it is not Diotima who speaks to us in her own voice. Yet, Diotima, whose existence is constantly questioned, might, paradoxically, be the only woman who is fully acknowledged in the philosophical discourse (cf. Chanter 1995, 162). It is the position of the teacher of love provided by Diotima with the fragments and traces of feminine life and expression, which offers Irigaray the possibility of entering into the discussion on love in a *new way*. She does not act as the beloved woman as she is positioned by man, but acts as someone who is able to criticize and question the already established truths about woman and about love. Moreover, she speaks as one who is able to create new truths. This is a position which one can take and cultivate without losing oneself as a woman. When the two mimetic positions—the beloved woman and the teacher in love—are combined, then a feminine authority of love can emerge: she arises from the practices of love in which woman has taken part only as a beloved woman and not as a lover and from the tradition of philosophical discourse which has authorized woman's expertise in love. Within the mimetic positions of woman, this is the only expertise a feminine person can have. But insofar as it is expertise, any expertise, it can provide an access to the public sphere of discourse.

So, Irigaray's writing forms a bridge that connects private amorous expressions to the public expertise on love, which also has been manifest in female mysticism, though in a different manner. The outcome is a feminine subject speaking and writing in love about love: in becoming wise love should not be given up (E, 27/ESD, 21). Rather, carnal love is cultivated to include a concept of love which includes both aspects of being human: embodiment and spirituality. Any lover striving for wisdom in love as Socrates teaches, has to take into account these two dimensions and their intertwinement in all relations, in her relations to herself, to the other, and to the world: "love was meant to be an irreducible mediator, at once physical and spiritual, between the lovers, and not already codified duty, will, desire" (ESD, 30/E, 36).

The Female Teacher Diotima and Her Feminine Style

The figure of Diotima is problematic as a feminine teacher insofar as her teachings are reported by male speakers and writers and handed down to other male speakers and writers. Her character is formed through sedimentations of male preconceptions of women and sexual love. The problem is dramatized by her absence in the situation in which her teachings are reported and defended. Irigaray writes: "She does not take part in these exchanges or in this meal among men. She is not there. She herself does not speak. Socrates reports or recounts her words. He praises her for her wisdom and her power and declares that she is his initiator or teacher when it comes to love, but she is not invited to teach or to eat" (ESD, 20/ E, 27). Moreover, Diotima's speech is repeated by a philosopher, Socrates, who seriously suspects and questions the capacity of writing to mediate truth in the teacher's absence. Thus, the problem of feminine teaching is serious from more than one aspect. The writer, Plato, and the speaker, Socrates, both fail their own Ideal of presence and fullness here. It is from this highly problematic position that Irigaray questions the hierarchy of carnal and spiritual love. And, again, her problematization of the setting of Plato's *Symposium* is intended to influence both Levinas's and Sartre's discourses and the whole Western philosophical and religious tradition.

Thus the very same text that establishes the metaphysical division between carnal and spiritual love includes an important trace or fragment which may allow the feminine style to become itself in several intentional relations. Through Irigaray's practices of speaking and writing in love about love as a woman, a new mode of femininity in the philosophical discourse is established: the words of Diotima obtain a new meaning. Diotima's discursive existence is crucial for Irigaray because Socrates's report on Diotima's teachings on love includes fragments of a feminine style of relationality (cf. Chanter 1995:162). We can only speak about fragments since Diotima's style, mediated by Socrates, cannot evolve coherently in a discourse dominated by male interests and needs.

Several explanations have been presented for this incoherence. Traditionally considered, the most obvious reason is Diotima as an instantiation of woman's essence, and as such expressive in an incoherent and senseless manner. As a priestess, furthermore, Diotima is claimed to serve religion and mysticism and avoid or neglect the goal of theoretical thinking. Irigaray questions this possible explanation, and shows how the traditional idea of feminine incoherence is based on a biased and limited view of the feminine. She does this by her careful readings of the canonical texts of the androcentric tradition, and in doing so, she also discloses incoherences in these texts, most clearly manifest in the relationship to the sexually other.

Irigaray Speaking as a Female Teacher

Irigaray starts to undermine the traditional prejudice about woman's incoherence and lack of style by emphasizing that Diotima is not present at the Symposium. Diotima was not invited or she did not want to accept the invitation; we do not know (E, 27/ESD, 20). Irigaray reminds the reader several times that Diotima's speech is mediated by Socrates, Diotima does not speak for herself (E, 27/ESD, 20; see also Chanter 1995, 161): "And Diotima is not the only example of a woman whose wisdom, especially about love, is reported in her absence" (ESD, 20/E, 27). While Socrates is usually known as a person who acknowledges the limits of his own capacities of knowing, he does not in this particular case express any doubts about his capacity of recollecting or grasping Diotima's words and style, or their significance. The idea implicit in Irigaray's reading is to point at a specific masculine incoherence: Irigaray asks whether the masculine philosophical subject is able to extend his (self-)reflective activity to his relationship to the (sexually) other.

In the beginning of the *Symposium*, it appears that the speech of Socrates is already mediated by several male persons. Thus, the truthfulness of the reported events in *Symposium* depends on several male persons, and on their capacities to recollect, listen and comprehend[2]. By emphasizing this, Irigaray urges us to question Socrates's capacity to comprehend a feminine style in its becoming and his capacity to listen and learn a concept of love that does not correspond to his expectations and anticipations. These expectations have several layers: personal, general (bound to his unacknowledged gender) and metaphysical.

In Irigaray's reading, the expressions and statements of Diotima, which traditionally have been considered as auxiliary or unconvincing, are studied as fragments and traces of an original and independent feminine style. For example, Irigaray emphasizes that Diotima laughs at Socrates' conviction that everyone [*tout le monde*] knows that Eros is a great God (ESD, 22/E, 28; *Symposium*, 202c–202d). Irigaray describes Diotima's response: "Her retort is not at all angry, the effect of hesitating between contradictory positions; it is laughter based on other grounds. While laughing, then, she asks Socrates what he means by everyone. Just as she ceaselessly dismantles the assurance or closure of opposing terms, she undoes all sets of units reduced to sameness in order to constitute a whole" (ESD, 22/E, 28; *Symposium*, 202a–202e).

Irigaray further describes Diotima's activity of questioning: "[. . .] she ceaselessly examines Socrates on his positions but without positing authoritative, already constituted truths [. . .]. And each time Socrates thinks he can take something as certain, she undoes his certainty. His own, but also all kinds of certainties that are already set in language. All entities, substantives, adverbs, sentences are patiently, and joyously, called into question" (ESD, 22/E, 28–29). The idea of Eros as the one who already possesses beauty and goodness, is easily questioned by Diotima: if Eros possessed all that he desires he would desire no more (E, 29/ESD, 22).

Later on Irigaray again notices that Diotima's laughter is reported but not interpreted by Socrates. This is how Irigaray interprets Diotima's laughter: "She continues to laugh at his going to look for his truths beyond the most obvious everyday reality, at his not seeing or even perceiving this reality. At the way in which his dialectical or dialogical method already forgets the most elementary truths. At the way his discourse of love neglects to look at, to be informed, about the amorous state. Or to inquire about its cause. Astonishingly, Diotima speaks about *cause*" (ESD, 26/E, 32–33). Irigaray wonders why Diotima fails in her own method and seeks cause from the animal world rather than emphasizes the fecundity between man and woman (ESD, 27/E, 33). Furthermore, Diotima's approval of pederasty does not sound convincing as woman's words in praise of eros to Irigaray's ear. Irigaray writes: "[L]ove between men is superior to love between man and woman. Carnal procreation is subordinated to the engendering of beautiful and good things. Immortal things. This, surprisingly enough, is the view of Diotima. At least as translated through the words of Socrates" (ESD, 31/E, 37).

The second possible reason for the incoherence of Diotima's speech is the fact that she operates in a situation which does not encourage the cultivation and development of feminine style, or its becoming to itself according to an internal ideal, but expects the feminine to serve the masculine Ideal (cf. Chanter 1995, 161). This kind of bias can be produced both for a feminine person herself and for a masculine person: the feminine can be expected to serve the masculine ideas and ideals. For example, in the following passage Diotima sacrifices fecundity between the two in love for reproduction as a third one:

> "Now those who are teeming in body betake them rather to women, and are amorous on this wise: by begetting children they acquire an immortality, a memorial, a state of bliss, which in their imaging they 'for all succeeding time procure.' But pregnancy of soul—for there are persons," she declared, "who in their souls still more than in their bodies conceive those things which are proper for soul to conceive and bring forth; and what are those things? Prudence and virtue in general [. . .]." (*Symposium*, 208–209a; ESD, 29)

In Irigaray's view, this tendency to favor the product of eros conflicts with Diotima's emphasis on the mutual becoming of two lovers. She argues that the incoherence results from Diotima's incapacity to become herself on her own terms. Diotima does not fully act as a woman, but only partially, insofar as the discourse needs feminine elements.

These problems can only be detected from the position of the full-fledged feminine subject established by Irigaray by articulating her relations to herself, to the world, and to the other. Through Irigaray's rereading of Diotima's speech two possible interpretations arise, which are both in agreement with Irigaray's project and with the genealogy of the feminine that she aims to institute. The first possibility is to emphasize that Socrates fails to follow Diotima's feminine way of thinking and speaking about love because he substitutes his own words for Diotima's expressions and because he cannot recognize the unity of her style. These points of failure are explicated by Irigaray.

The second possibility is to argue that Socrates while referring to a woman teacher—Diotima—when presenting his view of love, has managed to capture some fragments of a feminine style. If there were no fragments of femininity in Diotima's speech, then the reader would have difficulties in comprehending her as a woman teacher. As David Halperin, who believes Diotima to be Plato's invention, puts it: it is "by the virtue of the very language she uses to enunciate them [her erotic doctrines], she lets her audience know that a 'woman' is speaking—or, to be more precise, that Socrates is speaking in what he expects his audience to recognize as a woman's voice. At any rate, Plato clearly means us to notice that Diotima's conceptualization of eros derives from a specifically 'feminine' perspective" (Halperin 1990, 263).

Also these aspects of Plato's text are explicated by Irigaray. As said, both of these possible interpretations are equally in agreement with Irigaray's aim of tracing and instituting the genealogy of the feminine:

> I search for myself, as if I had been assimilated into maleness. I ought to reconstitute myself on the basis of a disassimilation. . . . Rise again from the traces of a culture, of works already produced by the other. Searching through what is in them—for what is not there. What allowed them to be, for what is not there. Their conditions of possibility, for what is not there.
> Woman ought to find herself, among other things, through the images of herself already deposited in history and the conditions of production of the work of man, and not on the basis of his work, his genealogy." (ESD, 10–11/E, 17)

The emphasis in Irigaray's reading of the *Symposium* differs from the traditional one, which focuses on Socrates' words and argument. Irigaray aims at identifying Diotima's own speech and her method of thinking about love. The method can be called dialectical, but Irigaray emphasizes that it is not dialectical in Hegel's sense, which reconciles the difference. Rather: "She presents, uncovers, unveils the insistence of a third term that is already there and that permits progression: from poverty to wealth, from ignorance to wisdom, from mortality to immortality. Which, for her, always comes to a greater perfection of and in love" (ESD, 20–21/E, 27). Irigaray further argues: "But contrary to the usual methods of dialectic, one should not have to give up love in order to become wise or learned. It is love that leads to knowledge, whether in art or more metaphysical learning. It is love that both leads the way and is the part. A mediator par excellence" (ESD, 21/E, 27–28).

According to Irigaray, the idea which is central to Diotima's speech, but which is least understood by Socrates and his successors, is the idea of fecundity of body and soul, the activity of loving. According to Diotima love is "engendering in beauty, with relation both to body and soul" (*Symposium*, 206; ESD, 25/E 31; *Le Banquet*, 205–206). Diotima further clarifies: "*The union of a man and a woman is, in fact, a generation; this is a thing divine; in a living creature that is mortal, it is an element of immortality, this fecundity and generation*" (Irigaray's italics) (ESD, 25/E, 32; *Symposium*, 206c–206; E, 32; *Le Banquet*, 206–207). Irigaray argues that Diotima is able to explicate this idea but that even she lets go of the possibility of fecundity in favor of reproduction by speaking about cause as we saw above. The problem of "losing the internal motivation" (*mobile interne*) or "internal fecundity" (*sa fécondité 'en soi'*) of love in emphasizing its external goal in reproduction can also lie in Socrates's report of Diotima (ESD, 27/E, 33). Irigaray writes: "This error in method, in the originality of Diotima's method, is corrected soon afterwards only to be confirmed later. Of course, once again, she is not there. Socrates retells her words. Perhaps he distorts them unwittingly or unknowingly" (ESD, 27/E, 33–34). Irigaray finds a deviation from Diotima's method in splitting the "subject" (*sujet*)[3] and "beloved reality" (*realité aimée*): immortality becomes the external goal of love. This division and putting into a hierarchy loses love as an "intermediary milieu" (*milieu intérmédiaire*) (ESD, 29/E, 35). According to Irigaray, here Diotima's method disappears: "love becomes a teleological quest for what is deemed a higher reality and often situated in transcendence inaccessible to our mortal condition" (ESD, 29/E, 35).

Irigaray's reading is motivated by the aim of being more faithful to Diotima's position as a woman than Diotima herself is able to be, or more faithful than Socrates who repeats Diotima's words for his own interests (cf. Chanter 1995, 161). It is from Diotima's speech that Irigaray finds an occasion to consider eros as a tension between two subjects—a difference that remains difference rather being overcome in a synthesis (cf. Chanter 1995: 163). This faithfulness allows us to shift the focus from a productive act to a relation. Rather than submitting eros to any external goal, Irigaray finds from Diotima's speech an idea of eros whose goal is inherent: the aim is to preserve its dynamism. Eros becomes richer in desiring and in this respect differs from need or lack to be fulfilled as in hunger or in thirst (or love of same, as Irigaray sees it). This aspect of eros can be found in Levinas's metaphysical desire, which Levinas defines as dynamism, which "becomes richer in desiring," but which is separate from need.

Irigaray's method has a double character: after problematizing the traditional view attributed to Socrates, she also shows an alternative way of presenting Diotima's teachings (cf. Chanter 1995, 159; Joy 2006, 37). By this double movement Irigaray questions the adequacy of Socrates' report of Diotima's teaching and the classical conception of love divided into two spheres: embodied and spiritual. Thus, Irigaray also questions Socrates' philosophical authority and asks if he is able to discover or present the non-habitual and the unexpected ideas of Diotima's teachings. More generally, Irigaray questions the capacity of the masculine subject to alone disclose the ideal as it is manifest in the perceived.

Irigaray's Daimonic Account of Desire

In order to have an idea of the influence of Diotima's speech on Irigaray's concept of desire, let us study closer Irigaray's formulations of desire.[4] Irigaray sees desire as a relation that allows distance and opens a space of freedom, a possibility of renewal, between the subject and the other, or between the subject and his or her world. Desire can even open the discourse to the other and resists the subject's reversal to itself (ESD, 76/E, 78–79). Desire for Irigaray is an intermediary. Desire is "situated in the attractions, tensions, and actions occurring between *form* and *matter*, but also in the *reminder* that subsists after each creation of a work, *between* what has already been identified and what still has to be identified, and so on" (ESD, 8/E, 16). Rather than a contact between stable identities, desire should be understood as "a changing dynamic whose outlines can be described in the past, sometimes in the present, but never definitively predicted" (ESD, 8/E, 16). Thus, Irigaray argues that desire cannot be grasped by the dualistic concepts of classical metaphysics: it should not be thought of as metaphysical (ESD, 8/E, 16). Its motivation lies "either in the passion of the subject or in the irresistible attraction of the object" (ESD, 76/E, 79).

No exact definition can be given to desire if love aims at its proper essence. This is because, for Irigaray, desire is the primordial movement which gives structure to time and space; desire is "a first movement *toward*, not yet qualified" (ESD, 76/E, 78–79). When not restricted by external interests, desire is, however, always double since it consists of two poles of attraction and support. Movement characteristic of desire includes two moments: the movement of going toward the other and the movement of coming back to oneself (ESD, 9/E, 16).

Irigaray's attacks both Sartre's and Levinas's accounts explicated above. She argues that desire cannot be understood in terms of "*envoutement*" and "possession" as Sartre proposes, and she shows that the object of desire is not the equivocal feminine (*le feminine comme équivoque*), as Levinas formulates. In Irigaray's view desire is not "a moment in history" nor "a moment of tension" as the descriptions based on the narrow notion of sexuality suggests (ESD, 8/E, 16).

Irigaray develops an account of desire as a tension between two irreducible subjects, neither oppositional nor complementary to each other. Commenting on the descriptions of the male phenomenologists, Merleau-Ponty included, she writes: "I would not say that desire makes the body ambiguous or equivocal, but rather that it renders I-me together with I-you. A double intention animates me: I want to return to myself, in myself and I want to be with you" (TBT, 28/ED, 55). Later on she continues: "Wanting to go towards you and still attempt the return in myself, I seek an alliance between who you are and who I am, in myself and in yourself" (TBT, 28/ED, 55).

According to Irigaray the idea of "equivocal" does not originate in any ambiguity or obscurity of the relation between the body and consciousness, nor in any confusion between subjectivity and objectivity or facticity, but is due to our ways of thinking and living the relation (TBT, 28/ED, 56). Thus, instead of differentiating between the opaque facticity of the feminine body and transparency of the masculine consciousness, we should conceive of desire as a relation between two bodily spiritual subjects—woman and man. This understanding and realization of desire, however, requires that we reflect on the relation that each gender has to maternal love (TBT, 31–32/ED, 58–59). This is necessary because desire is confused with a nostalgic attitude which fantasizes a paradise of the maternal womb or a symbiosis with the beloved woman. The task is to realize desire in the presence which is pregnant with the future and "enchanted" by the unexpected and becoming.

Desire in Irigaray's terms is not instinctual or structurally simple. Rather, the duality of subjectivity in desire requires a specific attitude, which consists of activity and passivity. In Irigaray's view the dynamics of desire include the activity of detaching oneself from the habitual to and with the other, and it also includes the passivity of listening to the other and letting him or her appear: it includes both activity and passivity, wakefulness and receptivity.

The active-passive attitude is strengthened by the experience of the other's specificity. Instead of trying to grasp the non-graspable Other, I must arrest my movement and halt before the other, leaving the other's transcendence intact. Only such a halt allows us to avoid the mistake of reducing the other to a fact or a thing, to an object of love, or an ensemble of qualities. The interrogative gesture of arresting one's movement when accompanied by an acknowledgment of the impossibility of actually possessing, grasping, and comprehending, allows the other to remain other.

The articulation of the other's specificity is necessary for the maintenance of the active-passive attitude: it culminates in the loving dialogue with the other. A dialogue between two expressing selves—persons—is required for the desired other is to remain alien and to resist all reductions to a not-me or to my nourishment. This attitude allows the other to remain other and allows the desire to grow as double: "The other is and remains transcendent to me through a body, through intentions and words foreign to me: 'you who are not and never will be me or mine' are transcendent to me in body and in words, in so far as you are an incarnation that cannot be appropriated by me, lest I should suffer the alienation of my freedom" (TBT, 18/ED, 39). Basically, Irigaray's claim is that sexual difference can only be established if the passions are cultivated so that they resist possession and appropriation.

Irigaray's Daimonic Account of Love

The lack of feminine self-expression leaves the feminine style and its amorous modifications partial. Yet, even if the sense of woman's being both for herself and man is constituted as partial and biased in carnal love, this is not inevitable or necessary. Fragments of expression in love reveal a feminine style, which is not part of or reducible to the dominant discourse. The cultivation of the feminine requires that the fragments of feminine amorous gestures are brought to their full extension, from private encounters to the public realm, from sensibility to writing (SP, 191, 193). Irigaray's own work is intended as a contribution to this task of cultivation of the feminine. Irigaray struggles to create feminine amorous gestures, starting from the specificity of the feminine body and aiming at speech and writing. In this way she unfolds the dynamic unity of the feminine style and its amorous modifications and invites other feminine and masculine persons to contribute to the constitution of a new type of ideality of the feminine and the amorous.

An amorous style covers a whole variety of different kinds of expressions, from movements and gestures to speech and writing. All types of relations, relation to the self, relation to the other, and relation to the world can be established by amorous expressions which aim at touching or caressing the beloved woman in his or her becoming. An amorous style includes both active and passive moments. In both cases the beloved woman's movement is not grasped, arrested, or circumscribed but is approached, touched, and followed in a way which leaves its movement free. The experience of loving is understood as covering the subject as a whole. Irigaray elaborates the temporality of love as duration that is neither a return to the past in the mode of nostalgia nor an appeal for the future on the cost of the present.

This way of understanding the love relation also has implications for our notion of the act of love as a sexual act. According to Irigaray it should be conceived of as a mode of becoming and indwelling, it is "dwelling with the self, and with the other—while letting the other go" (ESD, 212/E, 194–195). The act of love should be understood as a practice of inhabiting love and cohabiting in the house of flesh. In the act of love one's own body and the body of the other are both given anew, as if for the first time. The act of love is characterized by intensity, sensation, color, and rhythm, and not by the events of implosion and explosion, which Irigaray takes to dominate our practices and norms of erotic love (ESD, 212/E, 194). Carnal love is also connected to ideality and divinity, as is revealed by Diotima's dialectics of fecundity without production.

Irigaray elaborates this idea in *Éthique*: "the sexual *act* would turn into an act whereby the other gives new form, birth, incarnation to the self. Instead of implying the downfall of the body, it takes part in the body's renaissance. And there is no other equivalent act, in this sense. Most divine of acts. Whereby man makes woman feel her body as place. Not only her vagina or womb but her body" (ESD, 51/E, 55). What is at issue is the rebirth of woman's interiority: "I seek a complex marriage between my interiority and that of a *you* which cannot be replaced by me, which is always outside of me, but thanks to which my interiority exists" (ED, 28/ESD 55).

According to Irigaray, speech is constituted on the basis of our lived bodies, and our histories, in our unique subjectivities. As such speech—and writing modelled according to dialogic speech—makes possible concrete relations with others. The arresting in the face of the other, however, is not restricted to speech but also concerns movements and gestures. Since the other overflows my intentions, but can be addressed, unfamiliar, nonanticipated, and divergent meanings are a genuine possibility in the intersubjective order. For Irigaray, the question "Who are you?," and the recognition that "you not being me, mine or for me" is necessary for the other to remain other, instead of another not-me. Love is regulated by the singularity and the particularity of the other and the self. The preliminary gesture which makes possible the address of the other and the revelation of his or her particularity is the arrest of grasping movement.

Both Irigaray's descriptions of love and desire and her own activity of describing demonstrate how love can cover all the layers of subjective life and temporality. In other words, Irigaray's concept of loving is not confined or focused on the sexual act or its preconditions, in lack or fulfilment. Rather, Irigaray's concept and practice of love further develops the holistic conception of sexuality initiated by Merleau-Ponty.

This is why Irigaray can meaningfully claim that the sexual act—as an encounter between two spiritual and embodied persons and their sensible and the ideal lives—necessarily remains unfulfilled in the present state of affairs. In order to be fulfilled, the act of love must take place not only in the sphere of sexual practices but also in other spheres of life, most importantly in the acts of speaking and writing. However, in contrasting Merleau-Ponty's suggestion, Irigaray argues that sexuality should not be understood or characterized as an ambiguous or equivocal atmosphere, but as the dual of subjectivity. The other in love is another subject: an expressive unity, a person. In my view, Irigaray's relation to Merleau-Ponty is very critical with respect to his later work *Le visible et l'invisible*, but Merleau-Ponty's ideas of stylistic unities and amorous relations in *Phénoménologie de la perception* seem to anticipate Irigaray's ideas of love and desire. So Irigaray's relation to Merleau-Ponty is different, depending on which tendency, sameness, or difference, is, in Irigaray's view, the dominant tendency in his work.

Dynamics of Love of the Same and Love of the Other

Irigaray distinguishes between two possible attitudes of the lovers: the lover can strive to define the other's transcendence for his own purposes or he can struggle to let the other define herself, and thus to appear in her own intentional and motivational relations. The beloved woman can also be attended to as another person in her or his singular becoming, a co-lover. Irigaray calls the first attitude love of the same and the latter love of the other. Both these attitudes are analyzed in *Éthique*.

In her view both attitudes are possible in love. Both are also based on certain basic tendencies or dispositions inherent in subjectivity: the tendency to reduce the other or to the similar, on the one hand, and the tendency to open oneself to that which is new and surprising, on the other hand (cf. POP, 378/ PP, 434). Thus, the attitudes of love are not exclusive for but both are necessary constituents of love (cf. Korsisaari 2006, 48–49). Love of the other in Irigaray's terms has as its "object" an entire way or style of life rather than just certain aspects of it. Merleau-Ponty interestingly describes a mode of love close to Irigaray's idea of love of the other but in terms of true and mistaken love and without reference to sexual difference. He writes: "[T]rue love summons all the subject's resources and concerns him in his entire being, whereas mistaken love touches only one persona: 'the man of forty' in case of late love, 'the traveller' in the case of exotic appeal, 'the widower' if the misguided love is sustained by a memory, 'the child' where the mother is recalled" (POP, 379/PP, 434).

Instead of loving a person in this or that relation or as an aspect, one can love the entire style of a (feminine) person, which is constituted dynamically in the multitude of relations. Moreover, Irigaray argues that love of the other requires an intuition of the infinite, an opening toward that which cannot be achieved. The infinite can be comprehended as a divine principle, such as fecundity, as the struggle for objectivity or as the openness of life itself. If this condition is not met, then love remains self-centred and projective (E, 108–109/ESD, 111)

The actualization and fulfilment of love presupposes that the lover is able to suspend his habits and preconceptions and is also capable of opening himself to what is new and unexpected. However, no acquired or natural attitude or ability to balance one's own activities and passivities is sufficient for the actualization and fulfilment of love. Rather, this goal can be achieved only by concrete interaction and dialogue with the other or others. A concrete interaction and dialogue is necessary both for self-reflection and self-knowledge and for touching, rather than grasping, the other in his or her becoming. The relation between two only becomes possible through a specific form of activity: "It takes two to love. To know how to separate and how to come back together. Each to go, both he and she, in quest of self, faithful to the quest, so they may greet one another, come close, make merry, or seal a covenant" (ESD, 71/E, 73). This kind of movement, which can be found in the relation between persons, forms a precondition for loving wisdom with respect to the world and the relations constitutive of it.

As we have seen, the possibilities of love look very different depending on the (discursive) position of the lover. For genealogical reasons, the masculine and feminine perspectives open up the possibilities of love in different ways. The background of this difference is the fact that discourse is identified with the masculine but founded on the appropriation of the feminine. Moreover, because the masculinity of the discourse is not recognized, the masculine perspective on love has been identified with the phenomenon of love itself. To disclose and unravel this fundamental bias, Irigaray sets out to develop new modifications and practices of love on the basis of lacking, forgotten, or fragmented expressions of feminine modes of experience.

In this way Irigaray shows how the actualization and fulfilment of love requires distinct but interconnected movements and gestures on the part of women and men. In Irigaray's understanding the couple consists of two dynamic and temporalized subjects: it is a double dynamism. As in Irigaray's view, the inherent goal of love is to maintain its openness and dynamics; it corresponds to the temporally evolving style of a person. This conception of love Irigaray finds in Diotima's teachings but, as already mentioned, hints of it can also be found in Merleau-Ponty's phenomenology of sexual relations. As Merleau-Ponty sees it, love is potentially able to show us things, the world, the other as well as ourselves, not only as they or we are actualized but also in their or our potential/ideal.

This possibility also includes the unpredictable and open characteristics of style: the attitude of love corresponding to the ungraspable style of a person (and a generic style or any other style) is caressing rather than grasping. Only a caressing touch can abstain from arresting the movement of the dynamic style. This holds for all the relations, to the relation to oneself as well as other's freedom in his or her becoming. In Irigaray's conception of love the emphasis is on the potential truthfulness of perception and the means to achieve it in the subject's relations to itself, to the other, and to the world: both the self and the other should be perceived as expressive unities, styles, in their becoming.

Irigaray's discourse on carnal love seems to develop Merleau-Ponty's phenomenological account of stylistic unities, which remain undeveloped in Merleau-Ponty's own works, especially with respect to the topic of love. In Merleau-Ponty's view, carnal love reveals existence in a new way. In love, whether in respect to a person or to a writing, the fundamental affective and relational aspects of existence are accentuated. Affectivity is defined by Merleau-Ponty as attraction or repulsion toward an external "object," and thus it reveals existence as a relation to an active other rather than a self-inflected state. The transcendent other is necessary for the possibility of love, and this holds for self-love, love for the other, and love for wisdom. Insofar as the transcendent other in a love relation is usually and traditionally depicted as sexually alien, existence manifests itself as dual, as feminine and masculine. This duality as a structural feature of the subject of perception, affection, and knowledge is important also with respect to how objects, the relations between them and ultimately, the world, come to be for us. For these reasons, it is difficult to maintain the illusion of the self-sufficiency of the subject when reflecting on carnal love. This holds for many notions of the self-sufficiency of the subject: the subject as one, the subjects as neutral/of one sex and as purely spiritual. When opened toward the world and the other in the dynamic experience of loving, the subject finds itself as necessarily incomplete and perspectival.

An Effect of the Acts of the Woman Lover: An Opening for Self-Defined Feminine Expressivity

Irigaray's inquiries into love make the problem of woman more concrete but also create a possibility of actualizing the feminine style in concrete discussions between spiritual bodily persons. Irigaray addresses particular canonical writings which are constitutive of the philosophical discourse that presents woman, at best, as a lack or as lacking any original existence. The lack of feminine expression in the discourse distorts both the described content and the activities of description: the reader is assumed to be similar to the describer. The neglect of the specificity of the feminine lived body impairs the described content as well as the describing subject, and so it can be said to be doubled.

The meaning of love is constituted in the discourse, and through discourse it obtains its ideal existence in the discourse: in the "what" and "how" of speeches and writings. The influence between experience and discourse is two-way: the experience is structured by the discursive articulations and actual practices of love, but the discourse of love can be transformed by expressions of pre-discursive experiences. This duality is lost when love is subjected to a ready-made conceptual system or purified of content in abstraction. To resist this move Irigaray holds to the concreteness and singularity of experience in her investigations of the meaning of love. She finds such a resistance necessary for her both as a philosopher who studies the conditions of loving and as a lover who addresses the other in respect and wonder: they amount to the same thing.

Irigaray's writings disclose the close connection between discourse on love and the experience of love. Basing on this understanding of the interrelation between discourse and experience Irigaray also comments on Sartre's and Levinas's descriptions of love through her style of writing and not just by critical remarks on the intersubjective relations in *L'être et le néant* and *Totalité et infini*.

Sartre's position is that of a neutral observer and Levinas speaks in the first-person singular. By her interrogative and dialogical style, Irigaray questions the apparent neutrality of Sartre's descriptions, on the one hand, and the neglect of the duality of the subjects in Levinas's account, on the other.

To demonstrate how Irigaray's critique operates at the level of her style of writing, I first return to Irigaray's response to Levinas from the positions of a beloved one and a woman lover. She gives us her perspective to the mode of love relationship which Levinas describes: "When the beloved woman presents herself or appears to the male lover as a paradise to be referred back to infancy and animality, then the act of love does not lead only to profaning, but also to destruction, a fall" (ESD, 198/E, 183). In the last passages of her reading on Levinas's phenomenology of eros, Irigaray integrates the positions of the beloved woman and the self-defined feminine lover who takes into account the expectations of the male lover but refuses to fulfil these expectations. She writes: "The other cannot be transformed into discourse, fantasies, or dreams. It is impossible for me to substitute any other, thing or god, for the other—because of this touching of and by him, which my body remembers" (ESD, 216/E, 198).

Second, I will return to Sartre's account of the self-other relation, and study Irigaray's treatment of it by focusing on the stylistic and structural aspects of her writing. Irigaray begins the chapter by referring to her experience as a woman. Then she takes the position of a woman reader and lover and writes: "Given that consciousness is transcendent with respect to the body—as Sartre and the majority of Western philosophers think—the other exists beyond what is perceived as a fact. If this is the case, how do I desire and enter into a carnal relationship with him? In *Being and Nothingness*, Jean-Paul Sartre maintains that the only possible way is to enchant him. It is a matter of making his consciousness descend into his body, of paralyzing his liberty in the factuality of the body" (TBT, 18–19/ED, 36. Irigaray repeats Sartre's descriptions in a style which both assumes Sartre's use of the first-person pronoun but is different from Sartre's use in its dialogic mode: "Rather than grasping you—with my hand, with my gaze, with my intellect—I must stop before the inappropriable [. . .]" (TBT, 19 ED, 39).

Thus, in addition to her thematic concerns, Irigaray seems to challenge the assumed generality of Sartre's description—by writing as if Sartre himself, not the subject in general—was the subject implicit in his own descriptions on concrete relations. Thus she also points out the lack of self-reflection: Sartre does not include himself in the investigation. In Irigaray's view, the lover philosopher should include herself or himself in the investigation as a describer, as a singular man or woman but also as a person belonging to a masculine or feminine genre.

This is necessary insofar as the philosophical descriptions of love and desire aim at generality and truth. In contrast to the male phenomenologists, Irigaray does not try to take the position of an outside observer; she does not pretend to be neutral in her descriptions but struggles to mark her gender in her writing. She communicates her alternative concept of love in a specific, dialogical mode of communication, addressing the other as a concrete, specific person, a you. So Irigaray describes the relation between particular persons acting in love, and accordingly, she also directs her own words to particular philosophers who she also treats as masculine persons: to Emmanuel Levinas and to Jean-Paul Sartre.

Effects of Irigaray's Writing as a Woman Lover: New Standard for Truthfulness in Love and Wisdom

While the phenomenologists do not speak about love, they do not speak in love. Irigaray, however, argues that it is exactly the amorous mode of address that needs to be cultivated in the realm of *theoria* and *philosophia* where truth is. Her aim is to create new loving gestures on the part of woman in all dimensions of subjectivity (SP, 193). Through her own textual gestures and acts, Irigaray creates a new model for loving, a model that can be followed by anyone and as such is general and exemplary in a more powerful way than any private love relationship.

When written down, the model is available to anyone, even to readers who live in different times and places. The model can be followed and developed in many different ways in infinite variation. In this way Irigaray's textual work initiates a new mode of intersubjectivity, originating in the loving couple and referring to the past and the future without sacrificing the present for either dimension. Irigaray's criticism of concrete philosophical writings offers a possibility to reevaluate the assumed neutrality of the masculine subject and the generality of the conception of love originating in it.

Irigaray's alternative concept of love completes her explicit critique of Sartre's and Levinas's conceptions of love: the phenomenological descriptions of Sartre and Levinas remain perspectival despite their striving and pretence of universality. By articulating in a dialogical way the problems of the classical conceptions of love Irigaray offers textual and conceptual means for the masculine subject to become aware of himself. She argues that the masculine subject has forgotten the body as a threshold to the world, as a site of perception. The (masculine) subject is bound to the world but does not know himself as such, and refuses to think of himself as such. His existence and activity is restricted and dominated by a nostalgia for a womb or an inner universe, a closed whole that does not have an outside. This nostalgia restricts his self-knowledge in two related ways: his thinking about himself, others, and the world, but it also prevents him from entering into concrete, free interaction and dialogue with the other (gender). The masculine conceptualization of love is congruent with this illusion.

In this way Irigaray's work actualizes love in several dimensions of existence: she encourages the other to become him- or herself, she also returns to herself as a woman in her writing, and she establishes herself as a philosopher who belongs to a particular culture and tradition. This means that even acts of writing can operate as acts of love, and as gestures of caress (see Heinämaa 1996), in Irigaray's sense.

In my view, Irigaray understands "the two" or sexual difference as a duality constitutive of a couple, which, on the one hand, makes the gesture of caress possible, but, on the other, is also an aim which should be constantly strived for, and which cannot be completely achieved, not even in principle. What is at issue is the task that belongs to all lovers. Sexual difference becomes possible only if we abandon our preconceptions and habits when conceiving the sense of woman's being, on the one hand, and our preconceptions of the neutrality of the subject, on the other. In Irigaray's terminology the realization of love between two would mean the disclosure of "the material texture of beauty" or the *sensible transcendental*, constituted by the feminine and masculine styles. She believes that it is philosophy as a discipline that has to be questioned if this goal is to be approached.

Conclusions to Part II

In this part, we have focused on the dynamics of the habitual and the new as studied in the gradual evolution of the practices and conceptualizations of love and eroticism, starting from practices which establish a hierarchical relation between the feminine and the masculine, and proceeding to practices which are capable of opening a sexual difference as a constant interchange between the self and the other. This gradual evolution has been explicated by analyzing the figures, roles, and positions of the beloved woman and by inquiring into the possibilities of desire and love as discursive practices and pre-discursive lived experiences. Both dimentions can be exemplified by Plato's philosophy, criticized in the first part for their notion of fixed essence, but also by the classical phenomenology of the body. The next and final part of this book turns to Irigaray's dialogical reinterpretation of philosophy as love for wisdom.

Part III

Wisdom

In Irigaray's view philosophy as "the discourse on discourse" (le discourse des discourses) defines what is ideal in the two senses of the word—the universal and the perfect (TS, 74/CS, 72). In other words, philosophy defines what exists (ontology), what is valuable (ethics), and how we should strive for wisdom and truth with regard to them (epistemology). This is why, in order to develop the feminine style on all levels of discursive expression and to constitute a full feminine subject with all aspects of spirituality, one must understand and explain how it is possible to speak in philosophy as a woman and what the inclusion of the feminine speaking subject might mean for philosophy itself.

As already explained, in Irigaray's view, in order to obtain access to philosophical discourse, woman must assume a mimetic position. I have identified, mainly on the basis of Irigaray's work but also with the help of the works of other feminist philosophers that the three positions that are offered to women in philosophical discourse are the positions of the woman teacher, the philosopher's wife, and the oracle. Irigaray's work interestingly shows how these positions can be occupied mimetically in a productive way, in a way which opens up the possibility of developing a full-fledged feminine style of existence and a feminine philosophical style. We already saw how Irigaray, with the help of productive mimesis, transformed the figure and position of the beloved woman into a position of a partner in interaction and dialogue, into a woman lover. As we will see, this transformation is also part of the process of developing a full-fledged feminine existential style and a feminine subject of philosophy manifest in Irigaray's work.

A crucial aspect of philosophical discourse is writing. The inherent aim of writing is the widest possible audience and reception. The aim is to reach a large quantity of readers, but also the greatest qualitative variety of qualitatively different readings and the widest possible extension in time and space. These dimensions contribute to the ideality peculiar to writing itself, which, for Irigaray, forms the model of ideality in itself in being constituted by both sensibility and spirituality.

The constitution of the intersubjective philosophical community depends on our capacity to actualize the inherent aims of writing, and the truthfulness of the philosophical pursuit depends on our capacity to practice it in accordance with the model of ideality inherent in writing, the sensible ideality. From Irigaray's point of view, even the most effective writings lack an important aspect which contributes to their ideality, and this lack compromises their objectivity. Moreover, most writings, with the exception of, e.g., the writings of Husserl and Merleau-Ponty, also fail to recognize the intertwinement of sensibility and ideality, or corporeality and spirituality, as the necessary starting point for philosophizing and for the pursuit of self-knowledge of the philosophical subject.

Ultimately, Irigaray *questions* the idea of philosophy as the discourse of discourses. She does it by combining the transformed ideas and practices of love and writing, and their modes of ideality. The idea of a universal discourse correlates with the idea of the neutral subject, its ideal agent: the invisible and disembodied (male) god. Irigaray questions the neutrality of the philosophizing subject, its discourse, and its self-images by disclosing its expressive and embodied character. Irigaray does this with her the amorous modality of her style, which is based on the position of woman defined by the discourse, on the one hand, and on the neglected dimensions of embodiment and materiality, on the other. In distinction from dualistic metaphysics, phenomenologies of the body claim to take these dimensions into account. Yet, on the basis of what I have presented in this work, it seems that there is not only one but at least two ways of forgetting the embodiment of the philosophical subject. In addition to traditional metaphysical forgetfulness, manifest, e.g., in the radical distinction of the body and soul, we have also seen forgetfulness in phenomenological accounts, manifest in the forgetfulness of the philosophizing subject's own body and the masculinity of this body. Both of these problematic approaches are also manifest in the implicit notions of expressivity in the works of the philosophers studied in this book. Accordingly, two different but related conceptions of philosophy or philosophical discourse can be found in the masculine discourse as Irigaray conceives it: one ignores the connection between thought and expression (Plato, Sartre) and the other takes this connection seriously (Merleau-Ponty, Levinas). However, neither takes into account the possibility that a woman can take part in this discourse, either by speaking or by writing, nor do they problematize the identification between masculinity and neutrality in philosophizing.

On the basis of Irigaray's work it can be argued, however, that in both cases the (sexually) other is indispensable in the practices of striving for truth and objectivity. This indispensability can be demonstrated in two related ways: first, by making visible the limits of the received notions of philosophy and the philosophical discourse from the feminine point of view, and second, by showing how the idea of the separation of soul and body or embodiment and spirituality is manifest in philosophical writing.

13

Original Aspects of Woman in Philosophy

*Intermediating between
Materiality and Spirituality, Nature and Gods*

My inquiry into Irigaray's philosophy shows that in order to question the neutrality of philosophy and the disembodiment of the philosophical subject, it is not enough to demonstrate that the subject of personal love has been conceived as implicitly masculine by traditional philosophers. This is because of the crucial philosophical gesture of separating and distinguishing between the subject as an agent and patient of carnal love, on the one hand, and the subject as the self that philosophizes, analyzes, and conceptualizes the relation of carnal love, on the other. Thus, in order to institute a self-defined feminine subject, it does not suffice to assume the position of a woman lover in personal relations or to act as a feminine interlocutor in discussions concerning the topic of love. A self-defined feminine subject can only be instituted if her first-person expressive and self-reflective acts extend to philosophical discourse. Traditionally, philosophy as the crystallization of the rational activity per se is defined as the most "human" or spiritual of all activities, but at the same time is also defined in contrast with embodiment, woman, and the feminine. Ultimately, Irigaray questions this idea of philosophy and philosophizing with her explicit theses and through her performance as a feminine lover of wisdom.

∼

The analysis and interpretation of Irigaray's dialogue with Sartre, Levinas, and Plato (Socrates) on carnal love showed that these philosophers think that the one who needs material, spiritual, and emotional support and is temporarily dependent on the (sexually) other is a person and not a philosopher. The mimetic figure of the philosopher's wife, however, allows us to question this notion: the philosopher's wife supports the philosopher in his *contemplative* activity, which requires expression and address in order to be actualized as philosophy. When this idea is combined with the basic ideas of the phenomenology of the body, the conclusion is far-reaching: the embodied person cannot be separated from the writing and speaking philosopher.

As we have seen, and as other (feminist) philosophers have shown, there are several woman-figures in philosophy, but none of them is satisfying as a self-defined feminine subject of philosophy.[1] From the point of view of philosophical practice we must distinguish between the philosopher's wife, on the one hand, and the figures of the mystic and the oracle, on the other hand. Both types of female figures picture, in their own ways, embodiment and sensibility and modes of relationality typical of embodiment and sensibility. These dimensions of subjectivity are associated with the roles of the beloved woman, the wife, and the mother, and they can be forgotten, even opposed and rejected by the philosopher.

Yet, embodiment and sensibility are needed for contemplation and for practical life. The mystic, the oracle, and the sorcerer have the same function as a wife: all operate as a "passages" or as "guardians of perception" and "thresholds of the world" (cf. Le Dœuff 1989, 113). But, whereas the wife only contributes to the material conditions of philosophizing, the mystic, the oracle, and the sorcerer also contribute to the advancement of contemplation: they provide a "passage" between nature and gods, or spirit.[2] Both the figures of philosopher's wife and the oracle take part in a love relation.

From the point of view of the task of bringing the feminine style into the discourse, the problem, however, is that neither of these figures speaks nor writes for herself. The philosopher's wife remains silent, or her almost "meaningless" speech is merely reported in passing by a male-philosopher. The meaningful words of the oracle are also intermediated: they are reported and rephrased by a male-philosopher and his male pupils. The wife and the oracle both possess wisdom in one area of life, but they do not strive for general wisdom by giving up their possession of partial wisdom, e.g., wisdom on love and loving between persons.

By her discursive moves and expressive gestures Irigaray works to create a position of a feminine lover, a female lover of wisdom that is not reducible to either of the two positions, but includes both. By carefully weaving accepted meanings to new and unexpected expressions and articulations, Irigaray overcomes the limits of the positions of the wife and the oracle but is able include elements of both in the newly evolving position of the woman lover of wisdom. To understand how the position of woman lover of wisdom is constituted in Irigaray's textual practice, but potentially also in women's self-identities, we need study closer the figures and roles of the wife and the oracle and their modes of expressivity which can be localized in the same continuum as the figures of the hysteric, the beloved, and the mystic and their expressivity. We also need study Irigaray's modifications of these two positions and their transformed modes of expressivity.

A crucial step in Irigaray's attempt to unmask the neutrality and absoluteness of the (masculine) subject is to show that the contemplation and monologue of the philosophizing subject is supported in the tradition by either an imaginary or concrete woman-figure, the philosopher's wife and her mode of loving and supporting the philosopher.[3]

The Indispensability of the Philosopher's Women, and Their Self-Sacrificial Love for His Life and Work

A crucial step in Irigaray's attempt to unmask the neutrality and absoluteness of the (masculine) subject is to show that the contemplation and monologue of the philosophizing subject is supported in the tradition by either an imaginary or concrete woman-figure, the philosopher's wife and her mode of loving and supporting the philosopher.[3]

There are similarities in supportive functions of the philosopher's wife and that of the mother of a son. Yet, there is a crucial difference: the wife may carry the child of the philosopher, while the mother has carried the philosopher himself as a child. Both the wife and the mother may have philosophical aspirations of their own, but both may also lack such aspirations. Both represent a specific mode of love, unacknowledged, supportive, and self-sacrificing, love that confuses the identities of the two lovers despite the factual separation of their lived bodies. An example of a sister's self-sacrificial love, is the tragic figure of Antigone, prominent in the discussion of Irigaray's work (see Chanter 2011; Hom 2011).

This mode of self-sacrificial love differs from seduction, which is considered to be appropriate to the muse or the beloved woman. Both modes of love, matrimonial and seductive, however, constitute a totality of two complementaries or two opposites or remains as preparatory stage for the constitution of the ethical and philosophical subject. Because of the mode of love appropriate to the wife, she cannot occupy the position of a unique person loving and loved by the philosopher. Sadly, she cannot occupy the position of a person or a philosopher in her own right.

For the moment, let me focus on the male-defined meaning of the philosopher's wife and study it in two cases. The first is represented by the character of Xantippe; Socrates' spouse: she is a caretaker and provides for the philosopher's everyday life and existence; moreover, she stands for all the modes of experience and expression which are excluded from philosophical practice, e.g., the primitive modes of expression and speech such as chatter, gossip, nagging, and mourning. The second alternative is to work as a philosophical and theoretical helpmate or supporter: a philosophizing woman who restricts her philosophical capacities and aspirations to the tasks and questions which are given by a male-philosopher.[4] These two functions can even be connected and realized by one concrete woman. But in both cases, the philosopher's wife lacks a direct relation to philosophy: the philosopher's wife has only a relation to a philosopher-person (CS, 147, 148; cf. Le Dœuff 1989, 28, 118; Shapiro 2002, 197–200).

The philosopher's wife loves in a way that supports, and conditions, the other's spiritual achievements and provides him with resources for philosophizing. The wife can also support and assist the creating and maintenance of the works of the philosopher or their importance. An example, studied by Michéle Le Dœuff, is Simone de Beauvoir's role as an editor of Jean-Paul Sartre's works such as *Lettres au Castor* (see Lehtinen 2007). On the personal level the philosopher's wife supports the philosopher and provides the means of his well-being. She does this by acting in accordance with the wishes and expectations of the philosopher and by subjecting her own process of becoming to his need. Irigaray describes this situation by attributing to the male-philosopher a "narcissism which often extends onto a transcendental dimension" (TS, 151). The philosopher's wife, who functions as "reproductive material and duplicating mirror," underwrites this narcissm: "[c]ertainly without saying so, without knowing it. That secret in particular must never be disclosed. This role is only possible because of its ultimate avoidance of self-exploration: it entails a virginity incapable of self-reflection. And a pleasure that is wholly 'divine'" (TS, 151/CS, 147).

Yet, a constitutive possibility could be the way the wife, in practical, or partial, wisdom, can deviate from the philosopher's wishes and expectations. This support work includes the tasks of caring for the material, affective, and sensible dimensions of the philosopher's life in any way which advances his well-being and productivity. She also has to liberate the philosopher from his preoccupation with theory: "The philosopher's wife must also, though in a secondary way, be beautiful, and exhibit all the attractions of femininity, in order to distract a gaze too often carried away by theoretical reflections" (TS, 151/ CS, 148). Thus, the philosopher's wife is included in the practice of philosophy and strives for truth only indirectly and in a utilitarian way.

The philosopher's wife can advance the philosopher's work by offering practical assistance which does not require any philosophical education, for example, in documentation of his solitary contemplation by writing or typing. If the wife has philosophical aspirations and a philosophical education she can take care of the noncreative aspects of the philosophical work. She can comment on, repeat, and rephrase the philosopher's work both in private discussions and in professional events, and thus help in developing and maintaining its sense and importance.

These activities occur naturally, without recognition or acknowledgment from either party, the male-philosopher or the wife herself. In this case, the wife accommodates to the philosopher's wishes and expectations and works to protect the mixture of the personal and the philosophical. All this hinders her from becoming a woman philosopher in her own right. Her task remains that of support: she assists the philosopher in his pursuit of the Ideal, his Ideal, and his appearance in public life.[5]

Moreover, the philosopher's wife is also expected in both cases—in the case of the provider and in the case of the companion—to conceal her indispensable but neglected presence by distracting attention away from herself and toward the stereotypic characteristics of nagging, chatting, and gossiping. In this way the wife maintains the illusionary images of both parties. Irigaray describes the position of the philosopher's wife as follows: "That woman—and, since philosophical discourse dominates history in general, *that wife/woman of every man*—is thus pledged to the service of the 'philosopher's' 'self'' in all forms. And as far as the wedding celebration is concerned, she is in danger of being no more than the requisite mediator for the philosopher's celebrations with himself, and with his fellows" (TS, 151–152/CS, 148). In the last sentence, which can also be read as an implicit reference to the *Symposium*, Irigaray suggests that the masculine community of philosophers depends in its existence and function on the activity and operations of the wife. The wife mediates their relations of attraction and love but also covers the nature of the relations by her femininity.

Thus, three kinds of acts of concealment can be detected on the wife's part: that of concealing oneself as a person and a philosopher, that of concealing one's own indispensability for the male person and philosopher, and that of concealing the homosexual nature of the relationships constitutive for the community of male-philosophers.

The Partial and Mimetic Expressivity of the Philosopher's Wife

How then does the philosopher's wife (not) speak? The philosopher's wife does not have a position of speaking (in the discourse) for herself nor an acknowledged position as an interlocutor with the philosopher, especially not on philosophical matters. Insofar as she is able to discuss with the philosopher at all, the discussion must take place in privacy or, if in public, whether in an occasion of speech or writing, then the wife has to participate in it in a supportive function. Thus the wife remains a resource, unrecognized and unacknowledged as a person with her own stylistic unity and coherence, and a subject in the public sphere. She is not an *equal* interlocutor for the philosopher, either in the private or in public. Rather, her task is to repeat the philosopher's words without adding anything of her own (TS, 151/CS, 147; cf. Le Dœuff 1989, 125). As already emphasized, this also holds for the type of wife that has philosophical aspirations and a philosophical education.

Margaret Whitford (1991b, 8–9) finds that Irigaray mimics the role of the philosopher's wife in its "purest, unmixed form" in the text "Mére de glace," a reading of Plotinos in *Speculum*. In this reading, Irigaray quotes Plotinos, but does not comment on or question his views in any way. She just selects the passages to be quoted and puts them in order. Notwithstanding the title of the essay, she does not add a single phrase of her own. In *Ce sexe*, Irigaray also characterizes her mimetic position as the "philosopher's wife" by depicting her method of approaching the philosopher's texts as follows: she says that she questions philosophical discourse with "nuptial tools" (*outils nuptiaux*), and she claims that she has "a fling with the philosophers" (*faire la noce avec les philosophes*), and acts as "a philosophers wife" (CS, 147/TS, 150; see Grosz 1989, 138). Also the figures of the mother as sister are taken into account as mimetic positions in *Ce sexe*: "To go back inside the philosopher's house requires, too, that one be able to fulfil the role of *matter*—mother or sister" (TS, 151/CS, 147).

Like the beloved woman or mother or sister, the wife is situated in the sphere of private intimacy, in merely affective and/or sexual relationships where no discourse and no true words are needed. The difference lies in the public recognition of the wife's position in terms of marriage. Insofar as the figure of wife operates in a philosophical work, it provides a contrasting surface, material, or support for the philosopher's self-defined projects and aims.[6] It is worth emphasizing that one cannot transform the philosophical discourse if one faithfully assumes the position of the philosopher's wife. Yet, if the aim is to develop the feminine style of experiencing and intending, and to open a space for it, then the figure of the philosopher's wife cannot be neglected. In a similar way as the other feminine positions, such as the hysteric, the beloved, woman and the mystic, the figure of the philosopher's wife also offers a starting point to the possibility of questioning the sexual order and the discursive practice and as such includes an emancipatory potential A transformation toward self-definition would effect change in the character of the philosopher's wife and liberate it from the male-based definition.

For example, insofar as the philosopher needs to be and can be reminded of sensible and material reality, it can be questioned whether he really is independent of the material conditions of life and embodiment. The need to be reminded also implies that he is not totally independent of the (sexual) other, neither as a person nor as a philosopher. This means that the life of the philosopher, as well as his (self-deceptive) self-understanding and discourse, presupposes the operations of the philosopher's wife.

The function and role of the philosopher's wife is not acknowledged, as we have seen, on the basis of my explication of Irigaray's work. This indicates a problem in the constitution of philosophical discourse, practice, and its self-understanding. This problem and its solution have consequences for our understanding of materiality, embodiment, and affectivity in relation to spirituality.

Diotima: An Oracle/A Sorcerer

On the basis of our explication above, we can say that canonized philosophical discourse does not include a fully developed woman-figure that would have a direct relation to philosophy and an uncompromised position in the discursive practice of philosophizing.[7] The only figures that we find are related to a particular philosopher or to the work of a particular philosopher but not to philosophy as such. We can, however, find woman-figures with a direct relation to what ultimately exists in reality or ideally. In addition to the mystics described in Christian religious texts, the already mentioned priestess or oracle Diotima speaks to us through the texts that constituted the beginning of Western philosophy. According to Plato's *Symposium*, Diotima, in her knowledge and teaching of love, *precedes* Socrates, the first philosopher.

As we saw, our "knowledge" of this fact is based on Socrates's own words in *Symposium*, through Plato's written description: Socrates names Diotima as his teacher and reports their discussion in a detailed manner. Diotima's contribution to philosophy and its self-understanding is discursively acknowledged by Socrates and his interlocutors. Commentators largely agree about Diotima's fictionality, but evidence for her historical existence, assumably obliterated by the interpretative tradition from a certain historical point onward, has also been presented (Waithe 1987, 105, 106). Several possible explanations for why Socrates gives the floor to Diotima have been explored (Corrigan 2004, 112–118; for a feminist discussion see e.g., Nye 1989, 46, 58; Halperin 1990; Waithe 1987; Kuykendall 1989, 30). Socrates speech is widely paraphrased and is repeatedly explained and Diotima's teaching is treated as a pre-philosophical or preparatory mythical element (cf. Waithe 1987).

The fact is that whether Diotima is considered historical or imaginary, Diotima does not speak for herself despite the authority and expertise on love attributed to her.[8] As we have seen, Irigaray emphasizes this reality of absence and muteness. The artificial character of Diotima in *Symposium* is acknowledged by Irigaray in respect to the process of composing a dialogue in writing: "Often, in his own tongue, man describes, narrates, states, collects, organizes. He doubles the world or creates it. He may even happen to stage a dialogue" (ESD, 138/E, 131).

Irigaray also draws attention to the fact that there is a discord between Diotima and Socrates and/or Socrates and Plato: "But he remains the creator or engenderer of the universe, and of discourse, even when he mimes or repeats a truth that he does not really accept" (ESD, 138; cf. ML, 72–73/AM, 79). Nye (1989, 46), who criticizes Irigaray's view on Diotima, also notices this discursive discordance: "And what is Plato doing, letting Socrates repeat respectfully the teachings of a woman, teachings not always in keeping with Plato's own?"[9]

Feminist philosophers have argued that even though Diotima as a discursive figure offers us a dynamic conception of love, she does not present it as a result of a process of striving for wisdom by herself. Rather, her knowledge about the nature of love and wisdom and their correlates, beauty and good, originates in an external source: the divine. According to this line of argumentation Diotima is a mere intermediator between heavenly wisdom and earthly humans, an oracle (Songe-Møller 2002, 105; Le Dœuff 1998, 104, 107). In other words, she does not strive for wisdom or engage in intellectual work on her own, but, as Vigdis Songe-Møller states, "is wise already" (Songe-Møller 2002, 105).

Diotima's wisdom is based on her capacity to operate as a mediator between the divine and the human: she allows knowledge to overwhelm her and is able to mediate this to her pupils by her statements and questions. She has no particular skill in striving for wisdom or developing the results of her own approach. In this line of argumentation, Diotima is seen as a beloved woman, beloved woman by the gods, or a "figure of divine plenty," and her character is distinguished from the character of the Eros-philosopher Socrates, who is a lover, and is not wise, but is able to move between wisdom and ignorance (see also Corrigan 2004, 116; cf. 117–118). Waithe (1987, 105), for her part, argues that Diotima's ideas are distinct from those of Plato and Socrates and claims that Diotima has an erotic philosophy of her own.[10] The idea of the philosopher as a lover of wisdom is introduced in the speech by Diotima. Also the distinction between the feminine, passive and receptive beloved one and the active and masculine lover is established by her both in respect to love of persons and love for wisdom, as Irigaray sees it.

Yet, Irigaray claims that our understanding of Diotima's position as well as her relations to gods depends on how we conceive the dividing line between the divine/ideal and the real: "Unless what she proposes to contemplate, beauty itself, is seen as that which confounds the opposition between immanence and transcendence. As an always already sensible horizon on the basis of which everything would appear" (ESD, 33/E, 39). The idea of heavenly wisdom can be understood according to the Platonic tradition but it can also be comprehended in another manner. This other possibility would only appear if "one would [. . .] go back over everything to discover it in its enchantment," Irigaray writes (ESD, 33/E, 39). Irigaray's idea of "everything" is, in my view, to be reinterpreted as referring to our individual, philosophical, and cultural preconceptions as inheritors of the Platonic tradition.

For Irigaray, Diotima's words must be taken to mean that she is able to perceive the divine/ideal as inherent in the perceivable, or, in Irigaray's own words: "sensible transcendental, the material texture of beauty" (ESD, 32/E, 38). In this way Irigaray suggests that Diotima is more faithful to experience in her statements than the interpretative tradition, which prefers homogeneity and logical coherence, and too often neglects the writing of Plato and concentrates on the abstract construction of his doctrine of ideas and the presentation of Socrates as its spokesman and promoter.

An indication of Diotima's experiential approach can be seen in the passage that discloses her discordance or disagreement with Socrates on the topic of love's aim. Irigaray quotes from the *Symposium* in the passage where Diotima's explicit claim about the divinity of love is that the ideal of love is found in the fecundity of loving: "This action [suitable for a lover] is engendering in beauty, with relation both to body and to soul" (*Symposium*, 206, ESD, 25). Irigaray claims that Socrates does not capture the core of this claim but bypasses the idea of mutual conception and proceeds to develop his own dialectics. Irigaray writes: "But Socrates understands nothing of such a clear revelation. He understands nothing about fecundity of body and soul" (ESD, 25/E, 32). Yet, according to Irigaray, support for this alternative ideal of love can be found in the very same passage that Socrates ignores: "The union of man and woman is, in fact, a generation; this is a thing divine; in a living creature that is mortal, it is an element of immortality, this fecundity and generation" (*Symposium*, 206; ESD, 25).[11]

In Irigaray's reading the priestess Diotima, however, does not just serve as an access for woman to the (masculine) philosophical tradition. Diotima also belongs to a feminine genealogy of woman sorcerers and mystics that is not acknowledged or cultivated within the philosophical practice, but that supposedly has a privileged access to nature, on the one hand, and to the divine, on the other. Irigaray writes:

> The cultural functions that women might have performed have been judged asocial and hence have been barred to them. They were accused of being *witches*, or *mystics*, because of the potency of the relations they maintained with the cosmos and the divine, even though they lacked any extrinsic or intrinsic way to express them or to express themselves. Useful in the elaboration of the Other of the masculine world, women could have only a forbidden Other of their own. Which was often called demonic possession whereas in fact it involves an ability to perceive the divine (*daimon*) to which man in his shell, his various shells, remains a stranger. In so far

> as he is alien to a sensible transcendental—the dimension of the divine par excellence—and of its grace, man would remain a little outside the religious world, unless he is initiated into it by women. (ESD, 115/E, 111)

On the basis of Irigaray's work, it seems that Diotima's role is crucial, because it is part of the philosophical and metaphilosophical process of defining the scope of research and the methods of philosophy itself. But as emphasized, Diotima's speech is not given in the first-person mode of expression in the *Symposium* but is reported by several (male) persons. Such an expression cannot constitute a place for a feminine speaking subject in the (philosophical) discourse. This is the case with Diotima, who occupies the most influential and discursively acknowledged feminine position in Western philosophy.

Thus, it seems that the discourse only allows a meditative role for women: the philosopher's wife mediates between the private and the public and between the sensuous and the intellectual, and the oracle mediates between the divine and the human and between the ideal and the real. Neither of these roles or positions is discursively acknowledged and thus neither can be cultivated. Therefore, acting in either of these positions leaves the mechanisms of the discourse intact as well as the subject posited by it. Still, it must be emphasized that even though Diotima's words are just reported, fragments of feminine style of experiencing and thinking about experience are included in a canonical text. This inclusion is necessary for the plausibility of the narration, and it is the narration that sustains the arguments. To have a person, even a fictitious person, appear as a woman presupposes that something of the feminine style is brought into the discourse, even if woman herself is not.

My argument is that Irigaray's creative-philosophical work shows that the female figures of the philosopher's wife and the oracle, as traces and fragments, offer us a possibility to actualize, realize, cultivate, and develop the feminine style of intending and experiencing. The actualization and cultivation of these traces and fragments requires first-person acts of expression in the sphere of philosophy, where the ideal, what ultimately exists and what should be strived for, is constituted. These feminine figures crystallize and accentuate the meanings that women and the feminine have received in the tradition, and as such they offer specific points for a critical reflection in the philosophical tradition and its authority in defining the ideal (way of) being manifested by the subject of philosophy and by his works, or by his philosophical style. The wife and the oracle, both functioning in their own ways within the philosophical discourse, offer positions that can be mimetically transformed and cultivated into a style of philosophizing.

14

Irigaray as a Midwife for Diotima's Daimonic Philosophy of Eros

The mimetic figure of the oracle, again, and one more aspect of the wise woman Diotima of Plato's Symposium, *connects the feminine lover of wisdom to the feminine genealogy of wise women, i.e., mystics and sorcerers. By taking into account the association of the feminine with the mystical and nature, Irigaray connects the feminine genealogy to a particular philosophical approach, which she finds in Diotima's speech in* Symposium. *This approach values the role of the perceptual world and focuses on the ideality inherent in it (sensible transcendental). Irigaray's concept and practice of love seem to apply equally to erotic emotions directed at concrete particular persons and to spiritual love directed at philosophical speeches and writings. It is worth of emphasizing that instead of being focused on the* object of love, *Irigaray's work focuses on the* attitude of loving. *The cultivation of such love makes us more conscious of these relations and serves our becoming.*

∽

If my argument concerning the role of love in Irigaray's work as developed in the previous part is valid, love is, in her view, constitutive of the sense of woman and the feminine. Depending on the conception of love and desire in use, the dimensions of feminine and masculine, or embodiment and spirituality, can be understood either as mutually exclusive opposites or as related or even intertwined aspects. Furthermore, the understanding of the aims and nature of humanity varies in accordance with the accepted view of the nature of love and its constitutive parts. The determining aims of humanity can be taken to be external goals of production or self-sustenance and self-preservation realized either in carnal or in spiritual creations. Or, alternatively, the inherent aim of a human being can be seen to be the renewal of his or her own personal being and the personal being of others in the name of their future and fecundity.

In the classical conceptions of love and desire, the dynamic structure of eros, which takes place between the self and the other, is not restricted to carnal love but can also be found in spiritual love. For Irigaray's attempt to revert the sense of woman's being, the shift from carnal love as an inferior or preparatory phase for spiritual love to erotic love understood both as carnal and spiritual is crucial. Furthermore, eros understood as both carnal and spiritual is constitutive also of the sense of the material and the spiritual, of the process in which things come into being for us, as Irigaray understands it. For these reasons, i.e., its role in constituting the sense of woman's being and in constituting the sense of being in general, eros is crucial for the constitution of the woman lover of wisdom. As we have seen, Irigaray agrees on the role of love and desire in investigating existence with both Diotima and Merleau-Ponty. This means that eros is required for the inquiry into the dynamic essences or styles.

In Irigaray's view, this openness toward the future and the possible should also direct our philosophical acts of criticism and creation. This is why Irigaray, following both Merleau-Ponty's phenomenology and the feminine genealogy that she finds in the margins of Western thinking, from Diotima, gives precedence to eros both as a theme and as a philosophical method or practice (cf. Nye 1989, 46). Nye (1989, 55) also claims that "[f]or Diotima, love is not a recreation but permeates the whole of human activity."

On the basis of Irigaray's work, I argue that eros must be reinterpreted according to Diotima's idea of mutual conception and fecundity both in the case of loving another person and in the case of loving wisdom. The internal dynamism constitutive of eros strives merely for fecundity and not for any external goal. This goal can be posited in all dimensions of life and subjectivity. Thus, rather than leading to a hierarchy of the objects of love, Irigaray's/Diotima's eros leads to a recognition of difference and requires detachment from one's own habitual engagements. These engagements can be cognitive, but also sensible and affective.

Irigaray's Redefinition of Personal Love and Love for Wisdom

So, Diotima's/Merleau-Ponty's/Irigaray's conception of eros does not only have consequences for our understanding of personal love, as I pointed out in the previous part, but also for our understanding of love for wisdom. In personal love, as Irigaray understands it, concrete interaction and communication in dialogue with the (sexually) other is indispensable. A reading which also argues for the importance of this aspect in Diotima's speech can be found in Corrigan, though in terms of an idea of reality which is empirical rather than phenomenological:

> [. . .] Diotima points to a search that is simultaneously directed inward and outward. It is a way of living by transformation rather than by being filled with something that is useful and ultimately consumable or absorbable. In this sense, Diotima represents the living reality of dialogue itself, whether she is fictional or not, namely, that the other dialectical pole be really *other*, and not one's own voice or wishes masked as otherness, so that one can be genuinely changed by the experience of encounter and come to give birth to a reality that is not digestible, but that can be *tested*. (Corrigan 2004, 118)

The same holds for the relation between the philosopher and the world: not only interaction but also dialogue is needed. Both in the case of love for a particular person and in the case of philosophy as love for wisdom, the crucial role of eros implies that the lover is not able to disclose the other, the person or reality, by himself or by his own means. Communication with another philosopher-person is indispensable in both cases. In order for communication to be possible, the other philosopher-person must have and be able to occupy a position of his or her own, and must perceive herself or himself realistically and must strive for a realistic perception of the other. This includes the idea that the other with whom one communicates as a philosopher-person should not be reduced to or by one's own capacities or activities. For Irigaray, such an attitude discloses the other realistically: as he or she is in the network of his or her own intentional and motivational relations.

Love includes an exceptional potentiality to relate to the other person as an other *per se*, and not as an other of self. The potentiality of otherness and difference can be actualized in interactions with the other that takes into account his or her freedom and irreducibility. Also love for wisdom in Irigaray's account includes the possibility of loving the "object" of research as an other that cannot be reduced to one's own presuppositions and interests. The movement between "impoverishment" and "enrichment" of one's own presuppositions and interests, between the other's presence and his or her unattainability, can characterize personal love and loving wisdom. In philosophy, or love for wisdom, the other term of the love relation is the non-graspable evolving style of the world, the style of all possible styles, as Merleau-Ponty says (PP, 381/POP, 330)—and the unities of meanings (*styles*) constitutive of it. The erotic philosophical relation to the reality/world, in Irigaray's sense, presupposes the activity and passivity of touching and of being touched in its open infinity.

The relation between a solitary thinker, contemplator, or mediator, and reality is not adequate for the task of delineating the nature of reality: another philosopher is needed in dialogue with the first one. This is because the inherent tendency of the subject is to reduce everything alien to himself or herself. Only another lover of wisdom can question the philosopher's perception of reality and his conception of himself. Another lover of wisdom has her own relation to the multifaceted reality and, in the ideal case, also certain knowledge of the nature of subjectivity and a capacity for self-reflection as well. Objectivity can be aspired to only if the subject's conceptions of itself, of the other, and of the world can be radically questioned through concrete interaction and communication with the others and the world.

This challenge of self-questioning and self-problematization holds both for the subject in general and for every singular subject. The idea of constant movement between impoverishment and enrichment also implies that full objectivity remains an infinite aim and regulative principle and cannot be actualized, in the perception of reality or in the articulation of its ideal structures. This is due to the incompleteness and temporality, or openness, of the embodied, affective, and spiritual subject, and of the world. In my view, Irigaray's concepts of personal love and love for wisdom are related to each other in another way. One is conditioned by the other: the role of the persons concerned is fundamental in the practice of loving wisdom. This is because only another person—a parent or a teacher—can awaken our capacities to love. It implies that the movement characteristic of love for wisdom can already be activated in the love between persons. This is especially obvious in the case of the parent-child relation and in the teacher-pupil relation.

The difference in love between these two types of love—the love of persons and the love for wisdom—lies not only in the role of goal-oriented and methodologically supported activity of studying essences but also in the role of documenting this activity in writing. Between persons, love has to be expressed in words, acts, and gestures if it is not to remain just one person's dream or fantasy, but no written expressions are needed. However, if love for wisdom is to be actualized, writings are necessary. In accordance with Irigaray's idea of the dialogic nature of interaction as the basic mode of relation with other persons (and the world), the basic mode of writing that she proposes and develops in philosophy is dialogic. This is because the ideas of each person lack communal and universal validity as long as they remain unexpressed. To examine the ideas and to establish their validity, in principle, by anyone, writing is necessary.

The philosophical community is established in writings and the philosophical nature of the inquiries is negotiated, questioned, and/or affirmed in writing. This process is multilayered and temporal. Writing, as a practice of making one's views objective in the sense of being available to all, and potentially questioned by anyone, is indispensable for self-reflection. It provides the means to become conscious of one's engagements and the engagements of one's own genre (cf. Heinämaa 2009, 1).

In Irigaray's view, the positions of woman and man are the most distant and cannot be substituted by other positions. They are also the positions which are thematized and characterized in most habitual and prejudiced ways, at least culturally. In the current situation, taking into account the androcentric bias of philosophical discourse, the appearance and (be)coming of the feminine subject/lover is crucial for the rebirth of both personal love and philosophy. This is because the feminine subject has a specific relation to the possible, and is bypassed, neglected, or distorted by the discourse. Her genealogy has not been traced and has not been developed in the first-person point of view within discourse. Yet, the function of the maternal-feminine gives a foundation, not only for the "production" of the lived bodies and the symbolization of them, but also for the generation of the discourse itself.

As has been pointed out, this functioning is not recognized or acknowledged. The maternal-feminine which is constitutive of discourse includes not only the pre-discursive rhythmic and gestural expressions and speech considered to be "almost devoid of meanings," but also many forms of writings, such as fiction and poetry, which are considered to be inferior to the written documentation of the master discourse of Western philosophy. Even inside the philosophical discourse, some forms of writings are considered more central and more constitutive than others in respect to the meaning of philosophy. Thus, we find essays and dialogues overlooked and formal arguments and monologues privileged. Irigaray finds only an illusionary mode of dialogue from the dominant discourse, and says that it consists of "commands, prayers, appeals, [thanks], graces, cries, dirges, glorias, anger and questions," which take place not between persons, man and woman, but between man and his God, his ideal (ESD, 139/E, 132).

The material and sensible aspects of writing are identified with woman and the feminine, in Irigaray's view, and they have never been studied from her point of view in the discourse. This is why her freedom and her self-definition, if expressed, can have an unexpected and unanticipated effect on the discourse. Even if the discourse includes traces and fragments of the feminine subject, it has no means of predicting and no horizon for anticipating her birth as the *subject* of philosophy.

15

Writing

An Intervention into the Neutrality and Absoluteness of the Subject and a Model of Sensible Ideality

According to Irigaray, only a feminine style constituted in first-person expressions and extended to the philosophical discourse can show the masculinity and congruent partiality of the established discourse and open up the possibility of a new mode of philosophical practice: a dialogue in sexual difference. Irigaray's idea and practice of an amorous style of writing, based on her reinterpretation of personal love, questions the neutrality and absoluteness of the philosophical subject. This is done by showing that the philosophizing subject is again dependent on expressive embodiment, which always has an origin in a partial position or perspective. Irigaray's idea and practice of an amorous style motivates her philosophical reflections and operates also in her dialogic inquiries, as the analysis of the multilayered structure of Éthique de la différence sexuelle *will show. In* Éthique *Irigaray's amorous style obtains its full expression in its openness and dynamism.*

∽

According to Irigaray, the masculine style of existence does not appear as masculine in the discourse but appears as neutral. Irigaray writes: "scholars still claim that discourse and truth are neutral" (ESD, 133/E, 127). Irigaray continues: "The subject who enunciates the law is, they tell us, irrelevant, bodiless, morphologically undetermined" (ESD, 133/E, 127). Yet, "[t]he question of what the source of the subject's enunciation of this *episteme* might be fades away unanswered" (ESD, 133/E, 127). The neutral subject is secured, without his realization, by the "net of language which he believes he controls but which controls him, imprisons him in a bodiless body, in a fleshless other, in laws whose cause, source, and physical, living reason he has lost" (ESD, 133/E, 127).

Irigaray argues that the explication of the relation of the masculine subject to its other, its outside and/or woman does not suffice to point out the masculinity of the subject in carnal love: the fracture in neutrality and absoluteness has to be found within the subject of philosophy. In other words, the subject's relation to its other, the imagined "excluded" outside is constitutive of the subject itself and is its internal structure. As we have seen, Irigaray discloses the illusory nature of the neutrality and absoluteness of the masculine subject and discourse by showing how the female figures, the figures of the hysteric, the beloved woman, the female teacher, the philosopher's wife and the oracle participate in the constitution, not only of the sense of woman's being, and the male subject of carnal love but also of the identity and self-image of the (masculine) subject of philosophy.

Moreover, the type of unity and coherence which is associated with the masculine subject, operates as the model for the unity of discourse itself. Irigaray argues that this dominant model of coherence is founded on a mere archaic feminine form. More concretely, she works to find an internal fracture in the neutrality and absoluteness of the (masculine) subject and is able to identify such a fracture in the discourse concerning (carnal) love. Yet, while this fracture suffices to reveal that the neutrality of the (masculine) person/subject of personal love is illusory, it does not suffice to show that the autonomy and neutrality of the masculine subject of *philosophy* is illusory. This is because carnal love is conceptualized as a temporary degradation of the universal neutral subject from its proper spiritual existence to embodiment. In other words, the aspects of the subject which are needed for philosophizing are believed to be abandoned in the temporary falling under the influence of femininity and sensuality, as we have seen in the previous chapters.

The masculine subject of philosophy and its act of thinking are assumed to be neutral and completely disembodied. This can be seen, for example, in our way of understanding thinking, and conceptualizing and practising it, as a solitary contemplation and/or monologue. Writing which mediates the propositional content of contemplation is believed and claimed to be at its best when it is most "transparent," i.e., least visible and sensible as expression. In order for Irigaray to stick to her hypothesis about the illusory nature of the neutrality, autonomy, and absoluteness of the philosophical subject, she has to effect a change in the one activity and practice which is indispensable for thinking in several ways. This activity, constitutive of the philosophical subject, is philosophical writing. Philosophical writing is necessary for establishing a philosophical tradition, but it is also necessary in the process of striving for objectivity. Both one's own writings and the writings of others can serve the aim of distancing from one's own presuppositions and thus can help in obtaining self-knowledge both as a person and as a philosopher. Self-knowledge, on its part, is required for the attempt to distinguish that which is own and similar from that which is other and what is the relation between the two.

Irigaray works in a double fashion to disclose the illusory nature of the neutrality, autonomy, and absoluteness of the philosophical subject. The first task is to show that being a philosopher means essentially a relation to the writings of other philosophers, past, present, and future. We have seen how she has done this by criticizing the common, unacknowledged, presuppositions of the male-philosophers in their conceptualizations of carnal love. The second task is to show that writing always refers back to a (masculine or feminine) body. In what follows I will focus on how Irigaray, in my view, aims to proceed with both tasks by the amorous modality of her style of writing.

Let us first focus on the task concerning writing. Traditionally, the philosophical writings have concealed their temporality, materiality, sensibility, and stylistic nature and presented themselves as reports or documentations of the contemplation of the solitary and unitary subject. Yet, it is in connections and disconnections that prevail both within a singular writing and between singular writings where the philosophical subject can constitute itself. This process is temporal and occurs in the network of relations to and with other writers and writings, past, present, and future. Thus, in order to become part of the philosophical community or tradition, instead of functioning as an autodidact or an amateur, the subject of a solitary contemplation must explain his processes of research and its results in writing.

So, the processes of philosophizing and becoming a philosopher cannot be completed without writing that makes the "solitary" contemplation or meditation available to others and persuades us of its usefulness or its necessity. A perceivable expression of thought, formulated in writing and completed in words, is necessary if thoughts are to be available to the community, which is able to affirm the existence of the philosopher as a philosopher with an ideal position in the discursive field. Philosophical writings are public in a most precise sense, even when their topics concern private relations, as in case of carnal love.

In a similar way, as the relations between persons are supported by series of movements, gestures, "primitive" tonal expressions and speech acts, so too are writings supported by material signs, letters that are structured into words, phrases, passages, chapters, and complete philosophical works. All these signs are indispensable for the constitution of the open and dynamic unity of (philosophical) community. This holds for the unity of philosopher persons. It also holds for works of one single writer and for writings of larger unities, such as the unities of research fields and unities of a single genre. Thus, the philosophical subject is constituted both in a relation to itself, or to those similar to him or identical with him, and in relations to those that differ from him, including the world, which is given to him, and to all others.

The second task, which is related to the first, is to show that the philosophizing—contemplating or meditating—subject is necessarily embodied. This means that the philosophical subject has a body which, concretely speaking, is always either masculine or feminine or combines aspects of both. If this holds, then the masculine subject should not be thought to be merely temporarily embodied, i.e., only insofar as it is exposed to the corrupting influence of the feminine, as has been the case in the traditional discourse on carnal love.

The embodiment of the subject as co-extensive with his contemplative and meditative activities can be disclosed—but also concealed—by and in writing. This is because writing always refers back to a writing, inscribing, and moving hand, and further, to the organic whole of a writer: man, woman, or a combination of both. Thus, the philosopher as a writer who is constituted in his or her relations to all past, present, and future thinkers, is not only tied to other spirits but also to other bodies. The expressive—writing and speaking—body of the philosopher is inherently associated with other expressive bodies who can write and read. A similar network of potential and actualized connections is established between the bodies of writings.

It is important to notice that even the apparently neutral and monologic manner of philosophical writing addresses the reader from a certain position and with a certain figure. This position and figure are seemingly neutral, but are in Irigaray's view really masculine. For the reader who aspires to wisdom and truth, this mode of communication offers only two alternatives: the reader can either accept or deny the propositional content of the writing, but in both cases she accepts the fact of not being addressed as a person capable of self-reflection, a self-defined philosophical position, and a goal of her own.

Despite its neutralizing and idealizing self-representation, this position of the writer, and its correlate the reader, is also paradoxically constituted by textual means. The means used in and needed for its establishment and maintenance work to hide or cover the text's dependency on sensual-material signs as well as the bodily spiritual movements necessary for the act of writing. The essential materiality of writing, as well as the "solidarity" of thought and expression is explicated by Merleau-Ponty, but it has been neglected in favor of the maintenance of the illusory notion of philosophizing as a detached and autonomous activity.

Irigaray seems to maintain that the body is confused in philosophical discourse with the anonymous materiality which conceptually supports the philosophical discourse. The philosophical subject, and his writing, presents itself as disembodied and transparent instead of acknowledging its sensible-material aspects and making its expressivity explicit. On the one hand, Irigaray writes about the identification of woman and embodiment, but on the other hand she seems to think that the identification of neutrality and masculinity also applies to the body: the masculine body appears as a mere means of the spirit and the subject does not understand nor present himself as embodied. As mentioned earlier, this apparent tension in Irigaray's or in feminist thought has been recognized by the scholars. They point out that the masculine is more easily experienced and presented as a solid body with closed boundaries and unidirectional movements. The masculine body seems to be more easily controllable, and thus easier to forget than the lived feminine body identified with the narrowly understood sexual or nurturing aspects with its "fluid being" manifested in menstruation and pregnancy (Bergoffen 1997, 144; Heinämaa 2003, 72). Stone expresses this by writing that "male bodies are traditionally imagined to be uniquely so formed that their inhabitants can transcend them" (Stone 2006, 34). This experiential aspect of embodiment, given to the man and to the woman in the first person, is further consolidated by the dominant conceptualizations established from the male point of view.

In this scheme, when a nonspiritual dimension is needed for the constitution of the spiritual and when materiality cannot be denied or neglected, it is either not acknowledged or it is projected onto the feminine. My study has shown that this can occur in two different ways: as a projection onto the maternal-feminine, which is associated with anonymous materiality, or as a hierarchy of different modes of experience and expression. This is the case with a concrete body, as in descriptions of love, where masculine speech is contrasted with the "primitively" expressive feminine body.

So the neutrality, autonomy, and absoluteness of the philosophical subject, and also the presentation of ideas, have been created from and maintained by the raw material of language. Language as raw material consists not only of language as a system of phonemes and letters, words, and sentences, but also of the "inferior layers" of language such as rhythm and intonation, indispensable for fiction and poetry, and associated with the feminine. This has been possible because of the omission of woman's first-person perspective and the feminine style in discourse. In other words, the multiplicity of relations that can establish a feminine subject in discourse has not been cultivated to form points of comparison for the masculine subject. This is because feminine gestural unity with its morphology or form and its experiential content is excluded from discourse: "[. . .] women need to establish new values that correspond to *their* creative capacities. Society, culture, and discourse would thereby be recognized as sexuate and not as the monopoly on universal value of a single sex—one that has no awareness of the way the body and its morphology are imprinted upon imaginary and symbolic creations" (ESD, 68/E, 70).

How then can the masculine body (of writing) be recognized and encountered as such if it denies itself a body, especially a passive and receptive body? How can the (masculine) subject be identified in its embodiment and sexuality?

I argued that the possibility of this recognition and encounter, and the possibility of achieving a realistic conception of oneself, can be found in carnal love. This is because carnal love cannot sustain the pretence of neutrality and nonembodiment; they must instead be put aside, at least in a nonconscious and temporary manner. As we have seen in the previous part, however, it is not the philosophical subject who falls in (carnal) love with a woman, but a masculine person described by the philosopher. Irigaray argues, however, that the masculine lover is closely related to his describer and that the relation between the describer and the feminine beloved woman is very different. This is the fracture in the neutrality and absoluteness of the (masculine) subject of philosophy: instead of distancing himself from one of his topics—the masculine lover—he identifies with him and his acts, and presents the feminine beloved woman and her acts as its mirror image.

In my view, this fracture gives love a specific methodological role in Irigaray's examination of the assumed neutrality of the philosophical writing. The philosophical subject can perceive itself and its acts, thinking and writing, realistically only if another subject, different from it and its acts, is established. Realistic perception here implies that the subject would know itself as embodied, affective, temporally evolving and necessarily related to its exteriority. An embodied subject is necessarily temporal and perspectival and lacks completeness. The subject other to the masculine discourse can only be feminine, constituted of expressive acts with a nonanticipated structure and content. Irigaray combines this idea with the fracture in the neutrality of the subject found in the discourse on love. In my view, she argues that love can become a passage through which the feminine subject can enter the discourse and through which the constitutive relations of the feminine person can be transformed to serve woman's own becoming.

In the previous part we saw that Irigaray's work demonstrates that the primitive unity of feminine expressions is presupposed by canonical discussions of carnal love. Moreover, in these discussions also feminine expertise on love is recognized. Irigaray develops the fragments and traces of feminine expressions in her writings on love and desire. Love for wisdom in Irigaray's/Diotima's sense calls for a specific mode of philosophical writing capable of accounting for the feminine experience of the lived body and its expressions, which are both temporally founded on the genealogy of women. Only the cultivation of the mimetic dimension of feminine writing can—through a critically transformed conception of love—open the possibility for the development of a feminine style and its perfection and create a feminine philosophical style.

Irigaray works for this goal by describing and inventing caressing gestures on the part of woman. In *Sexes et parentés*, she claims to have created a new style of writing and thinking in *Éthique* (SP, 191). In her view, a new, amorous, style has to be created if we are to investigate and question the neutrality and masculinity of style(s): the aim is to reveal the masculine elements of style dominant in philosophical writing, which presents itself as neutral by contrasting it to her own feminine writing (SP, 184–185). Irigaray's amorous or caressing feminine style extends from the area of personal love to that of the theoretical: the presentation of the process of research, thinking, and writing. Understood in this way, love covers both the sensual and the intellectual dimensions of subjectivity.

Her style, by its amorous openness, reveals that we are always already tied, in all dimensions of subjectivity, to others and to the world whether we choose to be related or not. Irigaray writes that what is said in *Éthique* "moves through a double style: a style of loving relationships, a style of thought, of exegesis, of writing. The two are consciously or unconsciously linked, with a more immediately corporeal and affective side on one case, a more socially developed side on the other. But the language there is already allied with others" (SG, 177/ SP, 191). In cases of personal love, as well as in the case of love for wisdom exemplified in language, either speech or writing connects us to others and to the world (cf. Heinämaa 2000, 11; Vasseleu 1998, 15).

The Figure of a Rose: Multilayered Openings in *Éthique*

Irigaray's *Éthique* has four parts. The first part begins with a well-known lecture "Sexual difference" (*"La différence sexuelle"*). The first sentences of this lecture/essay anticipate a new era, and promise it on the condition that we manage to open up the potentiality of a now almost unrecognized sexual difference. This lecture/essay is followed by a discussion of Diotima's idea of eros under the heading "Sorcerer Love: A Reading of Plato, *Symposium*, 'Diotima's Speech'" ("L'amour sorcier. Lecture de Platon. Le Banquet, 'Discours de Diotime'"), and the theme of love is developed throughout *Éthique*. Three parts of the work begin with an essay that has the terms *l'amour de soi*, *l'amour du meme*, or *l'amour de l'autre* in its title. The work ends in a discussion about Lévinas's phenomenology of eros in an essay called "The Fecundity of the Caress: A Reading of Levinas, *Totality and Infinity*, 'Phenomenology of Eros'" ("Fécondité de la caresse. Lecture de Lévinas. Totalité et infini, Section IV, B, 'Phénoménologie de l'éros'"). Between the two lecture/essays on eros—"Sorcerer Love" and "The Fecundity of the Caress"—Irigaray investigates different philosophers with different topics: Aristotle's category of place, Spinoza's concept of God, Descartes idea of wonder as the first passion and Merleau-Ponty's concept of chiasm. All of these essays are connected together in complex ways.

Three parts of the work begin with an essay by Irigaray followed by discussions of three philosophical contemporaries: Plato and Aristotle, Descartes and

Spinoza, Merleau-Ponty and Levinas. *Éthique* is especially fruitful and important for the study of the feminine style in its state of becoming. Irigaray's amorous style of address makes the potential elements and constituents of the feminine style topical in a new way. *Éthique* seems to operate as an example of the feminine style, in its structural features, and in its relations to itself, to the other, and to the world. *Éthique* expresses the feminine subject in the process of its constitution.

In my view *Éthique* has a crucial position among Irigaray's works: through the opening of the potentiality of the feminine style that it affects, both Irigaray's earlier works and her later works can be read in a philosophically fruitful manner. Irigaray herself explains that *Éthique* is based on the cultural analysis that she has made in her earlier works: *Speculum, Ce sexe, Amante Marine, L'oubli de l'air*, and *Passions élémentaires* (SP, 191/SG, 177). Before *Éthique* the feminine style with its potential relations is only partially established and remains uncultivated, as the emphasis on mimesis, seduction, and "man's woman" in *Speculum, Ce sexe, Amante Marine, L'oubli de l'air*, and *Passions élémentaires* indicates: the feminine style is in the state of "budding" rather than in its full flourish.

After *Éthique*, the feminine subject of Irigaray's works is more in control of herself and her relations, but less is dynamic and less open (cf. Deutscher 2002, 18; Joy 2007, 4–5). This diminished potentiality and capacity for renewal means sedimentation of experience and increased rigidity of the experiential structures—habitualities—of the subject. This course of development of each (feminine) subject might be inevitable at least to some extent. This holds also for the generic feminine, understood as constituted by singular feminine styles of subjectivity in different phases of their evolution. In both, in the case of an individual style and in the case of a generic style, a specifically holistic attitude of love can help in questioning the habitual and can motivate a renewal. This attitude toward oneself, other, or others, that which is own and similar, consists of both critical and constructive gestures. It holds equally for persons and their works.

Éthique offers an exploration and a model of the feminine style and also a model of sexual difference as Irigaray sees it. This is concretized through a discussion of love and its operative aspect: the amorous or caressing attitude.[1] The main idea is that the related terms of love have been taken to form one whole, but Irigaray argues that the regulative ideal of love is to remain two. It is important to notice that two singular unique persons can conflate in the imaginary, but their lived bodies resist this conflation. Similarly, we can obtain a certain interpretation of a piece of writing or a body of texts, but the text as an original source of meanings is never reduced to our conception but can always open itself to us anew. As mentioned, this can occur through our personal evolution with the assistance of other persons or by the new perspectives offered by other readers of the texts or both.

The Speaking Subject of *Éthique*: The Relation to Oneself

Irigaray tells us that *Éthique* is based on the descriptions of the feminine body and the cultural analysis of Irigaray's previous works. In other words, after having written several works as a woman on the topic of woman, Irigaray has gained conceptual and textual resources both for reflecting on the being of woman and for developing a self-reflectively aware account of her own operation as a woman. Thus Irigaray has, throughout her work, developed her feminine style of existence and participated in developing the generic feminine also in the specific, but authoritative field of philosophy, where no "woman's woman" has been found.

As we have seen, the structure of my work reflects this evolution, which includes several phases. It started from the fragmentary expressions of the hysteric and the beloved woman in *Speculum*, *Ce sexe*, *Amante Marine*, and *Passions élémentaires*. In these works the relation to the male subject, an illusory absolute rather than a real lover, and his monologous discourse is dominant. Irigaray's critical attitude and her mimetic, more or less desperate, expressions reflect the biased situation. While pointing out the dominance of the male subject in defining woman and her mode of relating, she simultaneously points out woman's complicity in the situation. Moreover, she strives to describe feminine embodiment and experience from the first-person perspective already in *Speculum*.

The gradual increasing and widening of the variety of her diverse modes of expressions, the potentiality of feminine love of the self and love among women, and also the distance taken from the feminine condition granted her the possibility of becoming herself, of flourishing, in a multiplicity of relations. All these operations were guided by the aim of objectivity or love for wisdom and truth. As we will see, this multiplicity and flourishing can be perceived in the modes of addressing in *Éthique*. Futhermore, the aim of maintaining the tension between the habitual and the new, the male-defined feminine figures, the internalized roles of "man's woman" or, alternatively, the aim of self-definition and renewal are constantly negotiated. In this way, the same principle of love of wisdom as a movement in between poverty and richness, or between the habitual and renewal, unites, as a regulative principle, Irigaray's work as a whole.

Irigaray's amorous style in *Éthique* connects her speaking position to the mimetic positions of the beloved woman, the female teacher, and the philosopher's wife, and refers to the mimetic position of the hysteric through them. The amorous modality of Irigaray's style connects her speaking positions to the sphere of private intimacy to which these figures belong. Its background are also in the figures of the mystic and the oracle/sorcerer as intermediaries between nature and divine. However, a change in the role of mimicking the "man's woman" can be detected in *Éthique*. Carolyn Burke, for example, makes a distinction between the discourses of *Speculum* and *Éthique* by arguing that the former depicts the confusion of voices experienced in hysteria, while the latter develops a dialogic way of treating the classical texts (Burke 1994, 254; cf. Deutscher 2002, 162). In *Éthique* the fragmentary feminine self-expression of the hysteric or the muteness of the philosopher's wife has been developed into an integrated but open unity of expressions. This transformation has occurred with the assistance of the previous expressive acts but also by finding the constitutive possibilities offered by the masculine discourse and the feminine and masculine embodiment and affectivity.

On the one hand, Irigaray's style of writing manifests an awareness of the feminine genealogy and works for strategic aims. On the other hand, Irigaray's style of writing cannot be explained by any narrow or pre-posited aims. For example, as we already saw, Irigaray describes her first-person position of speaking and writing as a woman in an uncomplicated manner by saying: "I am a woman. I write with what I am" (JTNT, 53/JTN, 65). Yet, this apparent immediacy of feminine experience is always mediated by the dominant conceptual structures and available linguistic and stylistic formations of which Irigaray is constantly aware.

Another related aim is to develop the feminine style through feminine amorous gestures, which are "still to be created" (SP, 191) and bring into the discourse the feminine bodily morphology—which is given discursively not merely as a series of gaps and exclusions but also as a network of traces and fragments of lived experience and expression. The style of *Éthique* is formed in several dimensions, and the moves and gestures constitutive of it contribute to these two crucial aims of Irigaray's philosophical project.

Irigaray's activity of describing is always already founded on a network of multidimensional relations, and not in a frontal pose in respect to the world or to others. Her style is formed from the maternal-feminine element and it respects the structures of embodiment and sensibility and thus refers back to a shared life in which and of which we live pre-discursively. Breathing, for example, belongs to those modes of elementality which cannot be described in terms of the subject-object division, but which still constitute a relation that connects the subject to its exteriority.[2] These dimensions of subjective experience are thematized by Irigaray in *Passions élémentaires* and *Entre Orient et Occident*, but they are also discussed in *Éthique*.

Moreover, Irigaray's activity in speaking and writing originates in the pre-discursive experience and the elemental layer of the discourse: language and other speeches and writings. The affective unity of bodily expressions—singing, crying, and gesticulation—is presupposed in the constitution of the more articulate verbal unities of speaking and writing. Also, language as a system of intonations, melodies, and rhythms is presupposed by the language of propositional statements. To demonstrate the operations of this "elemental" mode of language, Irigaray writes in a way which highlights this elemental nature of writing and the connections between the expression and what is expressed. By her writing, she struggles to protect and accentuate this unity.

However, as established in writing, Irigaray's new style is not reducible to the primitive unities of amorous relations and their privacy and intimacy. Her way of establishing intersubjectivity creates a continuum between gestures, modes of vocal expression, and the "highest" forms of expression in speech and writing. Thus it connects the different layers of expressivity and aims at effecting a change in the constitution of intersubjectivity at all levels of existence, primitive and high. Therefore, no private-public dichotomy nor dichotomy between the intersubjectivity of the couple and broader intersubjectivity is established here (cf. Bergoffen 1997, 200, 207). This continuity is manifested in her writing: here she institutes and cultivates a loving attitude and introduces it into the context of philosophy, where ideals, that which is universal and that which is perfect, are defined and created. Verbal language presupposes gestural language, and all the writings, in their own specific modes of relating, serve as material for other writings by fertilizing and enriching one another.

By her amorous, i.e., intimate and interrogative modification of the philosophical style Irigaray marks the traditional relation of a woman to philosophy either as an object of love and desire or as a condition for the possibility of the masculine subject, both strictly distinguished from the activities of thought and meaningful speech. She develops descriptions of the body as it is lived by women, especially in encounters with the (sexually) other, beginning from the elemental affective and sensible dimensions of subjectivity. Thus she struggles to form a new feminine position and a point of view in the discourse on love, desire and wisdom.

The Relation to the Other Striving for Wisdom

In *Éthique*, Irigaray's feminine style is dynamically changing and moving, affective and passionate—in the sense of both receptivity/passivity and intensity—and it is poetic. It is characterized by openness and fragmentation but it is still identifiable. These features together form an informal and intimate mode of approaching, which is enforced by the conversational and interrogative, rather than affirmative, argumentative, or exegetic, manner of discussion. Through her style, Irigaray mimics not only the modes and areas of expression traditionally associated with the roles of the beloved woman and the wife, but also those of the teacher and the oracle.

On the other hand, she addresses a partner, another person engaged in the amorous relation, someone both capable of and willing to be involved in such a relation. As in any love relation, the amorous relation established in writing also includes two persons. In *Éthique* these are a woman and a man, Irigaray and the philosopher with whose writings she engages herself. The actualized dialogues in *Éthique* are based on Irigaray's earlier "dialogues" and her investigation into the ways how the actualization of a dialogue is made impossible by textual means in the canonical texts of certain male philosophers. For example, Ellen Mortensen explores Irigaray's practice of amorous "dialogue" with Nietzsche in Irigaray's *Amante Marine* (1989, 102–122). What is at stake is the possibility or impossibility of "dialogue" inherent in a philosopher's texts: Mortensen, in my view rightly, argues that Irigaray's "lover's discourse" falls on deaf ears with respect to Nietzsche (Ibid., 249).

However, Irigaray does not want to form a couple closed upon itself and separated from the sphere of the intersubjective. In *Éthique*, this attitude is evident in the way Irigaray does not direct her critique at any one person or work. The plurality of the relations to (sexually) other persons protects the writer from falling into the position of the beloved woman or the wife, which are defined exclusively in relation to one man. The distancing from these positions is furthered by Irigaray's way of addressing a singular philosopher-person, a "you" rather than a neutral non-person at one time. The pronoun "you" is an address of a unique person but not an exclusive one. Thus it allows Irigaray to discuss with several persons, each separately but not exclusively. Irigaray explains her way of reading other's text and the approach she wishes for her own texts: "The only response one can make to question of the meaning of the text is: read, perceive, experience . . . *Who are you?* is probably the most relevant question to ask of a text, as long as one isn't requesting a kind of identity card or an autobiographical anecdote. The answer would be: *how about you?* Can we find a common ground? talk? love? create something together? What is there around and between us that allows this?" (SG, 178/SP, 192)

As demonstrated by Irigaray's analysis of eros, loving a person is not separate from striving for wisdom: love at its most optimal means always already a process of striving for wisdom with the other. Moreover, love is plural and not one, in the sense that one mode of love does not exclude another mode, nor does one relation of love does not exclude another of a different kind. For example, feminine love of self is not excluded by love of another person: woman is not for anyone, she is, first of all, for herself in her multiplicity. Irigaray does not offer an exegetic reading or a scholarly interpretation with definite conclusions but engages herself in a dialogue with the texts, and their writers, and with the reader (cf. Kozel 2001, 115). In this intimacy, "you," the lover addressed, is connected to the reflective "I," which refers to the lover, the amorous interrogator, and to the reader. The amorous interrogator questions not only her partner and his perception of himself, but also herself and her realistic perception of the other and encourages the reader to engage with the same processes. All this questioning and self-questioning is needed because the writer and the reader can share prejudices and neglected possibilities that stem from the tradition of Western thinking, or their seemingly self-evident conceptions and practices may lie deep in unexamined "common sense."

So Irigaray mimics the expressions associated with the feminine in the tradition of philosophical writing, but she is not bound by the figures that she mimics. This is due to the positions occupied and relations modified in the earlier works and also to the constitutive possibilities offered by the specific philosophical texts. Rather, her special mode of writing in the first-person singular, when introduced in the realm of philosophy, opens a new possibility to question the masculine ideal of woman and the masculine as a norm of human existence and it establishes a beginning for the development of a generic feminine style. By connecting the topic of woman's being and her discursive position to the philosophical ideas of truth and wisdom, she effects a change in the situation of woman in philosophy. This leads to another transformation: the female speech position is cultivated so that it establishes a specific mode of philosophizing, a way of speaking through love about wisdom and truth. The transition from the position of an object or a resource to a position of a responsible and self-responsible speaking subject is effectuated by the amorous gestures constitutive of Irigaray's double style.

The Male Philosopher-Persons and the Tradition of Their Mutual Relations

In order to investigate Irigaray's philosophical style, and philosophical styles in general, it is crucial to pay attention to the dialogic relations established by Irigaray, i.e., her intimate discussions with classical and canonical philosophers. In her activity of writing, Irigaray also operates as a reader of the classical texts. The texts chosen and addressed by Irigaray are crucial moments in the development of the philosophical tradition in several ways. It is illuminative to study closer the titles of her dialogues with philosophers: in each case she associates a classical or canonical text with the body, with the name of the writer in her own title in parenthesis.

As we already saw, her lecture/essays are called, for example: "Fécondité de la caresse (Lecture de Lévinas. *Totalité et infini*, Section IV, B, 'Phénoménologie de l'éros' ") or "L'amour sorcier (Lecture de Platon. Le *Banquet*, 'Discourse de Diotime' "). The titles first name Irigaray's topical interest in the lecture/essay in question. The chosen topic correlates with Irigaray's interest in the position that the classical or canonical philosophical text has in the interpretative tradition. In "Sorcerer Love," for example, the main topics are the Platonic concept of eros and philosophy as the love for wisdom. However, Irigaray's thought about the feminine introduces a completely new aspect: the idea of love as the intermediary which cannot be reduced to dualistic oppositions and which is intimately linked to the feminine.

So the titles of Irigaray's lecture/essays provide a central topic and also indicate a whole body of work by presenting one of its parts. The philosopher's name refers to a whole corpus of work as well as to all interpretations attributed to it by the tradition. These references constitute the open whole in Irigaray's book, which then is brought into a transformative movement. In *Éthique*, discussions of the classics are followed by contemporary philosophers. This order implies a question about the unity of the tradition: has the tradition changed or remained the same in the different interpretations, recitations and modifications?

A further aspect of the philosophical tradition and its mode of constitution are disclosed by Irigaray's organization of the lecture/essays in pairs of two philosophical contemporaries: Plato and Aristotle, Descartes and Spinoza, Merleau-Ponty and Levinas. In each part of *Éthique* two philosophical contemporaries are juxtaposed and discussed in parallel. This form of organization accentuates and highlights the way in which the philosophical discourse and tradition is constituted as an interchange between masculine writers. This homogeneous and homoerotic intersubjectivity is made invisible by the supportive function of the maternal-feminine.

In all the couples—Plato and Aristotle, Descartes and Spinoza, Merleau-Ponty and Levinas—the successor can be seen as a critic and inverter of the predecessor's philosophy. The successor takes the other's philosophy to be something exterior to themselves and their thought and already constituted as such and tries to invert it (JAT, 108/ILTY, 63). Ultimately, the aim is to show the other philosopher and his work to occupy an inferior position in order to support the position occupied by oneself (Ibid.). The idea of inversion is affirmed by the canonical presentations of these couples in general accounts of history of philosophy, as well as in many specialized commentaries and encyclopedia.

Yet, the difference between the predecessor and the successor is not established as a hierarchical difference: readers and interpreters of philosophical texts accept and maintain the undecidability between two competing solutions. In the above mentioned cases the competing solutions are offered to fundamental metaphysical problems—dualism-monism, realism-idealism, immanence-difference—and they affirm this undecidability by producing more oppositional alternatives. Thus, the philosophical practices of commenting and interpreting guarantee, to different degrees, the permanent tension between two alternative fundamental metaphysical positions. These readings and interpretations constitute the philosophical tradition and they present the classical texts or specific formal arguments extracted from them as its solid foundation. One could think that Irigaray's aim is not to question any one alternative or phase in this edifice but to problematize its process of constitution as an interchange between males.[3]

Irigaray as a Woman Philosopher Striving for Truth

Irigaray, however, does not work to be included in this chain of male philosopher predecessors, nor could she be included. Her aim is not to invert any other philosophy. Instead, her aim is to invert herself (*renverse moi-même*) (JAT, 108/ILTY, 63). She examines and explores the structures of duality—couples—inherent in the constitutive processes of the philosophical tradition and their connections to sexual difference.[4] The inclusion of the idea of style of writing accentuates the necessarily unfinished and incomplete nature of writing. This openness depends on the temporality, affectivity, and embodiment of the philosophical subject, especially evident in relations of carnal love.

As a woman lover of wisdom, Irigaray does not operate from an "impartial" third-person perspective or report discussions of other people, speaking with, at least seemingly, unquestionable and "neutral" authority. Irigaray follows Merleau-Ponty's idea of the need to put essences back to existence in our inquiry into experience, and also in presenting the results of the inquiry for the readers. Irigaray does not abstract from her own experience to construe a theory of the universal features of experience in general or to discover the ultimate reality. Rather, she keeps her discourse open to include unexpected aspects both in her own experience and in the experience of the reader, thus developing the generic feminine in a manner which would not deny multitude or plurality. This experience is also constituted in relations to the sexually other.

By her style of writing and the composition of the structure of her work, I argue, Irigaray asks why the hierarchy of opposites is established only in the relations of man and woman. As we saw, on the basis of Irigaray's exploration of the dualities central to the philosophical tradition in *Éthique*, the structure of being in opposition as such does not lead to hierarchical difference. *Éthique* explores this duality as twofold: a tension, on the one hand, and duality, as a hierarchy of mutually exclusive terms, on the other. Irigaray studies different philosophical couples in order to show that duality can be conceptualized in several ways.

The most important couple of Irigaray's lecture/essays, however, is the problematic but also fruitful couple of Diotima and Socrates. Correspondingly, the methodologically most important reading is the reading of Socrates/Diotima's eros. The role of eros in *Éthique* is accentuated by the fact that the work ends with a discussion of Levinas's reinterpretation of eros. Irigaray shows how the shortcomings of Socrates' and Plato's concept of eros reappear in Levinas. This points to the task of once again returning to the beginnings of the tradition, with the aim of opening it up more fully by posing the question of sexual difference.

Irigaray's practice of eros-philosophy does not allow for any system building, its dialectics is not like that of Hegel's, she explains (ESD, 20/E, 27). The idea of a system is an idea of a finished and completed whole: untouchable, immovable, water tight, and without any gaps. Irigaray opposes the systematic notion of philosophical work to an organic one which includes the idea of an internal dynamics of renewal and rebirth. Irigaray's conception of philosophical work and writing has as its model the organic whole of the lived body and one of its imaginary representations: the rose. The ideal inherent in this sensuous figure can be found in the motto of the very first page of *L'oubli de l'air*: "The rose is without why; it flowers because it flowers" (cf. Krell 1992, 306).

Irigaray's dialogues differ from the paradigmatic Platonic dialogues in that they do not set the stage for several competing interlocutors. Moreover, she does not hide her interests as the stage manager. Rather, she makes her presence and her ways of questioning apparent through stylistic means. Also, the relations between Irigaray and her interlocutors—her reader and the other philosopher that she addresses—are made clear in their concreteness, openness, and dynamic nature. No relation is closed, sealed, or perfected. All remain in a state of becoming.

In this way we can become conscious of the multidimensionality of our relationships and be able to cultivate these relations. In order to effect a change in the value-hierarchy between reason and passion and to create a new mode of relationship—sexual difference—Irigaray argues that sensibility, passivity, and affectivity are indispensable elements of subjectivity in both its modes: feminine and masculine. She suggests that the condition for the possibility of the relationship of two subjects in philosophy and also in all other dimensions of existence, is in our capacity to be touched and moved by an other who is sexually different from us. Such a touching and moving can also happen through words and writing.

Irigaray's Address to the Reader in His or Her Multiplicity

Irigaray denounces the seemingly neutral or absolute position both for herself and for her reader. Her writing rejects all attempts to study and handle it in the third-person perspective of an observer. In her view, this kind of an attitude would put the reader in a position which cannot be maintained. As we have seen, in Irigaray's view we are always already engaged with the world and with others, their writings, but also with language as speakers, readers, and writers. These fundamental engagements motivate the central theme of distance in Irigaray's works. Writing can be a means of self-distancing and distancing oneself from one's self and gender both for the writer and for the reader.

In *Éthique*, Irigaray invites the reader to enter into a dialogue with the philosophical subject, which is constituted in these dialogues and in other writings which precede and follow them. Irigaray does this in an original and thorough manner. The texts discussed are identified but Irigaray's relation to them is not simply critical or simply constructive; instead it is both, or it changes from critical to constructive and back again. Irigaray's way of posing questions to the text, suggesting answers, and abstaining from closing the discussion establishes a special dynamic relationship with the original texts and their writers. It is not always easy to see where the source text ends and where Irigaray's own commentary begins.

Tina Chanter characterizes Irigaray's way of writing in the following manner: "As is typical of her textual readings, her strategy is to quote a passage, and then comment on it, in a commentary that will sometimes include other words that are direct quotes from Merleau-Ponty, but that are not marked as such—are not enclosed within quotations marks" (Chanter 2000, 235–236 fn15). Tina Chanter identifies this way of writing as mimicry. I, however, argue that it has an aspect and aim which can be identified with neither the reproductive nor productive mimetic function: instead of having seduction as its aim, it strives for a genuine dialogue by making different perspectives available to the reader. It is the reader who can open the possibility of genuine intersubjectivity and help in building up the tension which prevents the woman-man couples formed by Irigaray from collapsing into hierarchy or closure.

This occurs in a way that Irigaray's manner of assimilating parts of the other's texts requires the reader to be responsible for differentiating between the voices of Irigaray and the philosophers' ideas, which are commented upon, and their styles. Furthermore, in this way she invites the reader to study the original texts that Irigaray comments on in person in order to take his or her own position in relation to them, and, also, to identify Irigaray's voice and position more clearly (cf. Whitford; Chanter 2000, 236). Thus, another dialogic couple, in addition to that formed by Irigaray and the male-philosopher, is formed: the couple consists of the male-philosopher and the actual reader. The reader is invited to form her own conception of the original text as well as Irigaray's approach to the text, and this distancing and reflective exercise makes the specificity of Irigaray's methodology and variety of topics become clearer.

The aim is to encourage and help the reader to make a new beginning in her own philosophizing, and to consciously relate both to the tradition and to Irigaray's inquiries. This opening of the discourse/tradition implies an awareness of woman's position as well as an awareness of its modification in Irigaray's writings. The reader forms a dialogue between herself and Irigaray (cf. Kozel 1996, 120). This dialogic relation presupposes that the reader has taken a path that is analogous to the one that Irigaray has taken in her work, although starting from the reader's own life. This common voyage, in the end, offers an opportunity to distinguish oneself from the tradition, and also from Irigaray's approach, which challenges the tradition and helps define one's own position with respect to both. The multilayered dialogues invite the reader to enter into an analogous process of self-reflection and self-constitution which has been instituted by Irigaray. The materials studied are canonical philosophical writings, so the self-reflection happens not only in respect to oneself but also in respect to oneself as an inheritor and builder of the philosophical tradition.

These characteristics of Irigaray's work as a specific kind of facilitator of change and transformation is recognized already by the pioneering Irigaray scholar, Margaret Whitford (1991, 5), who writes that the way Irigaray's work is written allows for the possibility of change in the reader over a period of time, "or of being changed as a result of reading, not as an immediate slash but in a slow process of making connections." Moreover, she argues that inherent in Irigaray's work is the need for readers and interpreters, who also facilitates change (Whitford 1991, 5). This idea is also put forward in the recent works on Irigaray's philosophy such as Rachel Jones' *Irigaray* (2010) and the edited anthology *Thinking with Irigaray* (2011), which both demonstrate by acts and arguments how to carry Irigaray's thought forward.

Self-reflection also shows new, possible modes of engaging with or distancing oneself from the tradition of thought. The reader can identify herself or himself with Irigaray, a singular woman who is aware of her position as a woman. Or she can find her position differs from that of Irigaray's as a singular woman who is aware of being woman but who has a different relation to the generic feminine than Irigaray has. The reader can also be a man, who is unable to identify himself as a woman. Yet, he can become aware of his position as a singular man perhaps devoid of the generic masculine to which he could relate. Ideally, the reader, whether a man or a woman, is a lover-philosopher who strives for the good and the beautiful and is able to question her or his own motives and affections. This, however, presupposes not only that the philosopher-lover understands her- or himself as an embodied person with perspectival experience, but also that she or he welcomes other experiences and their articulation. It is only by bringing the feminine body-spirit unity and its amorous modifications into the discourse that the feminine style in its potentiality can be identified and cultivated. (Feminine) body-spirit unity is necessarily open, dynamic, and temporal, both in the case of persons and in the case of writings.

This requires an illumination of the relation that the self has to itself, as well as the genealogy of its genre and other embodied spiritual unities of women. By making explicit these relations to oneself, to the other, and to the world, Irigaray also indicates someone who is sexually other to herself. This non-neutral, masculine bodily subject can only be revealed, and encountered, when feminine subjectivity—a feminine subject conscious of herself—has been established in discourse. Irigaray carefully outlines the possibility of feminine subjectivity and, correspondingly, the possibility of masculine subjectivity, instead of being satisfied with the repetition of the notion of an absolute and neutral subject and the practices supporting this notion. It is through the actualization of the perspective on feminine style that the possibility of the non-hierarchical relation of sexual difference opens up.

The Feminine Philosophical Subject
Constituted by Feminine Acts of Writing

- Irigaray's philosophical style covers all the central aspects of feminine style or feminine subjectivity. It gives us a model of a feminine subject with philosophical authority. Lacking an authoritative feminine philosophical tradition, Irigaray attempts to demonstrate two processes at the same time: how the forming of the tradition has become impossible because of the lack of feminine expressions, and how it can be formed from mere fragments of expressions and traces of genealogy. As we have seen, in this attempt at love has a crucial role to play.

In her writing, Irigaray gives expression to a woman who is conscious of herself as a woman. Consciousness of one's being a woman does not presuppose any philosophical work, but feminine "style" must be brought in contact with philosophy if feminine style is to be fully actualized. Irigaray defines her writing as philosophical through her statements, through her choice of the material of research, and through her formulation of the tasks and the problems of inquiry.

If woman is properly distinguished from the maternal and from man's image of woman, then the masculine view of the self and the masculine ideal of alterity are brought into transition. Irigaray writes: "If man achieves autonomy from a maternal that supports him, from the kind of all-powerful Other that is finally extrapolated into God, then perhaps he will discover that there is something inhering in the female that is not maternal? Another body? Another machine? (At worst?) A machine that uses a different sort of energy? Which would oblige man—humanity—to glimpse something other. Something not of his world. Not built to his specifications" (ESD, 145–146/E, 137). Irigaray continues:

> Perhaps man might then discover that something of another world persists in the female. Something that lives, that is neither plant nor animal, neither mother nor child simply. Irigaray asks whether this feminine other is [s]o very different that he can have no idea of it? Or else that—by bending that something to his idea—he loses its power? Something so different that he has not thought of it? Even in his sexual period? Which he still interprets in terms of erection, ecstasy, going out of himself (in the Other?), ejaculation, out of himself into the other.
>
> Man, mankind, might take out a new lease on life if he were not to exploit something (notably something vegetal) that is neither this nor that. Nothing that man has ever thought of or conceived: in self for self for him. Immanence, in-stance [*l'instance*] in the feminine?" (ESD, 147/E, 138)

In all her works Irigaray addresses herself most directly to the male philosophers, critics have pointed out. The writings of women are not completely absent, however, but operate implicitly in Irigaray's work, as already suggested in connection to the female mystics.[5] Both knowledge of one's own gender and knowledge of the other's gender are necessary for the development of the self-knowledge of a person.

The central role of heterosexual love is also based on her view of the nonreciprocity of the prevailing sexual hierarchies. Irigaray's attempt to problematize the traditional positions of woman and man and their interrelations is intended to open up the possibility of thinking anew the distinction between heterosexual and homosexual love. Instead of focusing on the womanhood or manhood of the partners in a love relationship, we can focus on the mode of loving. This is because the same pursuit of remaining or becoming two holds equally for hetero- and homosexual love even though the ways of remaining or becoming two may differ.

In principle, all the relations constitutive of the feminine style are mutually implicative. These relations also refer to the masculine style and to the open and dynamic generic masculinity.[6] Addressing a masculine person and intending masculinity as a stylistic unity contributes to the possibility of cultivating the masculine style, in contrast to masculine subjectivity as a fixed and closed totality. Irigaray writes to the other, the masculine subject, indicating a possibility of transformation of the relations to himself, the world, and the divine/ideal: "In all his creations, all his works man always seems to neglect thinking of himself as flesh, as one who has received his body as that primary home [. . .] which determines the possibility of his coming into the world and the potential opening of a horizon of thought, of poetry, of celebration, that also includes the god or gods" (ESD, 127–128/E, 123).

On the other hand, for the masculine to appear as masculine, sexed instead of neutral and absolute, the alternative feminine ideal is required. It is the interaction and dialogue between these two multidimensional stylistic unities, the generic feminine and the generic masculine that, for Irigaray, conditions the ideal immanent in the perceivable but can also be found in the perceivable. The fully developed masculine style would include the different alternatives "woman's man," "woman's man internalized by man," and "man's man." On the basis of Irigaray's work, we can say that the relations constitutive of the sense of man are biased in a way that corresponds to the omissions and biases in the constitution of the senses of woman and the feminine as the complement or negation of man and the masculine. The articulation of the masculine as a stylistic unity reveals new ways of conceptualizing sexual difference.

By her multidimensional activity Irigaray shows how the presumed formless and maternal-feminine can, through woman's first-person expression, become a stylistic whole and a constitutive norm for itself. The effects of this transformation are already described in *Ce sexe*: women, when fully occupying the position of speaking subjects, would "challenge the discourse that lays down the law today, that legislates on everything, including sexual difference, to such an extent that the existence of another sex, of an other, that would be woman, still seems, in its terms, unimaginable" (TS, 85/CS, 82). Irigaray's own inquiries into love contribute to this task of questioning; they make visible two basic ways of forgetting the feminine in philosophy: the metaphysical and the phenomenological.

Conclusions to Part III

This part studied the feminine relation to wisdom, as it is lived by women on the one hand, and as it is conceptualized as an indirect relation by the masculine discourse, on the other. The phenomenological idea of a dynamic essence or style allows us to understand how this relation to wisdom can be modified so that the existential relations that we have to ourselves, to the other, and to the world will be renewed, and conceived as constitutive of ideality which has its model in the complex relationality manifest in (Irigaray's amorous style of) philosophical writing. This also includes the possibility of understanding the world as a style of all styles. Irigaray finds this notion of the world as a style of styles from the works of Plato and the phenomenologists of the body. In these works she also discovers the idea that dynamic essences *must* be studied with the assistance of love and desire, understood and lived in a daimonic way. So, the phenomenology of the body provides here the background against which the philosophical originality of Irigaray's overall project becomes articulate. Yet, instead of being satisfied with either the alternative offered by Plato or the male phenomenologists, Irigaray develops a third alternative.

Conclusions

One of the main tasks of my exploration was to provide an account of the crucial discordances between Irigaray's own writings and the interpretations that have been given of her works. The discordances crystallize in the disputes concerning Irigaray's arguments about central issues: the sense of the "traditional woman" in the philosophical discourse and pre-discursive female and male experience, the mechanism and activity of mimesis, the specificity of the feminine lived body and its expressivity, and the idea of sexual difference as a backdrop of all of the previous issues. Based on my original explication and interpretation of Irigaray's philosophy, I have challenged accusations about her claimed neglect of the multiplicity and plurality of women and about the claimed prescriptive, normative function of her concept of woman.

The clarification of the existential-phenomenological background of Irigaray's work offers, in my view, a new basis for a critical evaluation of her claims about femininity and sexual difference. Ultimately, Irigaray's account of feminine being urges us to reflect critically on our ideas of philosophical activities and practices and ourselves as philosophizing persons. By inviting us to perform this task, Irigaray's work contributes to the development of the philosophy instead of remaining merely as a philosophy of gender.

Irigaray's writing was explored as a paradigmatic example of the feminine style of existence, of intending being, acting, and reacting in relation to oneself, to the (sexually) other, and to the world. Three central types of relationality—embodiment, desire, and wisdom—were focused on. In each part of the book, I delineated and characterized the mimetic positions which Irigaray assumes and from which she operates in order to modify feminine expressivity, affectivity, and the practices of loving wisdom. The explications showed that these mimetic figures provide access to discourse and make it possible to speak as a woman.

The first part of my work studied the specific mimetic figure, role, and position of the hysteric and mystic and explicated the relationality characteristic of embodiment and expression. The second part focused on the mimetic positions of the beloved woman and the woman teacher and discussed the relationality of desire. The third part clarified the mimetic figures, roles, and positions of the philosopher's wife and the oracle and studied the relationality of (philosophical) writing. By her mimetic activity, Irigaray discloses and develops possibilities which are inherent in mimetic woman-figures and in their modes of relating, but which lack articulation in the dominant discourse.

First, mimetic occupation of the position of the hysteric allows Irigaray to show that the ideas and ideals of woman and the feminine are dominantly male-defined. Thus, the figure of the hysteric points to a problem in the discourse, which has been, and still is, considered sexually neutral. Furthermore, the paralyzed and fragmented expressions of the hysteric indicate a possibility of a gestural unity of the feminine lived body. Through her mimetic writing, Irigaray gives expression to the feminine body from the first-person point of view. I argued that she finds the means of exploring feminine gestural unity in the phenomenology of the body.

Second, Irigaray also assumes the position of the beloved woman. From this position she is able to question the preconceptions that the male lover/philosopher has about himself and about carnal love. The central target of Irigaray's critique is the strict distinction which is made between the male subject of love, on the one hand, and the masculine subject who conceptualizes, explores, and theorizes love, on the other.

Assuming the mimetic position of a woman teacher, exemplified by Diotima in Plato's *Symposium* and basing on Merleau-Ponty's phenomenology of sexual relations, Irigaray is able to articulate a conception of carnal love and desire which allows a feminine subject and the specificity of her stylistic unity. From this position Irigaray is able to undo the hierarchical relationship between carnal love and spiritual love, and between their objects, and is able to substitute for it a variety of loving attitudes.

Third, the mimetic position of the philosopher's wife and the relationality characteristic of writing allows her to disclose the materiality and affectivity inherent in philosophy and its subject. The function of the philosopher's wife is to provide the material and emotional, even spiritual, support for a philosopher's contemplative and meditating activities without any acknowledgment. The need for support is contrasted to the idea of the self-sufficiency of the male-philosopher. The oracle Diotima exemplifies a mimetic position of a wise woman but also establishes a connection to the feminine tradition of mystics and sorcerers. In Irigaray's reinterpretation of Diotima's discourse, wisdom is not defined as detachment from our carnal condition, or our sensible relations to ourselves, to the (sexually) other, and to the world. Instead, loving wisdom means striving for wisdom in all of these sensual-transcendental relations.

This work suggested that writing is indispensable for the temporal persistence of philosophical ideas. Writing also refers back to an expressive body. Through her amorous style of writing, Irigaray addresses philosophical writings that indicate expressive bodies, which differ from her own body. Ultimately, Irigaray's reinterpretation of philosophy as the love of wisdom discloses the ideal as immanent in the perceivable. Writing exemplifies the mode of ideality emergent in the perceivable: the sense of a specific piece of writing or series of writings is formed in multiple relations. These relations Irigaray makes visible by her amorous style.

Sexual difference in Irigaray's sense must be understood as a difference between two dynamic and continuous ways of relating and changing rather than as a hierarchical dualism of two opposites or complementaries. The beginning of sexual difference, in Irigaray's sense, presupposes different kinds of gestures and movements on the side of woman and on the side of man: woman and man are the two subjects either manifest or implicit in the philosophical discourse and its positings of being and beings. So, to summarize, the main transformative gesture of Irigaray's work is the gesture of opening up the possibility of sexual difference by instituting and constituting a feminine subject and by problematizing the neutrality and absoluteness of the subject who is able to love wisdom and generate this pursuit also in his or her interlocutors.

The corresponding gesture on the part of man may have been invented and manifested in reality. However, it still lacks expression in the philosophical discourse, which is considered paradigmatic in loving wisdom, and which traditionally has assigned the position of speaking the truth to the neutral subject that in reality has been masculine. This gesture of instituting and constituting masculine subject should be expressive of masculine existential style, which is aware of itself as masculine, and reflective of its constitutive relations, as well as of its specific relation to the issue of being and becoming. By such an exemplary gesture made in the transtemporality and generality of the philosophical discourse, the possibility of sexual difference would actualize itself more fully. This should be done from at least two different perspectives: the masculine and the feminine. So, after Irigaray's initiation of phenomenology of feminine being, a significant future task would be to initiate a phenomenology of masculine being in its embodied, affective, and spiritual dimensions.

Notes

Introduction

1. An influential example of dismissal of this type is made by Judith Butler (Cheah and Grosz 1998:27–28).

2. The relationship between Irigaray's thought and Husserlian phenomenology has been originally recognized by Sara Heinämaa, who emphasizes that Irigaray's relation to Husserl's phenomenology is not direct but is mediated by the commentaries of Maurice Merleau-Ponty, Jean-Paul Sartre, and Emmanuel Levinas (Heinämaa 1996, 1997, 1999, 2003, 2006). Irigaray's relationship to the phenomenological tradition with a focus on post-phenomenological and existential sources has been explored by Mortensen (1989), Chanter (1995), Vasseleu (1998).

3. While, in my view, Irigaray's work is heavily indebted to Simone de Beauvoir's phenomenological—fictional and philosophical—work on the multifaceted manifestations of the feminine, this characteristic of *identifying with the feminine* with her own name and identity in the sphere of the philosophical distinguishes Irigaray's work from de Beauvoir's.

4. The idea of gender as an existential style does not distinguish between matter and idea or form, and as such it is an alternative for the sex/gender distinction, which seems to be continuous with the metaphysical idea of strict discontinuity of matter and idea (or form) criticized by Irigaray (see Jones 2010).

5. Several commentators have focused on the fact that the "essentialism" of Irigaray's work has been criticized much harder than that of the male philosophers, whose methods she is assumed to apply to the question of woman (e.g., Derrida), and that Irigaray's role in the discussions in contemporary discussion in the history of philosophy is unjustifiably less significant than for example Foucault's (Braidotti 1989, 99; Whitford 1991a, 126; Songe-Møller 2002, 153–154).

6. Some commentators have pointed out problems is Derrida's deconstructive method and his idea of woman's style congruent with it: deconstruction questions the ideal generalizations and woman as genre, and accordingly finds woman defining herself as a woman is unacceptable, i.e., as a metaphysical conception (Derrida [1978] 1979, 70–71; Joy 1995, 278). For the close relation of Nietzsche's (Dionysian) woman and Irigaray's account of woman see Joy (1995, 277); Nesbitt Oppel (2005, 4). For the

feminist criticisms on the relationship between Nietzsche's conception of woman's style, i.e., woman idolized by man and actual women aiming at emancipation see Joy (1995, 277); Heinämaa (2003, 128–30).

Chapter 1

1. For Irigaray's critique of Lacan's "feminine" position of speaking and writing, see Jones (2010, 144, 152–159).

2. Commentators have pointed out that Irigaray's idea of woman's style is reminiscent of Derrida's concept of style developed on the basis of his readings of Nietzsche. Derrida writes: "There is not such thing as the essence of woman because woman averts, she is averted of herself. Out of the depths, endless and unfathomable, she engulfs and distorts all vestige of essentiality, of identity, of property" (Derrida [1973] 1979, 51). However, Derrida's woman is a *textual* figure detached from feminine persons and feminine embodiment. The problem of not being able to theoretically distinguish woman writing as a woman and man writing as a woman dogs commentators of Irigaray who interpret her work in Derridean terms, detaching woman from the feminine lived body. For Irigaray's woman in relation to Nietzsche's Platonism and Nietzsche's account of woman as a style, see Mortensen (1989, 204); Joy (1995, 277); and Nesbitt Oppel (2005, 4).

3. This way of comprehending gender identity is an alternative to the conceptual framework of sex/gender—distinction, which seems to stem from the same source as the other conceptual distinctions established by the hylomorphic tradition (Jones 2010, 4–6; cf. Poe 2010, 111).

Chapter 2

1. For a recent philosophical explication of Irigaray's readings of Plato, Plotinos, Aristotle, Descartes, Kant, Hegel, Freud, and Lacan, and the connections between these thinkers in relation to the feminine, see Jones (2010).

2. In her later works Irigaray also focuses on "the practical concerns arising from the fact that women had not contributed to the formation and development of the public institutions they entered in the twentieth century," as Deutscher (2002, 13) puts it.

3. My interpretation differs from Naomi Schor's influential interpretation of Irigaray's mimesis in its emphasis on the intertwinement of the discourse and pre-discursive experience and in the accentuation of the continuity of the male-defined femininity and self-defined femininity (Schor [1986] 1994, 66–67). Moreover, my interpretation is based on an explication of the Platonic background and it observes the relationships of diverse modes of mimesis from the perspective of feminine existential style.

4. Judith Butler (1993) articulates these two modes of the feminine as *the specular feminine* and *the excessive feminine* in her deconstructive reading of Irigaray.

5. In the discussion of the philosophy of arts, the difference of reproductive mimesis is usually connected to Plato and the productive mimesis to Aristotle (see Kuisma 1991; Melberg 1995).

6. Nesbitt Oppel (2005, 22) argues that Nietzsche also articulates this aspect of woman as an actress of man's ideal.

7. In the same male-defined continuum of woman's roles are also the virgin and the prostitute. Irigaray argues that along with mother these are the allowed social roles of women from which the characteristics of (so-called) feminine sexuality are derived (TS, 186/CS, 181). However, in my view no specific forms of feminine expression stems from these three roles; instead, they are either silent or if they are not, they overlap with the roles of the beloved woman or the wife.

8. The Platonic essence functions in two ways: as an idea for a thing and as an ideal, a norm, for a thing. In order to include both aspects to one word, and to denote to the dualistic metaphysics of Platonism, I use the term Ideal.

9. An association of women and the material and sensible aspects of being can be found, for example, from Nietzsche. He writes: "When we love a woman, we easily come to hate nature because of all the repulsive natural functions to which every woman is subject; we prefer not to think about it at all, but when our soul for once brushes against these matters, it shrugs impatiently and, as just said, casts a contemptuous look at nature: we feel insulted; nature seems to intrude on our property and with the most profane hands at that. In cases like this one refuses to hear anything about physiology and decrees secretly to oneself, 'I will hear nothing of the idea that the human being is anything other than soul and form!'" (Nietzsche 2001, 70; cf. ML, 108/AM, 115; see also Nietzsche 2001, 71–73)

10. This is a crucial theme of *Speculum*, and has been extensively explored by Jones 2011, and Sandford 2010. For the Nietzschean variation of usurping feminine generative powers into artistic creation, see Baracchi 2005.

11. This quotation can be found in the very last page of *Speculum*, which has no page number neither in the French original text nor in the English translation.

12. Alison Stone (2006, 36) argues that the defenders of strategic or political essentialism affirm this division of passive and indeterminate body matter and the spirit by attributing a one-directional shaping force to cultural and social practices and symbolic structures and misleadingly attribute this view to Irigaray. The problem is that, without reconsidering the nature-culture distinction, the hierarchical difference between them remains in force. In her view, German philosophy of nature can provide a solution to this problem by providing a conception of active matter which, on the one hand shapes culture by its expressions and vice versa, and on the other hand has an inherent shape and dynamic character. Even if our solutions differ, the emphasis on dynamic nature of Irigaray's "essentialism" and critical attitude toward the "hylomorphic model," in which we have indefinite matter and form which give it shape, connects my reading and that of Stone's, and also Jones (2010). For an extensive analysis of Irigaray's criticism of the hylomorphic model, see Jones (2010).

13. An important female predecessor of Irigaray, Simone de Beauvoir, finds and inquires into two ways of loving: feminine and masculine based on a hierarchical division of the sexes in *Le deuxième sexe* ([1949] 1976, 519–586). All the three positions of *la narcissiste*, *l'amoreuse*, and *la mystique* connect to the feminine condition and love in as far as it is possible for woman subordinated and subordinating herself to man and his ideals. Beauvoir's position differs from Irigaray's in that she does not open up possibilities for developing feminine subjectivity from these "feminine" positions, but instead

suggests that these positions should be rejected and left behind in order to become equal companions with man. Insofar as we have internalized one or more of these positions, an internal contradiction is formed within Beauvoirian frame. In Irigaray's case, the positions can be reconciled and developed into more self-definitive ones with no pathologization or self-accusations of having non-feminist characteristics. Yet, in the end of the *Second Sex*, Beauvoir hints at a possibility of love which would allow two subjects, a line of thought extensively developed by Irigaray. Moreover, Beauvoir does not extend her analysis of these positions into the practice of philosophy as Irigaray does.

Chapter 3

1. Irigaray divides her work into three phases. The first phase concentrates on articulating "how a single subject [. . .] has constructed the world and interpreted [it] according to a single perspective" and criticizing this state of affairs (JLI, 97). The second phase consists of creating mediations that could "permit the existence of a feminine subjectivity" (JLI, 97). The third phase entails the construction of "an intersubjectivity respecting sexual difference" (JLI, 96).

2. A throrough comparison of the female mystics' positions in the patriarchal church and monastery institution and women philosophers' positions as Irigaray sees them would be illuminating due to similarities in the constitution of patriarchal authority.

3. We also have phenomenological inquiries into mysticism, which could be of help in tracing these possibilities. For an illuminative phenomenological inquiry into the mystical experience as exemplifying religious experience in general, see Steinbock (2007). According to Steinbock Teresa's writings are especially fruitful for the aims of phenomenological research for "their attention to experiential detail," and "for having character of being 'raw,' honest, direct, unpretentious, and expressive of profound sensitivity to the complexities and nuances of spiritual experience" (Steinbock 2007, 50–51).

4. For a similar point, and a discussion, on Irigaray's and Beauvoir's relationship and ourselves as interpreters detecting—or not detecting—the implicit connections between female thinkers, see Heinämaa (2006, xix).

5. Jonna Bornemark's phenomenological reading of Mechthild of Magdeborg's writings discloses striking similarities between Mechthild's and Irigaray's ideas. These entail Mechthild's relationship to God, her daimocentric position—not supported by the dominant monastery institution—and Diotima's/Irigaray's daimonic philosophy of eros. The connections include the emphasis on love and the soul-body union along the lines of the *Song of Songs*. For instance, for Mechthild, the erotic, in her relation to God, does not transcend the body but intensifies it and divinity is associated with the relation rather than the lover or the beloved (Bornemark 2009, 346, 347). Moreover, according to Bornemark, the male and female mystics also have different experiential relations to embodiment: for women embodiment plays a more significant role, which affects the way how the transcending toward the divine or God is interpreted (Bornemark 2009, 341, fn 375).

6. For the phenomenological discussion of place in Irigaray's commentary on Aristotle's "place" in Irigaray's *Éthique* see Casey (1998, 322–332); in relation to Heidegger's interpretation of "place" in Aristotle, see Chanter (1995, 151–159). For a dis-

cussion of one's own body and the body of the other and their places in Irigaray's philosophy, see Heinämaa (2007, 243–266). For a psychoanalytic approach to Irigaray's "place," see Weiss (1999, 79–83).

Chapter 4

1. Excerpts from this interview by Alice A. Jardine and Anne M. Menke were first published in *Yale French Studies*. In Irigaray's *Je, tu, nous* (1990) this interview is included with the title "Écrire en tant que femme," and under the title "Luce Irigaray" in *Shifting Scenes: Interviews of Women, Writing, and Politics in Post-68 France* (1991). As I do not have the French original, I compare the translations and use the one which exemplifies my points better.

2. For a recent and extensive explication of the constitutive significance of embodiment in Husserl's philosophy, see Taipale (2013).

3. The English translation is based primarily on a text edited by Professor S. Strasser and published in the first volume of Husserliana and secondarily on a "Typescript C" (Haag, Martinus Nijhoff).

4. Commentators have pointed out the relations of Nietzsche's and Derrida's philosophies to Merleau-Ponty's conception of the lived body. About Merleau-Ponty's own philosophical style and its relation to Derrida, Grosz (1994, 94) writes: "[. . .] Merleau-Ponty's work, in ways that surprisingly anticipate Derrida's supplementary readings of dichotomous polarizations, attempts to take up and utilize the space in-between, the 'no-man's land' or gulf separating oppositional terms."

5. Lisa Käll (2008, 124) argues that the reversibility of the bodies, the main point of Irigaray's critique, is, for Merleau-Ponty, always incomplete. This incompleteness forms the distance (*écart*) between the bodies and gives more room to alterity than Irigaray admits, claims Käll (cf. Halsema 2008, 74).

Chapter 5

1. Levinas has named the relation to the elemental to be a relation *enjoyment* (*jouissance*) (TI, 117–118/TIE, 114–115). An element allows bathing or navigating but cannot be surrounded, controlled, or submitted to the subject's intentions. The relation of enjoyment differs also from the non-relation established, e.g., in hunger or need (*besoin*), in which that which needs assimilates into itself that which is needed (TI, 121/TIE, 116). This kind of non-relation of need, characterizes, for example, hunger and thirst.

2. For an attempt to think sexual indecidability within the conceptual framework of philosophy of sexual difference and Merleau-Ponty's philosophy of the body, see Salamon 2010.

3. Compare Irigaray's idea of woman's sexuality to an idea of feminist philosopher Shulamith Firestone with an intuition of holistic conception of sexuality (1979, 147): "When we demand the elimination of eroticism, we mean not the elimination of sexual joy and excitement but its rediffusion over—there is plenty to go around, it increases with use—the spectrum of our lives."

4. The figure of lips and its literal and referential readings is analyzed by Margaret Whitford in a classical article "Irigaray's Body Symbolic" (1991). In her view, Irigaray's point is not exhausted by neither kinds of readings, instead the point is the proliferation of new readings (1991c, 101).

Chapter 6

1. An example of this kind of conceptualization making woman's (self-)love in Irigaray's view impossible can be found in Hegel's work (JAT, 44).

2. Because modification in the practices of listening, not only in expressing, is demanded for interaction to actualize, Irigaray also explores also these practices. According to her, listening to the other is a combination of activities. It involves abstaining from one's own presuppositions in letting, even encouraging, the other to speak for her/himself (JAT, 179–185/ILTY, 115–119).

Chapter 8

1. This aim is evident in an example that Sartre takes from Proust's *In Search of Lost Time*. In Proust's work the character Marcel has made his beloved woman Albertine completely dependent on him economically and has installed her at his home. Despite the possibility of possessing her physically at any hour of the day, Marcel is anxious, because he cannot possess the "consciousness" of his beloved woman (EN, 406/BN, 478).

Chapter 10

1. For the relation of writing to the ideas of masculinity and seduction in Sartre, see Boulé (2005, 36, 105, 151–154).

2. The passage in Irigaray's *Etre deux* to which I refer here starts in this way: «Jean-Paul Sartre ne désigne pas le sexe de l'autre dans ce passage décrivant la relation charnelle. Il est possible d'imaginer que cette autre est une autre mais aucune allusion n'est faite à la différence des sexes.» The passage is omitted from the English translation.

3. In Irigaray's critical comments the capital O of Sartre's Other indicating radical alterity is replaced by a lowercase o.

4. Bergoffen (1997, 217) derives the idea of the ethics of love from Simone de Beauvoir's work.

5. Stella Sandford (2000, 5) argues that "[i]n the early work eros performs the phenomenological function of what will later be called 'ethics,' and the idea of the Other is articulated through what will appear to be one particular sort of Other, the feminine."

6. Perpich's interpretation of the caress as the perfect model of transcendence in Levinas's work is restricted to his early work.

7. Sandford (2000, 31) argues that the roles of eros and the feminine have been underestimated in Levinas's scholarship but argues for their importance in Levinas's ethics as a whole.

8. For problems of this view as a conception of loving an individual, see Vlastos (1973) and Nussbaum (1979, 132–134). Nussbaum also offers an overview of the discussion on Vlastos's view.

9. This idea of the assimilation of the self and the beloved also can be found also in Aristophanes's speech in the *Symposium*. In this androgyne myth, eros is motivated by the initial fusion of the two sexes into one being. After the fusional state of "paradise," the revengeful gods separated the beings into two. In this myth eros is defined as lack: it means searching for one's missing half, one's complement, and its aim is to become fused with him/her. This myth is crucial for Freud's and Lacan's psychoanalytic interpretations of eros. For a feminist analysis of this aspect of eros in the *Symposium*, see e.g., Songe-Møller (2002, 101–103); Korsisaari (2006, 69–77).

Chapter 11

1. Stella Sandford (2000, 95) argues for the importance of the myth of the origin of eros for Levinas's conception of eros in *Totalité et infini*.

2. I capitalize Eros here because the topic refers to the god as discussed in the Socrates/Diotima's speech in the *Symposium*.

Chapter 12

1. In Sartre's case this omission is especially striking since his companion Simone de Beauvoir was herself a philosopher who reflected and described the same phenomena.

2. For a detailed account of the seemingly insignificant prologue of the *Symposium*, in which it is argued that the report of the *Symposium* is presented inside the narrative, see Corrigan (2004, 7–20).

3. Irigaray acknowledges that the word "subject" is inadequate for Plato's philosophy (E, 35).

4. Irigaray studies the topic of desire also with respect to Descartes's theory of passions. However, for Descartes desire is secondary and wonder is primary in his classification of passions, while for Diotima desire is primary and possibly includes a component of wonder.

Chapter 13

1. For Michéle Le Dœuff's account of the available positions for women in philosophy and a comparison between Irigaray's and Le Dœuff's philosophical styles congruent with their respective ontological convictions, see Lehtinen (2007, 109–125).

2. For woman's position as a mediator between nature and spirit see Chanter (2011, 265–292) on Irigaray's relationship to Hegel's philosophy and his "woman." Hegel's discussion on Antigone also heavily mediates Irigaray's account on Antigone, a woman-figure, which also exemplifies these characteristics of being between nature and spirit, or gods. Antigone is sometimes presented as a subversive figure who could be

a heroine, or female subject; however, she seems not to be self-defined, but is rather expressing her mother's desire, and moreover, is directed toward death rather than life (see also Hom 2011, 247–263).

3. The philosopher's wife is a well-known figure in feminist philosophy, and my explication her supporting activities is informed not only by the preceding argumentation of this book but also by Le Dœuff's idea of *Heloïse Complex*, an analytic tool for comprehending the different tendencies of the philosophical careers and philosopher-images of women and men. I have argued elsewhere that Irigaray's and Le Dœuff's diagnosis of the relationship of women and philosophy, both made in terms of amorous relations, converge, even if their solutions diverge (Lehtinen 2007, 109–125).

4. While this setting is not a problem if it is restricted to a certain phase of the philosophical career, the beginning, it becomes a problem if no development is shown or allowed. The same problem holds for a male student, or a member of a philosophical school. However, because of the diverse genealogies of females and males, the male student is a son or a follower occupying the place of the male teacher. The female student, however, easily fills the functions of a wife because of the expected and internalized expectations of feminine behavior (Le Dœuff 1989, 106–107; Lehtinen 2007, 109–125).

5. Michéle Le Dœuff's analysis includes a figure accepted by the philosophical institutions of France, which is continuous with that of a philosopher's wife and that of an oracle; a female scholar in history of philosophy, who is faithfully devoted to one male-philosopher's work.

6. Sandford detects this relationship of conditioning from Levinas's *Totalité et infini* (Sandford 2000, 45–46; cf. Firestone 1979, 121).

7. This is not to say that no such *individual* female philosopher could be found; Hannah Arendt is an example of such a canonized female philosopher.

8. Halperin argues that not only does Diotima not speak for women but she also silences them by lending the feminine authority and the reciprocal erotic practices, as well as terminology of procreation associated with women's sexuality in Greek culture, to what turns out to be only a projection of male experience onto women (Halperin 1990, 289; cf. Songe-Møller 2002, 110). In Halperin's view, also with reference to Irigaray's *Speculum*, the speech of Plato's Diotima only helps in studying the male imaginary, the "specular poetics of male identity and self-definition," and not in studying attitudes toward real women (Halperin, 289, 297). Halperin's book was published after Irigaray's *Éthique*, but he does not refer to Irigaray's reading of the *Symposium*.

9. New readings of Diotima's philosophy, have been developed by feminist philosophers either through arguing for Diotima's historical existence or her own philosophical position. But she has also been criticized as Plato's invention. For the former see e.g., Mary Ellen Waithe (1987), Andrea Nye (1989); for the latter see David Halperin (1990) and Vigdis Songe-Møller (2002). Diotima also has a position in the interpretations made of the *Symposium* in psychoanalytic discourse. For example, Chiesa (2006, 66) points out that in Lacan's interpretation, which focuses on Alcibiades's speech, Diotima represents the unconscious of Socrates, or the feminine in Socrates (see also Corrigan 2004, 113fn 26). Kuykendall (1989, 28–30) takes the psychoanalytic approach in her commentary on Irigaray's "Sorcerer love" as a starting point, and argues that "Irigaray both presupposes and seeks to disclose a female unconscious" and in doing so distances herself from Freud and Lacan.

10. Waithe (1987, 107–111) argues that if we assume Diotima's views to be identical with those of Plato, this implies a problem in respect to the consistency of Plato's views in the *Symposium*, on the one hand, and in other dialogues, on the other. According to Waithe (1987, 91), the relevant key conceptions, in which Diotima's philosophy can be distinguished from Plato's and Socrates' philosophies, are the concepts of the good and immortality, the theory of personal identity, the doctrine of ideas, the doctrine of transmigration of souls, and the role of reason.

11. Nye finds these possibilities of Diotima as a feminine philosopher from Diotima herself. Nye thinks she does this despite the misleading translations and Irigaray's prejudices as an inheritor of the Platonic tradition. Nye sees Irigaray's treatment of Diotima's speech as deconstructive in the Derridean sense and criticizes Irigaray's approach as ahistorical (Nye 1989, 45–58).

Chapter 15

1. An important passion, which is related or even included in the amorous attitude from the gestures to thinking, is the passion of wonder, which Irigaray finds from Descartes's *Passions de l'âme*. For wonder, in Irigaray and Descartes and Irigaray's relation to Descartes's philosophy more broadly, see Heinämaa (1999, 277–290; 2000, 45–71), Joy (2006, 36–55), and Jones (2010, 100–114).

2. For a reading which explores the relationship of Irigaray's idea of the practice of breath and the phenomenological methodology see Oksala (2006, 43–46).

3. Rachel Jones's interpretation of the connections between the founding fathers and canonized philosophers in *Speculum* provides a new perspective also in respect to the organizational structure of *Éthique*. Jones finds surprising contacts and contiguities between seemingly oppositional philosophies. For example, in Jones's interpretation of *Speculum*, Plotinos's philosophy forms a culmination point Plato's and Aristotle's philosophies on the topic of matter (Jones 2010, 98, 99).

4. For mother-daughter couples in Irigaray, see Bergoffen (2007, 152).

5. An important example in this sense is the role of Beauvoir's phenomenology of eroticism in Irigaray's thought (see e.g., Bergoffen 1997, 206).

6. For the constitution of masculinity described in its dominant and subordinate forms, see e.g., Boulé (2005, 4–5).

Bibliography

Ainley, Alison. "The Invisible of the Flesh: Merleau-Ponty and Irigaray." *Journal of the British Society for Phenomenology* 28, no. 1 (1997): 20–29.
Baracchi, Claudia. "Elemental Translations: From Friedrich Nietzsche and Luce Irigaray." *Research in Phenomenology* 35, (2005).
Beauvoir, Simone de. *Le deuxième sexe I & II*. Paris: Editions Gallimard.
Bergoffen, Debra B. *The Philosophy of Simone de Beauvoir: Gendered Phenomenologies, Erotic Generosities*. Albany: SUNY Press, 1997.
———. "Irigaray's Couples." In *Returning to Irigaray: Feminist Philosophy, Politics and the Question of Unity*, edited by Maria Cimitile and Elaine Miller. 151–172. Albany: SUNY Press, 2007.
Bornemark, Jonna. *Kunskapens gräns, gränsens vetande: en fenomenologisk undersökning av transcendens och kroppslighet*. PhD diss., Södertön University College, Stockholm: Södertörn Philosophical Studies 6, 2009.
Boulé, Jean-Pierre. *Sartre, Self-Formation and Masculinities*. New York, Oxford: Berghahn Books, 2005.
Braidotti, Rosi. "The Politics of Ontological Difference." In *Between Feminism and Psychoanalysis*, edited by Teresa Brennan, 89–105. London and New York: Routledge, 1989.
Butler, Judith. *Bodies that Matter: On the Discursive Limits of Sex*. New York and London: Routledge, 1993.
Canters, Hanneke, and Grace M. Jantzen. *Forever fluid: A reading of Luce Irigaray's Elemental Passions*. Manchester and New York: Manchester University Press, 2005.
Casey, Edward S. *The Fate of Place: A Philosophical History*. Berkeley, London: University of California Press, 1998.
Chanter, Tina: *Ethics of Eros: Luce Irigaray's Rewritings of the Philosophers*, New York, London: Routledge, 1995.
———. "Wild meaning: Luce Irigaray's reading of Merleau-Ponty." In *Chiasms: Merleau-Ponty's notion of flesh*, edited by Fred Evans and Leonard Lawlor. 219–236. Albany: SUNY Press, 2000.
———. 2011. "Antigone's Exemplarity: Irigaray, Hegel and Excluded Grounds as Constitutive of Feminist Theory." In *Thinking with Irigaray*. Edited by Mary C. Rawlinson, Sabrina. L. Hom and Serene J. Khader, 265–292. Albany: SUNY Press.

Cheah, Pheng, and Elizabeth Grosz. "The Future of Sexual Difference: An Interview with Judith Butler and Drucilla Cornell." *Diacritics* 28, no. 1 (1998): 19–24.
Chiesa, Lorenzo. " 'Le ressort de l'amour': Lacan's theory of love in his reading of Plato's Symposium." *Angelaki* 11, no. 3 (2006): 61–81.
Chisholm, Diane. "Irigaray's Hysteria." In *Engaging with Irigaray*, edited by C. Burke, N. Schor, and M. Whitford. 263–284. The Series Feminist Philosophy and Modern European Thought. New York: Columbia University Press, 1994.
Corrigan, Kenneth, and Elena Glazov-Corrigan. *Plato's Dialectic at Play: Argument, Structure and Myth in the Symposium*. Pennsylvania: Penn State Press, 2004.
Derrida, Jacques. *Spurs—Nietzsche's Styles/ Éperons—Les Styles de Nietzsche*, translated by Barbara Harlow. Chicago and London: University of Chicago Press, [1978] 1979.
Deutscher, Penelope: *The Politics of Impossible Difference: The Later Work of Luce Irigaray*. Ithaca, London: Cornell University Press, 2002.
Easlea, Brian. *Witch Hunting, Magic and the New Philosophy: An Introduction to Debates of the Scientific Revolution 1450–1750*. New York, London: Harvester Wheatsheaf, 1980.
Fielding, Helen. "Only Blood Would Be More Red: Merleau-Ponty, Irigaray and the Ethics of Sexual Difference." *British Journal of Phenomenology* 32, no. 2 (2001): 147–159.
Firestone, Shulamith. *The Dialectic of Sex: The Case for Feminist Revolution*. London: The Women's Press, [1971] 1979.
Folkmarson Käll, Lisa. "Spår av könsskilnad: Luce Irigaray i dialog med Maurice Merleau-Ponty." *Agora: journal for metafysisk spekulasjon* 26, no. 3 (2008): 114–133.
Freud, Sigmund. "General Remarks on Hysterical Attacks." In *Collected Papers Volume II*. Authorized translation under the supervision of Joan Riviere, 100–104. The International Psychoanalytic Library No. 8. New York: Basic Books, 1959a.
———. "On the Theory of Hysterical Attacks." In *Collected Papers Volume V*, edited by James Strachey. 27–30. The International Psychoanalytic Library No. 37. New York: Basic Books, 1959a.
Gallop, Jane. *The Daughter's Seduction: Feminism and Psychoanalysis*, Ithaca, NY: Cornell University Press, 1982.
Grosz, Elizabeth. *Sexual Subversions: Three French Feminists*. St. Leonards: Allen & Unwin, 1989.
———. *Volatile Bodies: Toward a Corporeal Feminism*. Bloomington and Indianapolis: Indiana University Press, 1994.
Halperin, David M. *One Hundred years of Homosexuality and Other Essays on Creek Love*. New York, London: Routledge, 1990.
Halsema, Annemie. "Phenomenology in the Feminine: Irigaray's Relationship to Merleau-Ponty." In *Intertwinings: Interdisciplinary Encounters with Merleau-Ponty*, edited by Gail Weiss. 63–84. Albany: SUNY Press, 2008.
Heinämaa Sara: *Ele, tyyli, sukupuoli*. Helsinki: Gaudeamus, 1996.
———. 1997. "Pinnan liikettä: Luce Irigarayn ajatus naisellisesta tyylistä" *niin&näin*, no. 3: 21–26.
———. "Wonder and (Sexual) Difference: Cartesian Radicalism in Phenomenological Thinking." In *Norms and Modes of Thinking in Descartes*, edited by Tuomo

Aho and Mikko Yrjönsuuri. 277–296. Acta Philosophica Fennica 64, Helsinki: Hakapaino, 1999,

———. *Ihmetys ja rakkaus*, Helsinki: Nemo, 2000.

———. *Toward a Phenomenology of Sexual Difference: Husserl, Merleau-Ponty, Beauvoir*. Lanham, Maryland: Rowman and Littlefield, 2003.

———. "On Luce Irigaray's Phenomenology of Intersubjectivity: Between the Feminine Body and its Other." In *Returning to Irigaray: Feminist Philosophy, Politics and the Question of Unity*, edited by Maria Cimitile and Elaine Miller. 243–265. Albany: SUNY Press, 2006.

———. "A Phenomenology of Sexual Difference: Types, Styles and Persons." In *Feminist Metaphysics: Explorations in the Ontology of Sex, Gender and the Self*, edited by Charlotte Witt, 135–155. Dordrecht: Springer. 2011.

Hollywood, Amy. "Beauvoir, Irigaray and the Mystical." *Hypatia* 9, no. 4 (1994): 159–185.

Hom, Sabrina L. "Antigone Falters: Reflections on the Sustainability of the Revolutionary Subjects." In *Thinking with Irigaray*, edited by Mary C. Rawlinson, Sabrina. L. Hom, and Serene J. Khader. 247–263. Albany: SUNY Press, 2011.

Husserl, Edmund. [1913] 2002: *Ideas Pertaining to a Pure Phenomenology and to a Phenomenological Philosophy, Second Book: Studies in the Phenomenology of Constitution. Collected Works, Volume III*, translated by Richard Rojcewicz and André Schuwer from German *Ideen zu einer reinen Phänomenologie und phänomenologischen Philosophie, Zweites Buch: Phänomenologische Untersuchungen zur Konstitution, Husserliana, Band IV*, Dordrecht, Boston, London: Kluwer Academic Publishers, [1950] 1995.

———. *Cartesian Meditations: An Introduction to Phenomenology*, translated by Dorion Cairns from German original *Cartesianische Meditationen und pariser Vorträge, Husserliana, Band I)*, Dordrecht, Boston and London: Kluwer Academic Publishers.

Jones, Rachel. *Irigaray: Towards a Sexuate Philosophy*. Key Contemporary Thinkers. Cambridge, Malden: Polity Press, 2011.

Joy, Morny, and Eva K. Neumaier-Dargyay, eds. *Gender, Genre and Religion: Feminist Reflections*. Waterloo, Ontario, Canada: Wilfried Laurier University Press for the Calgary Institute for the Humanities, 1995.

Joy, Morny. *Divine Love: Luce Irigaray, Women, Gender and Religion*. Manchester Studies in Religion, Culture and Gender, Manchester, New York: Manchester University Press, 2006.

Joy, Morny, Kathleen O'Grady, and Judith L. Poxon, eds. *French Feminists on Religion: A Reader*. London and New York: Routledge.

———. "Autonomy and Divinity: A Double-Edged Experiment." In *Thinking with Irigaray*, 221–243. 2011.

Korsisaari, Eva Maria. *Tule rakkaani: naisen ja miehen välisestä etiikasta kirjallisuuden rakkauskuvauksissa*. Helsinki: Teos, 2006.

Kozel, Susan. "The Diabolical Strategy of Mimesis: Luce Irigaray's Reading of Maurice Merleau-Ponty." *Hypatia* 11, no. 3 (1996): 115–129.

Krell, David Farrel. *Daimon-life: Heidegger and life-philosophy*. Studies in Continental Thought. Bloomington: Indiana University Press, 1992.

Kuisma, Oiva: *Platon, Aristoteles ja Plotinos taiteellisesta mimesiksestä*. A Licenciate Study in Aesthetics. University of Helsinki, 1991.
Kuykendall, Eleanor H. "Introduction to 'Sorcerer's love' by Luce Irigaray," *Hypatia* 3, no. 3 (1989): 28–61.
Laba Cataldi, Suzanne. "The Philosopher and her Shadow: Irigaray's reading of Merleau-Ponty." *Philosophy Today* 48, no. 4, (2004): 343–354.
Lacan, Jacques. *On Feminine Sexuality, the limits of Love and Knowledge. 1972–1973: The Seminar of Jacques Lacan (Encore) (Vol. Book XX)*, edited by Jacques-Alan Miller, translated by Bruce Fink from French *Le Séminaire, Livre XX: Encore*, 1975, New York: Norton, 1998.
Langer, Monika. "Sartre and Merleau-Ponty: A Reappraisal." In *The Debate between Sartre and Merleau-Ponty*, edited by Jon Stewart. 93–117. Evanston, IL: Northwestern University Press, 1998.
Le Dœuff, Michèle *The Philosophical Imaginary*, translated by Colin Gordon from the French *Recherches sur l'imaginaire*. Les Editions Payot, 1980. London: Athlone Press, 1989.
———. *Le Sexe du Savoir*, Alto Aubier, Paris. 1998
Lehtinen, Virpi. "Eettinen rakkaus: rakastajien sukupuolen merkitys Luce Irigarayn ajattelussa," [Love and Ethics: the Significance of the Lover's Gender in Irigaray's Thought], in *Rakkaudesta toiseen: kirjoituksia vuosituhannenvaihteen etiikasta*, edited by Sara Heinämaa and Johanna Oksala. 167–184. Helsinki: Gaudeamus, 2001.
———. "On Philosophical Style: Michèle Le Dœuff and Luce Irigaray." In *European Journal of Women's Studies* 14, no. 2 (2007): 109–125.
———. 2012. "Luce Irigaray on Love and Political Behavior: Reading Enrico Berlinguer and the Julian Assange Affair." The Recent Work of Luce Irigaray, edited by Heidi Bostic. *L'Esprit Créateur* 52, no. 3 (2012): 99–112.
Mazis, Glen A. "Touch and Vision: rethinking with Merleau-Ponty Sartre on the Caress." In *The Debate between Sartre and Merleau-Ponty*, 1998.
Melberg, Arne. *Theories of Mimesis*. Series Literature, Culture, Theory 12, Cambridge, New York, Melbourne: Cambridge University Press, 1995.
Moi, Toril. *Sexual/Textual Politics: Feminist Literary Theory*. New York, London: Routledge, [1985] 1995.
Mortensen, Ellen. *"Le Féminin"and Nihilism: Reading Irigaray with Nietzsche and Heidegger*. PhD diss. University of Wisconsin-Madison, 1989.
Nagl-Docekal, Herta. *Feminist Philosophy*, translated by Katharina Vester. Boulder, CO and Oxford: Westview Press, 2004.
Nesbitt Oppel, Frances. *Nietzsche on Gender: Beyond Man and Woman*. Charlottesville, London: University of Virginia Press, 2005.
Nietzsche, Friedrich. *Gay Science*. Cambridge Texts in the History of Philosophy, edited by Bernard Williams and translated by Josefine Nauckhoff and Adrian Del Caro. Cambridge: Cambridge University Press, 2001.
Nussbaum, Martha. "The Speech of Alcibiades: A Reading of Plato's Symposium." *Philosophy and Literature* 3, no. 2 (1979): 131–172.
Nye, Andrea. "The Hidden Host: Irigaray and Diotima at Plato's Symposium." *Hypatia* 3, no. 3 (1989): 45–61.

Oksala, Johanna. "From Sexual Difference to the Way of Breath: Toward the Feminist Ontology of Ourselves." In *Sex, Breath and Force: Sexual Difference in Post-Feminist Era*, edited by Ellen Mortensen. 33–48. Boulder, New York: Lexington Books, 2006.

Perpich, Diane. "From the Caress to the Word: Transcendence and the Feminine in the Philosophy of Emmanuel Levinas." In *Feminist Interpretations of Emmanuel Levinas*, edited by Tina Chanter. 28–52. University Park, PA: Pennsylvania State University Press, 2001.

Plaza, Monique. " 'Phallomorphic' Power and the Psychology of 'Woman.' " *Ideology and Consciousness* 4 (1978):4–36.

Plotinus. *The Enneads*, translated by Stephen Mc Kenna, Burdett, NY: Larson Publications, 1992.

Poe, Danielle. "Can Luce Irigaray's Notion of Sexual Difference Be Applied to Transsexual and Transgender Narratives?" In *Thinking with Irigaray*, edited by Mary C. Rawlinson, Sabrina L. Hom, and Serene J. Khader. 111–130. SUNY Series in Gender Theory. Albany: SUNY Press, 2011.

Poleshchuk, Irina. *Temporality of the Face-to-Face in Levinas' Ethics*. Philosophical Studies from the University of Helsinki 27. Helsinki: Helsinki University Press, 2009.

Salomon, Gayle. *Assuming a Body: Transgender and Rhetorics of Materiality*. New York: Columbia University Press, 2010.

Sandford, Stella. *Metaphysics of Love: Gender and Transcendence in Levinas*. London and New Brunswick, NJ: Athlone Press, 2000.

———. *Plato and Sex*. Cambridge, Malden: Polity Press, 2010.

Schor, Naomi. "This Essentialism which is Not One: Coming to Grips with Irigaray." In *Engaging with Irigaray*. 57–78.

Shapiro, Lisa. "Princess Elisabeth and Descartes: The Union of Soul and Body and the Practice of Philosophy." In *Feminism and History of Philosophy*, edited by Genevieve Lloyd. 182–203. Oxford Readings in Feminism, Oxford, New York: Oxford University Press, 2002.

Sjöholm, Cecilia. "Crossing Lovers: Luce Irigaray's *Elemental Passions*." *Hypatia* 15, no. 3 (2000): 92–112.

Songe-Møller, Vigdis. *Philosophy without Women: the Birth of Sexism in Western Thought*, translated by Peter Cripps. New York, London: Continuum Press, 2002.

Steinbock, Anthony J. *Phenomenology and Mysticism: The Verticality of Religious Experience*. Bloomington and Indianapolis, IN: Indiana University Press, 2007.

Stoller, Silvia. "Asymmetrical Genders: Phenomenological Reflections on Sexual Difference," translated by Camilla R. Nielsen. *Hypatia* 20, no. 2 (2005): 7–26.

Stone, Alison. *Luce Irigaray and the Philosophy of Sexual Difference*. Cambridge, New York: Cambridge University Press, 2006.

Taipale, Joona. *Phenomenology and Embodiment: Husserl and the Constitution of Subjectivity*. Evanston, IL: Northwestern University Press, 2013.

Tallon Russel, Helena. *Irigaray and Kierkegaard: On the Construction of the Self*. Macoa: Mercer University Press, 2009.

Vlastos, Gregory. "The individual as an object of love in Plato." In *Plato 2: Ethics, Politics, Religion and the Soul*. Oxford, New York: Oxford University Press, 1973.

Witt, Charlotte. *Ways of Being: Potentiality and Actuality in Aristotle's Metaphysics*. Ithaca, London: Cornell University Press, 2003.
Vasseleu, Cathryn. *Textures of Light: Vision and Touch in Irigaray, Levinas and Merleau-Ponty*. Warwick Studies in European Philosophy, New York, London: Routledge, 1998.
Waithe, Mary Ellen. "Diotima of Mantinea." In *A History of Woman Philosophers Volume 1*, edited by Mary Ellen Waithe. 83–116. Dordrecht: Martinus Nijhoff Publishers, 1987.
Weed, Elizabeth. "The Question of Style." In *Engaging with Irigaray*. 79–110.
Weiss, Gail. *Body Images: Embodiment as Intercorporeality*. New York and London: Routledge, 1999.
Welton, Don. "Affectivity, Eros and the Body." In *Body and Flesh: a Philosophical Reader*, edited by Donn Welton. Malden, MA: Blackwell, 1998.
Whitford, Margaret. *Luce Irigaray—Philosophy in the Feminine*. London: Routledge, 1991a.
———. 1991b. "Introduction." In *The Irigaray Reader*, edited by Margaret Whitford. Oxford and Massachusetts: Basil Blackwell.
———. 1991c. "Irigaray's Body Symbolic." *Hypatia* 6, no. 3 (199c): 97–110.
———. 1994. "Reading Irigaray in the Nineties." In *Engaging with Irigaray*. 15–33.
Wyschogrod, Edith. *Emmanuel Levinas: The Problem of Ethical Metaphysics*. New York: Fordham University Press, 2000.
Xu, Ping. "Irigaray's Mimicry and the Problem of Essentialism." *Hypatia* 10, no. 4 (1995): 76–83.

Index

absolutely contrary contrary *(le contraire absolument contraire)*, 105–106
abstractions, concepts and theoretical discourse. *See also* dualisms; Eternal Feminine, man's woman *and other concepts;* the generic; ideas, doctrine of (Plato) *and other theories;* metaphysics; norms; the pre-conceptual; roles
    Diotima and, 148, 161, 175
    discourse and, 39
    embodiment and, 57, 70–71, 94, 187
    experience and, 1, 24
    feminine style and, 16, 17, 19, 27–29, 87, 90, 99–100, 142, 161, 189, 192
    gender identity and, 212*ch*1*n*3
    indexing this book and *(see, or better, dialogue with* the Indexer)
    Irigaray's work and, 8, 31, 40, 72, 189, 192, 197
    Levinas's Other and, 133
    love and, 159
    masculine subject of philosophy and, 167, 184, 185, 205, 208
    maternal-feminine and, 32–33
    Merleau-Ponty's account and, 44, 55, 60, 64
    mimesis and, 9
    phenomenology and, 2, 55
    philosophical discourse and, 23, 24, 25
    Platonism and, 5, 23, 27–29
    poetry *versus,* 73
    the pre-discursive and, 159
    reality and, 39
    Sartre's, 120, 124
    sexual difference and, xi, 8, 120, 177–178, 202, 215*n*2
    the wife and, 170
    writing and, 64, 114, 190, 192
active-passive attitude, 102, 110, 154, 155, 157, 179
actualization
    Aristotle and, 5
    of the feminine, 40
    of feminine existential style, 15–16, 21, 24, 25, 84, 159, 176, 200, 201
    the hysteric and, 41
    of Irigaray's work, 2, 162, 193–194
    listening and, 216*n*2
    of love, 92, 146, 157–158
    of love between women, 103
    of love of wisdom, 180
    mimesis and, 25, 41
    of philosophical discourse, 6, 21, 145, 166, 168, 193–194
    of relations, 179
    of self-love, 92, 96
    sexual difference/sameness and, xi, 209
    writing and, 186, 193–194
affectivity. *See also* auto-affection
    as dimension of existential style, 11
    experience and, 80

actualization *(continued)*
  genealogy of, 124
  language and, 62
  lived body and, 58
  love and desire and, x
  Merleau-Ponty and, 54, 59, 158
  passivity and, 57
  perception and, 5, 61
  phenomenology of the body and, 5, 57, 59
  philosophy and, 208
  self-reflection and, 61–62
  Speculum and, 41
  subjectivity and, 198
Alcibiades's speech, 218*n*9
Amante marine (Marine Lover of Friedrich Nietzsche) (Irigaray), 29, 32–33, 78, 97, 190, 191, 194
l'amoreuse, 213*n*13
amorous state/relation, 149, 150, 193, 218*n*3
amorous style. *See also* the caress
  beloved woman and, 97
  bodies and, 185, 192
  discourse as texture and, 24
  Éthique and, 46, 190, 191, 192, 193–194
  feminine body-spirit unity and, 200
  interrogator and, 194
  Irigaray's, 155, 161–162, 188–189
  love of wisdom and, 161
  Merleau-Ponty's anticipation of, 156
  mimesis and, 191
  neutral discourse and, 166, 187
  philosophical discourse and, 166, 183, 189, 193, 195, 208–209
  private/public expressions and, 147, 155, 191, 193
  reinterpretation of philosophy and, 208–209
  renewal and, 205
  the seductive *versus*, 45
  sexual difference and, 190
  Symposium and, 4
  wonder and, 219*n*1
  writing as emergent in perceivable and, 209

amour de soi. See love of self (feminine) and love among women; love of self (masculine) and love between men
"L'amour sorcier. Lecture de Platon. Le Banquet, 'Discours de Diotime'" ("Sorcerer Love: A Reading of Plato, *Symposium*, 'Diotima's Speech'") (Irigaray), 135, 189, 195, 218*n*9
animality, 129, 130–131, 141, 160
Antigone, 169, 217*ch*13*n*2
Aphrodite, 143
Arendt, Hannah, 218*n*7
Aristotle
  category of place of, 189
  essence and, 4, 5
  female/male hierarchies and, 22
  importance of, 23
  Irigaray's reading of, 212*ch*2*n*1
  mimesis and, 212*n*5
  "place" and, 214*n*6
  Plato and, 189–190
  Plotinos and, 219*n*3
authority, feminine, 146, 147
authority of male philosophers, 23, 29–30, 152–153
auto-affection (auto-eroticism), 77, 78, 81, 94

beauty
  Diotima's account, 174
  Eros and, 143
  the face and, 129
  masculine desire and, 92
  Socrates' discussion and, 135–136
  texture of, 24, 162, 175
  truth and, 135
  the wife and, 170
Beauvoir, Simone de
  eroticism in Irigaray's work and, 219*n*5
  ethics of love and, 215*ch*10*n*4, 216*n*4
  Irigaray on, 85
  Irigaray's work distinguished from, 211*n*3, 213*n*13, 214*n*4
  on love, 213*n*14
  mysticism and, 34
  on neutral discourse, 2–3

phenomenology of eroticism of, 219*n*5
as philosopher's wife, 170
Sartre and, 217*ch*12*n*1
becoming. *See also* potential
  amorous style and, 155
  attitude of loving and, 177
  being and, 10
  the body and, 71
  the caress and, 110
  desire and, 113–137
  Diotima's account and, 150
  existential stylistic unity and, 14
  feminine style and, 190
  Ideal of Woman and, 28
  of Irigaray's work, 76
  love and, 158
  love wisdom and, 181
  masculine need and, 170
  mimesis of Diotima and, 146
  phenomenological method and, 55
  relations and, 198
  self-reflection and, 11
  stylistic unities and, 14
being (Being), 1–2, 10, 11, 23, 56
Being and Nothingness (Sartre), 160
beloved woman. *See also* carnal love; man's woman
  amorous style and, 155
  beauty and happiness and, 143
  becoming and, 155, 157
  the caress and, 109–111, 127–128
  carnal love and, 139–143, 208
  desire and love and, 11, 36, 91–98, 207–208
  Diotima as, 174
  the face and, 130
  female body and, 32–33, 50–51
  feminine expressive body and, 75
  feminine self-love and, 92–93, 94, 99–104
  the hysteric and, 48, 98
  inadequacy of, 113
  Irigaray's style as, 97–98, 106, 145–162, 194, 208
  Levinas's account and, 113, 125–134, 127–128, 129, 130, 131–132, 133, 160

lived feminine body and, 75
love and desire and, 162
love of self and, 92–93
male desires/expectations and, 34–35, 50–51, 91–93, 94, 98
as man's woman, 91–98
masculine subject and, 95, 184, 188, 191, 208
maternal love and, 154
mimesis and, 26, 48, 69, 89–90, 143, 146, 147, 165, 188, 207–208
as mirror image, 188
"passages" to the divine and, 82
philosophical discourses and, 4, 113, 139–143, 168
Plato and, 113
"primitive" expression and, 37, 48, 82, 106, 109, 113, 146
roles of women and, 11
Sartre and, 107, 113, 115–116, 120, 216*ch*8*n*1
seduction and, 95–96, 169
singularity of relations and, 194
spiritual embodiment and, 107
Symposium and, 135–137
as unique, 106, 145
unity of expression and, 106–107
Bergoffen, Debra, 122, 215*ch*10*n*4, 219*n*4
Bernini, Lorenzo, 34, 46
the (in-)between, 5, 14, 126, 133–134, 215*n*4
biases. *See also* perspectives (points of view); presuppositions
  carnal love and, 155
  feminine incoherence and, 148, 150
  gendered being and, 1, 2–3
  love and, 158
  love between women and, 103
  man's woman and, 51, 92, 202
  the masculine and, 202
  masculine body and, 94
  mimesis and, 21, 191
  phenomenological method and, 2, 56, 69
  philosophical discourse and, 6–7, 181

biology/physiology, 4, 7, 8, 71, 77, 213*n*9
   see also nature; reproduction; science
"The Blind Spot of an Old Dream of Symmetry" (Irigaray), 41
Bornemark, Jonna, 214*n*5
breathing, 192, 219*n*2
Burke, Carolyn, 191–192
Butler, Judith, 211*n*1, 212*n*4

Canters, Hanneke, 80
the caress. *See also* amorous style
   amorous style and, 155
   beloved woman and, 127–128
   desire and, 109–111
   dynamic style and, 158
   holistic sexuality and, 109–111
   intersubjectivity and, 107
   Irigaray's account of, 107–108, 110–111
   Irigaray's style as, 90
   Levinas's account and, 127–128, 130–134, 131, 133–134
   masculine desire and, 94
   opening and, 111, 128
   renewal and, 133–134
   Sartre's account and, 107, 119–120, 122, 128
   style of Irigaray and, 90
   subjectivity and, 110
   writing as, 162
carnal love. *See also* beloved woman; eroticism; love and desire (eros); lovers, masculine; pleasure; sexuality
   embodiment and, 186
   eros and, 178
   feminine style and, 95, 114
   gestural unity and, 74
   ideality and, 139, 155
   Levinas's account and, 105–106, 107–108, 124–134, 139, 140
   masculine (philosophical) discourse and, 86, 113–137, 185
   Merleau-Ponty's account and, 146, 158
   mimesis and, 89–90, 97, 98, 146
   neutral discourse and, 188
   personhood and, 140
   Platonism and, 114, 134–137
   Sartre's account and, 106–108, 115, 120–124, 134, 139, 140
   sexual difference and, 89
   spirituality and, 82, 137, 145, 146
   subjectivity and, 95, 139–143, 159, 184
   uniqueness of woman and, 105–108, 113–114
   wisdom and, 141–142, 147
Cartesian Meditations (Husserl), 57–58
cause, 150, 152
Ce sexe qui n'en est pas un (Irigaray). *See also* "La 'mécanique' des fluids"; "Quand nos l èvres se parlent" (Irigaray)
   in context of Irigaray's works, 190
   male norm and, 33, 191, 202–203
   mimesis and, 25, 27, 40, 97, 172, 191
   transparency and, 76
"Ce sexe qui n'en pas un" (Irigaray), 76
change and development, xi, 4–5, 10, 19, 28, 51–52, 71
   see also the new; transformation
Chanter, Tina, 43, 44, 46, 134, 199, 211*n*2, 214*n*6, 217*ch*13*n*2
cheerfulness, 60–61
Chiesa, Lorenzo, 218*n*9
coherence, 31, 106, 184
communication, 18, 73, 79
   see also dialogue
communities. *See* intersubjectivity; the private and public; readers
concealment, 171
concepts. *See* abstractions, concepts and theoretical discourse; intertwining
consciousness, 56, 71, 106–107, 115, 116, 117, 122, 124
   see also soul–body distinction; souls, feminine; spirituality; subjects and subjectivity
le contraire absolument contraire (absolutely contrary contrary), 105–106
le corps machinique (the mechanical), 83–84, 93, 96

Corrigan, Elena Glazov- and Kenneth, 178–179, 217*ch*12*n*2
crying, 35, 91, 97–98, 106, 192
culture
  destructive tendency of, xi
  duality of bodies and, 9
  feminine existential style and, 5
  hysteria and, 34
  imagination and, 3
  morphology of women and, 8
  mother-daughter relations and, 100
  nature and, 213*n*12
  self-reflection and, 19

daimon, 175
daimonic conception of eros, x, 1, 153–156, 177–181, 205, 214*n*5
"daimonic possession," 214*n*5
death, 57, 79, 123, 218*n*2
deconstructive readings, 8–9, 39, 41, 49, 211*n*6, 212*n*4, 219*n*11
  see also Derrida, Jacques *and other deconstructionists*
demonic possession, 175
Derrida, Jacques, 8, 211*nn*5,6, 212*ch*1*n*2, 215*n*4, 219*n*11
Descartes, René, 189–190, 196, 212*ch*2*n*1, 217*ch*12*n*3, 219*n*1
desire. *See* love and desire (eros)
desire, expectations and needs, masculine. *See also* carnal love; norms; roles
  beloved woman and, 34–35, 50–51, 91–93, 94, 96, 98
  carnal love and, 139
  Eros and, 149
  female embodiment and, 50–51, 71
  feminine becoming and, 170
  feminine desire and, 95
  gestural unity and, 101
  God and, 94
  the hysteric and, 34, 42
  ideal of woman and, 25
  Irigaray's account and, 160
  jouissance and, 79
  Levinas's account and, 124–134, 152, 153, 215*ch*5*n*1

materiality and, 172, 208
maternal-feminine and, 32, 33
metaphysical, 124–125, 153
mother-daughter relations and, 103
la "mystérique" and, 37
narrow notion of sexuality and, 93–95
Sartre on, 117
the wife and, 170
desire, feminine, 34, 79, 95, 98
détente-décharge, tension-décharge (relaxation-discharge model), 93
Deutscher, Penelope, 114
Le deuxième sexe (de Beauvoir), 213*n*13
dialectical methods, 151, 197–198
dialogue. *See also* intersubjectivity; readers
  active-passive attitude and, 153, 157
  the caress and, 111
  carnal love and, 114
  Éthique and, 191–192, 193–194, 198–199
  interrelation and, 98
  Irigaray's account and, 156, 160
  Irigaray's style as, 74, 108, 161, 194, 198
  love and, 90, 178
  love of wisdom and, 179–180, 187
  the masculine and, 202
  masculine subject and, 161
  Merleau-Ponty's account and, 63
  objectivity and, 86
  Symposium and, 135
  variety of styles and, 86
difference and sameness. *See also* hierarchies; love of same/love of other; sexual difference
  Diotima's account and, 152
  embodiment and, 22
  feminine-masculine, 33
  Irigaray's mimesis and, 44
  love of, 101
  man's woman and, 83
  need and, 125
  philosophical subject and, 185, 188
  self-knowledge and, 185
  strategic essentialism and, 8
  of styles, 18
  between women, 28, 104

"*La différence sexuelle*" ("Sexual difference") (Irigaray), 189
Dionysian woman, 211*n*6
Diotima. *See also* the oracle/sorcerer; *Symposium* (Plato)
  as couple with Socrates, 197
  expression of, 173–174, 176
  feminine style and stylistic unity and, 176, 208
  fragmentation and, 148, 149–150
  genealogy of women and, 188
  historical existence of, 218*n*9
  Irigaray's account of, 145, 146–159, 177–181
  as oracle, 174
  'poverty' of Eros and, 143
  silence and, 218*n*8
  Socrates' account and, 136, 173–174
  "texture of beauty" and, 24
discourse. *See also* dialogue; discourse (dominant masculine philosophical); perspectives (points of view); philosophy; writing
  beloved woman and, 36
  constitutive outside of, 9
  (dis)unity of, 49
  experience and, 159
  the feminine and, 30
  feminine body and, 13–14
  feminine style and, 25
  intersubjectivity and, 89
  intertwining and, 24
  language, identity and face and, 131
  Levinas's account and, 131
  love and, 159
  love between women and, 103
  maternal-feminine and, 181
  mimesis and, 14, 212*ch*2*n*3
  the mystic and, 37
  neutral, 22
  non-unity of, 86
  personhood and, 127
  philosophy as, 24–29
  the pre-discursive and, 56
  self-definition and, 167
  truth and, 49, 84
discourse (dominant masculine philosophical). *See also* neutral discourse; phenomenology; wisdom and its lovers
  actualization of, 6, 21
  amorous style and, 166, 205
  beloved woman and, 36
  bias and, 6
  carnal love and, 113–137
  Ce Sexe and, 202–203
  deconstructive readings and, 8–9
  Diotima and, 145, 147–148
  disembodiment of subject and, 74, 141–142, 146, 166, 184, 186–187
  dominance of, 48–50
  embodied–spiritual unity and, 114
  embodiment and, 21–37
  essences and, 21
  excess and, 16
  excess of, 15–16
  exclusion of the feminine from, 24
  experienced *versus* ideal reality and, 24
  expressions of women and, x
  feminine embodiment and, 3, 61, 114
  feminine existential style and, 3
  feminine speech and, 50
  hierarchies and, 22
  the ideal and, 140
  Irigaray's work and, 1, 3–4
  language and, 75
  materials of, 6
  maternal origin and, xi
  mimesis and, 40, 42, 48
  'poverty of Eros' and, 143
  reproductive mimesis and, 24–28, 26
  sexual neutrality and, 26
  soul and, 82
  Speculum and, 41
  thought and, 166
  woman's essence and, 27–28
  women in, 5–7, 167–176
  women's perspectives and, ix
disembodiment, feminine, 28, 83, 136

disembodiment of male philosophical subject, 74, 141–142, 146, 166, 184, 186–187
the divine. *See also* the infinite; the sensible (sensual) transcendental (ideal)
  Diotima and, 174, 175
  eros and, 46, 79
  female, 47
  feminine soul and, 81–84
  "primitive" expressive unity and, 82
  sensuality and, 79
  sexual acts and, 155, 156
dominance, masculine, 48–50
dualisms, 9, 115, 134, 153, 177, 196, 197, 213n8
  see also hierarchies; the (in-)between *(under B)*; mind–body distinction *and other metaphysical distinctions*
dynamic essence. *See* style, existential
dynamism, 152

Earth, xi
"The Ecstasy of Saint Teresa" (Bernini), 34, 46
eidetic variation (imaginary variation), 54, 55
the elemental, 69–70, 72, 73, 75, 98, 100–101, 110, 192–193, 215ch5n1
  see also materiality
elle-même avec elle-même ("herself with herself"), 71
embodiment and bodies. *See also* affectivity; the caress; carnal love; disembodiment, feminine; disembodiment of male philosophical subject; embodiment and bodies, feminine; embodiment and bodies, masculine; flesh; gestural unity; lived body; phenomenology of the body; the pre-discursive; soul–body distinction; writing
  abstractions and, 57, 94, 187
  Derrida's account and, 212ch1n2
  desire and, 153

as dimension of existential style, 11
duality of, 9
Husserl's account and, 215ch4n2
Levinas's account and, 127
masculine (philosophical) discourse and, 21–37, 87, 114, 185
materiality confused with, 186–187
Merleau-Ponty's account and, 10, 62, 71, 215ch5n2, 215n5
perspectives and, 117, 188
phenomenology and, 87
the philosopher and, 168, 182, 186
productive mimesis and, 39–52
reflexivity and, 57–58
relations and, 186
reversability and, 215n5
Sartre's account and, 106–107, 115, 118, 119, 120
sexual act and, 156
sexuality and, 93–95
Socrates' account of love and, 137
speech and, 123
spirituality and, 4, 5, 75, 81, 87, 107, 114, 147, 166, 200
subjectivity and, 57, 62, 71
writing and, 10, 186–188
embodiment and bodies, feminine. *See also* disembodiment, feminine; gestural unity; reproduction
  as alternative norm, 52
  beloved woman and, 90, 91, 106
  essentialism of Irigaray and, 7, 8
  Éthique and, 191
  as expressive, 13–14, 22
  feminine existential style and, 15–19
  feminine lived bodies, 59–86
  first-person style and, 14, 53–54, 191, 208
  Irigaray's style and, 10, 85
  male desire/need and, 50, 71
  male discourse and, 61, 98
  man's woman and, 50–52
  Merleau-Ponty's account and, 65
  the mystic and, 214n5
  philosophical discourse and, 3

embodiment and bodies *(continued)*
   self-love and love among women and, 99–104
   subjectivity and, 91
embodiment and bodies, masculine. *See also* disembodiment of male philosophical subject
   forgetting of, 187
   hysteria and, 47
   identity and, 81
   Irigaray's account and, 85
   male lover and, 93–94
   mediation of woman and, 83
   projection on feminine other of, 141
   the sensible and, 139
   subjectivity and, 85, 161
the "emergent in perceivable," 209
enchantment, 121, 154, 160, 174
Encore (Lacan), 34
end-point *(telos)*, 5
enjoyment *(joissance)*, 18, 32, 80, 215*ch5n*1
   see also pleasure
Entre deux (Irigaray), 65, 215*ch10n*2
"L'entrelacs–le chiasme," 65
Entre Orient et Occident (Irigaray), 192
entwinements. *See* intertwining *and don't ask why*
epistemology, 6
"equivocal," 152–153, 156
erection, masculine self-, 83, 89, 94, 101
eros. *See* love and desire (eros)
Eros (god), 216*ch11n*2
eroticism. *See also* auto-affection; carnal love; sexuality
   Beauvoir's account of, 219*n*5
   elimination of, 215*ch5n*3
   evolvement of, 163
   as mechanical, 83–84
   the new and, 162
   phenomenology of, 219*n*5
   sexuality and, 59, 60
essences. *See also* essentialism of Irigaray's work; Eternal Feminine; metaphysics; style, existential (dynamic essence)
   alternative accounts of, 7–9
   Aristotelian/Platonic, 5, 213*n*8
   bias and, 6
   biology and, 8
   Derrida on, 212*ch1n*2
   differences between women and, 28
   Diotima and, 148
   existence and, 65
   the feminine and, 10, 30–31
   feminine style and, 17
   genetic conception of, 55
   of humanity, 33
   Levinas's account and, 127
   the maternal-material and, 101
   Merleau-Ponty's account and, 197
   mimesis and, 21
   phenomenological method and, 55
   phenomenology and, 56, 87
   phenomenology of body and, 3–4
   philosophical tradition and, 29, 30
   Plato and, 5, 162, 213*n*8
   Platonic, 5, 27–30, 213*n*8
   prejudices and, 8
   as stylistic unities, 55
essentialism of Irigaray's work. *See also* the generic feminine
   debate about, 1, 4, 7–9, 53, 211*n*5
   inexistence of woman and, 13–14
   political or strategic, 213*n*12
   strategic, 19
   unjust criticism of, 211*n*5
Eternal Feminine, 7, 30
ethics (of love), 122, 126, 127, 215*ch10n*4
   eros and, 215*n*5
   Levinas's account and, 130, 132, 133–134, 215*n*7
Éthique de la différence sexuelle (Irigaray). *See also* "The Invisible of the Flesh: A Reading of Merleau-Ponty"; "Questions à Emmanuel Lévinas sur la divinité de l'amour"; "Sexual difference"; "Sorcerer Love: A Reading of Plato, *Symposium*, 'Diotima's Speech'"
   amorous style and, 46, 187, 188–189, 190

in context of Irigaray's works, 4, 40, 46, 190, 191, 214n1
dialogue and, 198–199
dualities and, 197
eros and, 197
Irigaray's style and, 188–189, 191–194
lips and, 78
on love, 189–190
love of same/other and, 157–159
Merleau-Ponty's account and, 43–44, 65
mucous and, 77, 83
organizational structure of, 219n3
sexual act and, 156
étonnement (wonder), 54, 159, 189, 217n4, 219n1
L'être et le néant (Sartre), 97, 115, 116–117, 121, 159–160
excess (that which is left outside of; "more")
    beloved woman and, 37
    of common sense, 27
    desire and, 153
    the elemental and, 70
    of feminine desire, 79
    feminine style and, 15–16, 30
    the gaze and, 116
    the hysteric and, 35
    maternal-feminine and, 32
    productive mimesis and, 21
    recognition of other and, 96
the excessive feminine, 212n4
existence
    affectivity/sexuality and, 54
    body as expression of, 60
    discourse and, 49
    essence and, 65
    phenomenological method and, 55
    phenomenology and, 54
    sexuality and, 59, 60
existential style. *See* style, existential (dynamic essence)
expectations, masculine. *See* desire, expectations and needs, masculine
experience. *See also* lived body; the preconceptual and the pre-discursive; reality

    Diotima and, 175
    discordant interpretations of, 207
    discourse and, 159
    first-person expressions and, ix
    Irigaray's work and, 1
    masculine, 207
    phenomenology and, 54
    practices of love and, 158
    sensible, 5
expression. *See also* dialogue; discourse (dominant masculine philosophical); expression, feminine; the face; gestural unity; language; "primitive" expression; speech; writing
    discordant interpretations of, 207
    Levinas's account and, 134
    Sartre's account and, 117
    sexually other and, 134
    soul–body distinction and, 22
expression, feminine. *See also* Diotima; gestural unity; gestures; "primitive" expression; style, feminine
    diverse modes of, 73
    embodiment and, 22, 29
    feminine identity and style and, 48
    feminine lived body and, 72–77
    the hysteric and, 49
    intentionality and, 58
    Irigaray's work and, 1, 11
    Levinas's account and, 129–130
    love between women and, 103
    man's woman and, 33–34, 51
    the maternal and, 101
    maternal-feminine and, 44
    the mystic and, 36–37
    non-discursive modes of, 73
    as norm, alternative, 52
    opening and, 62
    opening for, 159–162
    philosophy and, x, 22
    possibility and, 50
    sexuality and, 60, 61
    unity of, 98
expression, "primitive." *see* "primitive" expression

fabric, 24
the face, 125, 126–127, 129, 130, 131, 132, 139
faces, smiling, 61
facticity, 118, 121, 123, 153
"Fécundité de la caresse. Lecture de Lévinas. Totalité et infini, Section IV, B, 'Phénoménologie de l'éros'" ("The Fecundity of the Caress: A Reading of Levinas, *Totality and Infinity*, 'Phenomenology of Eros'") (Irigaray), 189, 195
fecundity. *See also* generativity; reproduction; the son
  the caress and, 110
  Diotima and, 150, 151–152
  eros and, 178
  as ideal of love, 175
  the Ideal *versus*, 135
  the infinite and, 157
  intersubjectivity and, 111
  Levinas's account and, 126, 130, 133
  reproduction and, 155
"The Fecundity of the Caress: A Reading of Levinas, *Totality and Infinity*, 'Phenomenology of Eros'" ("Fécundité de la caresse. Lecture de Lévinas. Totalité et infini, Section IV, B, 'Phénoménologie de l'éros'") (Irigaray), 189, 195
the feminine *(le féminine)*, femininity and woman *(la femme). See also* beloved woman *and other mimetic figures;* embodiment and bodies, feminine; essentialism of Irigaray's work; feminine style *(le style féminine);* gender; gestural unity; sexual difference; style, feminine
  actualization of, 40
  Butler on, 212*n*4
  denial of, 26
  dialogue with masculinity, 11
  discordant interpretations of, 207
  discourse and, 30
  eros and, 126–127
  exclusion of, 49
  generic, 5
  Irigaray's terminology and, 15
  Levinas's account and, 106, 127, 215*n*7
  love and, 89, 177, 195
  male-defined, x, 212*ch*2*n*3
  male definitions of, x, 212*ch*2*n*3
  masculine discourse and, 24
  masculinity and, x–xi, 7–8
  metaphysical hierarchies and, 22
  metaphysics and, 30–31
  neutral discourse and, 122–124
  other women, 75
  philosophers and, 212*ch*2*n*1
  productive mimesis and, 40
  self-defined, 212*ch*2*n*3
  Socrates and, 218*n*9
  specular versus excessive, 212*n*4
  as theoretical entity, 72
feminine style *(le style féminine). See also* amorous style, Irigaray's; the feminine *(le féminine)*, femininity and woman *(la femme);* mimesis, reproductive
  discourse and, 25
  excess of masculine discourse and, 15–16
  exclusion of the feminine and, 49
  feminine expression and, 48
  fragmentation of subject and, 142
  the hysteric and, 35
  Irigaray's, 47
  Irigaray's work as example of, 10
  of men, 5
  mimesis and, 24–25
  reproductive mimesis and, 25, 26
  the wife and the oracle and, 168
  wisdom and, 165
feminists, 4, 7–9, 8, 46–50, 168, 216*n*9, 218*n*9
  see also Le Dœuff, Michèle *and other feminists*
fiction, 23, 181
Fink, Eugen, 54
Firestone, Shulamith, 215*ch*5*n*3
first-person expressions/perspective
  bodily origins of, 72
  the elemental and, 72

exclusion of, 187
female embodiment and, 191
feminine being and, 6
feminine embodiment and, 14, 53–54, 69, 71, 208
feminine style and, 5
feminine subjectivity and, 76, 84
gestural unity and, 91, 102
the hysteric and, 49
Irigaray's, ix, 9–10, 54, 106, 145
Levinas and, 160
love and desire and, 61–62, 143
the masculine and, 195
maternal-feminine and, 202
the mystic and, 42–43
objectivity and, 86
phenomenological description and, 2
philosophy and, 176
productive mimesis and, 40
readers and, 10
Sartre's, 160
sexuality and embodiment and, 54
stylistic unities and, 202
transformation and, 87
unity of feminine expression and, 98
writing and, 16
flesh. *See also* the fold; lips
  bodies and, 120
  the caress and, 110
  the Ideal and, 136
  Irigaray's account and, 155
  masculine self-understanding and, 202
  Merleau-Ponty's account and, 44, 55, 66, 71
  Sartre's account and, 117–120
  writing and, 184
flourishment, ix, xi, 40, 84, 190, 191
the flower, 80–81
fluidity. *See also* mucous
  concepts and, 1
  female embodiment and, 51, 82, 187
  feminine existential style and, 16–17
  the hysteric and, 35
  ideality and, 55, 76–77
  lips and, 81
  metaphysics and, 30
  openness and, 10, 82

poetry and, 73
styles of perceptual objects and, 55
woman as, 31
the fold, 81
forgetfulness
  beloved woman and, 130
  body of philosophical subject and, 166
  Eros and, 143
  of lived embodiment, xi
  of masculine body, 187
  practices of love and, 158
  two kinds of, 203
form (idea), 16, 27, 30, 32, 33, 211n4, 213n8
  see also ideas, doctrine of (Plato)
the for-the-other, 96
Foucault, Michel, 211n5
founding fathers, 219n2,3
fragmentation (incoherence). *See also* "primitive" expression
  beloved woman and, 141
  Diotima's style and, 148, 149–150
  feminine style and, 142, 155
  gestural unity and, 208
  the hysteric and, 48, 49, 73–74
  Irigaray's style and, 193
  lips and, 79
  masculine perspective and, 143
  masculine philosophical subject and, 148–149
  the mystic and, 48
  practices of love and, 158
  versus the "primitive," 106
  "primitive" expression *versus*, 106
  of unities, 106
freedom. *See also* grasping; possessing
  desire and, 153
  feminine subjectivity and, 142–143
  Irigaray's work and, 10
  Levinas's account and, 124–125, 128, 131
  lived body and, 71
  love and, 91, 106–107
  male-defined spirituality and, 82
  other's, 121–122
  perception of lover and, 96

freedom *(continued)*
  Sartre's account and, 115–116, 117, 118, 119–120, 123, 160
  seduction and, 116
  sexuality and, 85
  writing and, 181
Freud, Sigmund and psychoanalytic discourse, 4, 33–34, 35, 41–42, 103, 212*ch*2*n*1, 218*n*9
fusion, 216*n*9
future, 18, 126, 128, 131, 132, 140, 153, 178, 209
  see also temporality

Gallop, Jane, 42
the gaze, 115, 116, 123–124, 170
gender and gendered being
  as existential style (dynamic essence), 4–5, 211*n*4
  existential style and, 10
  existential styles and, 4–5, 18–19
  identity and, 212*ch*1*n*3
  objectivity and, 2–3
  openness and, 104
  oppression and, 9
  perception and experience and, 5
  readers and, 76
  self-knowledge and, 202
  sex/gender distinction and, 212*ch*1*n*3
  styles and, 19
gender-blending identities, x–xi, 18
genealogy, 130–134
genealogy, feminine
  Beauvoir's account and, 214*n*4
  cyclical temporality and, 71
  Diotima and, 175, 177, 188
  Eros and, 143
  Irigaray's account and, 47, 150, 151
  Irigaray's style and, 192
  Levinas's account and, 131
  mimesis of Diotima and, 146–147
  mucous and, 84
genealogy, masculine, 218*n*4
generativity, x, xi, 2, 10, 30, 47, 175, 213*n*10
  see also fecundity; the new

the generic feminine. *See also* identities, feminine
  the caress and, 158
  characterized, 5
  community/intersubjectivity and, 85–86
  Irigaray's style and, 191, 195, 197, 200
  mimesis and, 3, 37
  openness and, 5, 190
the generic masculine, 5, 202
German philosophy of nature, 9
geste-parole (gesture-word), 111
gestural unity
  beloved woman and, 36, 91
  exclusion from discourse of, 187
  existential style and, 58
  feminine style and, 105, 114
  feminine "style" and, 16, 30, 75
  feminine writing and, 75
  first-person expression and, 102
  the hysteric and, 73–74, 106, 208
  language and, 62, 63
  Merleau-Ponty's account and, 61
  speech/writing and, 192
  subjectivity and, 142
gestures. *See also* amorous style; the caress; the gaze; gestural unity
  amorous, 155
  the elemental and, 70
  emotions and, 60–61
  fulfillment of love and, 158
  Irigaray's style and, 11
  mucous and, 83
  sexual difference and, 209
  style and, 18
  writing and, 193
gesture-word *(geste-parole)*, 111
God. *See also* the Ideal; Mechthild of Magdeburg
  female body and, 51
  Levinas's account and, 131, 133
  love of wisdom and, 181
  man's woman and, 82
  the maternal and, 201
  (M)other and, 94–95

the mystic and, 36–37, 43, 46
Spinoza's account and, 189
the good, 219*n*10
grasping. *See also* possessing; the ungraspable
  arrest of, 156, 160
  beloved woman and, 127–128, 155
  the caress and, 120, 122
  essences and, 27, 55
  Irigaray's account and, 156
  the other and, 154
  other's freedom and, 122
  Sartre's account and, 116, 117, 120, 160
  Socrates and, 149
Grosz, Elizabeth, 8

habits. *See also* repetition
  after *Éthique*, 190
  awareness of, x
  beloved woman and, 130
  desire and, 153
  development and, 71
  distancing from, 90
  feminine sexuality and, 77
  Irigaray's account and, 132
  Irigaray's style and, 191
  love and, 90, 157, 162
  new, 85
  the non-habitual, 152–153
  positions of woman and man and, 180–181
  reality and, 49
  self-reflection and, 18
  sexuality and, 78
  speech and writing and, 64
  tension and, 11
Halperin, David, 151, 218*n*8, 218*n*9
Hegel, Georg Friedrich, 23, 151, 197, 212*ch*2*n*1, 215*ch*6*n*1, 217*ch*13*n*2
Heidegger, Martin, 23
Heinämaa, Sara, 19, 51, 58, 59, 61, 66–67, 211*n*2, 212*n*6, 214*n*4, 215*ch*3*n*6, 219*n*1
Heloïse Complex, 218*n*3
the here, 58
  see also place

"herself with herself" *(elle-même avec elle-même),* 71
heterosexual love, 202
hierarchies. *See also* dualisms; sexual difference
  carnal/spiritual love and, 208
  change and, 198
  female-male sexuality and, 42
  feminine-masculine, 7–8, 22–23, 33, 162
  ideal of subjectivity and, 142
  Irigaray's account and, 197
  Levinas's account and, 130–134
  of love, 143, 148, 152
  the maternal and, 101
  maternal-material and, 101
  mucous and, 77
  nature and, 213*n*12
  projection and, 187
  sexual, 202
  Symposium and, 135
  undecidability *versus,* 196
history, 156
  see also the past
holistic attitude, 190, 215*ch*5*n*3
  see also stylistic unities, perceptual
Hollywood, Amy, 46
homosexuality, 202
human beings, xi, 33, 177–178
  see also persons and personhood; subjects and subjectivity
humanity, 27–28, 29, 107, 137, 139, 142
Husserl, Edmund, 10, 54, 57–58, 67, 80, 86, 166, 211*n*2, 215*ch*4*n*2
  see also phenomenology of the body
"hylomorphic mode," 213*n*12
hylomorphic tradition, 212*ch*1*n*3
hysteria, repression of, 47
the hysteric
  amorous style and, 191
  beloved woman and, 48, 98
  desire and, 36
  disturbance of discourse of, 35–36, 37, 48–49
  embodiment and expression and, 207

the hysteric *(continued)*
  fragmentation and, 48, 70, 74
  Freud on, 33–34
  gestural unity and, 73–74, 106
  God and, 37
  Irigaray's writing as, 41–42, 48–49, 192
  male desire and, 92
  man's woman and, 34–36
  masculine norm and, 49
  masculine subject of philosophy and, 184
  mimesis and, 26, 34–35, 41–42, 47, 48–49, 73–74, 191
  mimesis by men of, 47
  the mystic and, 36
  neutral discourse and, 208
  repression of, 47

idea (form), 16, 27, 30, 32, 33, 211n4, 213n8
  see also ideas, doctrine of (Plato)
the Ideal. *See also* God; the ideal and ideality
  defined, 213n8
  Diotima's account and, 150
  Levinas's account and, 134
  man's woman and, 82
  masculine subject and, 142
  of masculinity, 28
  Socrates' discussion, 135–137
  transcendence and, 134
  of Woman, 27–28, 29–30
the ideal and ideality. *See also* beloved woman *and other ideals of woman;* the Ideal; ideas, doctrine of (Plato); perfection; the sensible (sensual) transcendental (ideal); transcendence
  carnal love and, 139, 143, 155
  Diotima's account and, 178–179
  essence and, 213n8
  fecundity and, 175
  of femininity, 26, 92, 213n6
  fluidity and, 55, 76–77
  hierarchies and, 142
  Irigaray's work and, 1, 7
  Levinas's account and, 134

  of lived experience, 28–29
  male erotic, 96
  masculine subject and, 153
  Merleau-Ponty's account and, 158
  the perceivable and, 47
  phenomenological description and, 2
  philosophy and, 165–166
  reproductive mimesis and, 25, 26, 27–28
  the sensible and, 81–83, 156, 166
  of subjectivity, 54
  of woman, 27, 37, 140
  women and, 82, 85
  the world and, 55
ideas, doctrine of (Plato), 21, 22–23, 25, 27, 175, 219n10
identifying with the feminine, 211n3
identities. *See also* self-definition (self-image)
  beloved woman and, 140
  desire and, 153
  Diotima and, 219n10
  female body and, 51
  feminine expression and, 48
  gender and, 212ch1n3
  gender-blending, x–xi
  Irigaray's style and, 9–10, 43–46, 194
  Irigaray *versus* de Beauvoir on, 211n3
  Levinas's account and, 128, 131
  lips and, 81
  love between women and, 104
  lovers and, 169
  lovers or wisdom and, 168–169
  male bodily experience and, 81
  male desire and, 92
  masculine, 30, 45, 140
  mimesis and, 45–46
  mother-daughter relations and, 103
  sexual, 19
imaginary variation (eidetic variation), 54, 55
imitation. *See* mimesis
immanence, 47, 66, 133, 174, 196, 201
immortality, 219n10
imperfection, 22, 49, 56
  see also perfection

incoherence. *See* fragmentation (incoherence); "primitive" expression
"L'incountournable volume" (Irigaray), 77
individuals. *See* specificity (particulars, singulars, uniqueness); substitution
individuals, problems of loving, 217n8
inexistence of woman, 13–14
infancy, 130–131
the infinite, 79, 82, 140, 157, 179
inner life, 63–64, 83, 95
"innerness for herself" *(l'intériorité avec soi),* 71
In Search of Lost Time (Proust), 215*ch*8n1
instrumentality, 50, 93, 94, 100, 110, 116, 120
see also *telos*; usefulness
intentionality
  bodies and, 58
  body-subject and, 71
  the caress and, 128
  double, 152–153
  experience and, 80
  feminine lived body and, 70
  intersubjectivity and, 107
  language and, 73
  Levinas's account and, 125
  mother-child relation and, 124
  of the other, 63
  perception and, 54–55
  reciprocity of gestures and, 60
  sexuality and, 60
  subject–body and, 57
l'intériorité avec soi ("innerness for herself"), 71
intersubjectivity (community). *See also* dialogue; private and public; readers
  the caress and, 107, 109, 110–111
  dialogue and, 98, 108
  discourse and, 89
  feminine freedom and, 142–143
  feminine generic style and, 84–86
  homoerotic, 196
  Irigaray's style and, 161, 193, 194
  Levinas's account and, 129–130
  meanings and, 156
  readers and, 199

  Sartre's account and, 101
  seduction and, 122–123
  sexual difference and, 214n1
  voluptuousness and, 129
intertwining. *See also* the sensible (sensual) transcendental (ideal); style, existential (dynamic essence); "texture of beauty" and "style of (all possible) styles"
  discourse and, 24
  ideal/sensible, 82–83, 166
  Irigaray's style and, 75, 107, 147
  lips and, 81
  love and, 177
  Merleau-Ponty's account and, 59, 66
  mimesis and, 212*ch*5n3
  oppression and, 9
  philosophy and, 29
  religious experience and, 47
  Sartre's account and, 123
  Socrates' account and, 177
  style and, 18
  unity of style and, 5, 76
"The Intertwining–The Chasm" (Irigaray), 43–44
"The Invisible of the Flesh: A Reading of Merleau-Ponty" (Irigaray), 43–44, 65
Irigaray (Jones), 200
"Irigaray's Body Symbolic" (Whitford), 215*ch*5n4
Irigaray's style (writing). *See also* amorous style; beloved woman; dialogue; first-person expressions/perspective; the hysteric; mimesis; the mystic (sorcerer); the teacher, female; the wife (philosopher's); wisdom and its lovers (philosophers)
  as acts of writing "in love," 41
  concepts and, 192, 197, 202
  development of, 4, 40, 46, 190, 191, 214n1
  distancing and, 199
  as embodied, 10, 85, 145
  as female lover, 41, 145–162, 146, 168–169 (*see also* beloved woman)

242 Index

Irigaray's style (writing) *(continued)*
   feminine being and, 1–2
   feminine existential style and, 2, 4–5, 15–19, 207
   feminine genealogy and, 192
   as feminine lived body, 69–72, 75–76, 145, 212*ch*1*n*2
   feminine subjects and, 11, 76, 201
   generativity and, x, 2, 10
   identity and, 9–10, 43–46, 194
   intertwining and, 75, 107, 147
   language and, 192–193
   Levinas's account and, 114, 159–161
   masculine-embodied lover and, 139
   material of, 3–4
   as maternal-feminine, 45
   methodology and, 2–3, 40–41
   phenomenological tradition and, 211*n*2
   as primitive unity, 106
   the private and public and, 147
   the private/public and, 98
   quotations and, 31, 71, 199
   relation to oneself and, 191–193
   Sartre's account and, 114, 159–161
   self-reflection and, 199–200
   Symposium and, 135
   titles of Irigaray's works and, 195–196
   transformation and, 200, 201–202
   truth and, 6–7, 160–161
   the wife and, 172
   as woman lover, 145–162
irréfléchi (the nonreflective), 118

Jantzen, Grace M., 80
Jardine, Alice A., 215*ch*4*n*1
Je, tu, nous (Irigaray), 215*ch*4*n*1
Jones, Rachel
   on generativity, 213*n*10
   on hylomorphic model, 213*n*12
   on Irigaray's style, 40–41
   on Lacan, 46, 47, 212*ch*1*n*1
   on lips, 80
   on male body/identity, 84
   on the maternal, xi, 101
   on matter, 219*n*3
   on Plotinus, 219*n*3
   on readers, 200
jouissance, 79–90
Joy, Morny, 46–47, 141, 211*n*6, 212*n*6

Käll, Lisa, 215*n*5
Kant, Immanuel, 23, 212*ch*2*n*1
Kuykendall, Eleanor H., 218*n*9

Laba Cataldi, Suzanne, 44
Lacan, Jacques, 34, 46, 47, 79, 212*ch*1*n*1, 212*ch*2*n*1, 216*n*9, 218*n*9
Langer, Monika, 107, 115, 118, 119, 121
language. *See also* discourse; expression; meaning; speech; writing
   carnal love and, 129–130
   feminine/masculine, 83
   freedom and, 117
   God and, 95
   intentionality and, 73
   Irigaray's account and, 131
   Irigaray's style and, 192–193
   Levinas's account and, 131
   as masculine, 75
   Merleau-Ponty's account and, 62–65
   mimesis and, 41
   openness of, 56
   perspectives and, 117
   as raw material, 187
   Sartre's account and, 116–117, 122
   unity and, 51–52
   women and, 26, 73
laughter, 35, 42, 149
Le Dœuff, Michèle, 3, 30, 170, 217*ch*13*n*1, 218*nn*3,5
Lettres au Castor (Sartre), 170
Levinas, Emmanuel. *See also* discourse (dominant masculine philosophical); phenomenology; phenomenology of the body; *Totalité* et infini (Levinas)
   body of woman and, 32
   on the caress, 215*n*6
   the caress and, 107
   on carnal love, 139–143

Index 243

on desire and need, masculine, 124–134, 152, 153, 215*ch*5*n*1
the elemental and, 69
on enjoyment, 215*ch*5*n*1
on eros, 152, 197, 215*n*7, 216*ch*11*n*1
Éthique and, 189–190
on the feminine, 215*n*7
first-person discourse and, 160
homogeneity of discourse of, 114
importance of, 23
Irigaray's critique of, 106, 130–134
Irigaray's style and, 159–161
on love and eros, 124–134
man's woman and, 90
Merleau-Ponty and, 196
mimesis of beloved woman and, 97
Sartre's account and, 196
sexual difference and, 89
on subjectivity's failure, 139
uniqueness of woman and, 105–106
writing style of, 114
le lien natal ("natal bond"), 56
lips, 65, 66, 78–81, 109, 215*ch*5*n*4
listening, 215*ch*6*n*2
lived body. *See also* embodiment and bodies; the face; gestural unity
affectivity and, 58
beloved woman and, 36
the caress and, 111
Derrida and, 212*ch*1*n*2
expression and, 5, 72–77
forgetfulness of, xi
gendered being and, 2
holistic sexuality and, 77–81
the hysteric and, 208
idealization of, 28–29
Irigaray's style as, 69–72, 75–76, 145, 212*ch*1*n*2
masculine, 14, 94
meaning and, 49
the mother and, 123–124
phenomenology and, 55, 57–58, 69, 84–86
productive mimesis and, 114
renewal and, 198

Sartre's account and, 123–124
the soul/divine and, 81–84
style and, 5, 16
writing and, 84–86
the look, reversability of, 67
love. *See also* affectivity; beloved woman; carnal love; love and desire (eros); love of self and love among women
disinterested, 125–126
dual perspectives and, 86
the feminine and, 89
Irigaray's writing as acts of writing "in love," 41
Levinas's account and, 125
limits of thought and, 45
mimesis and, 45
mucous and, 83
narrow sense of, 91
the oracle and, 168
roles and, 11
self-sacrificial, 169
subjectivity and, 90
the wife and the oracle and, 168
love and desire (eros). *See also* beloved woman; carnal love; daimonic conception of eros; desire, expectations and needs, masculine; desire, feminine; eroticism; love; *Symposium* (Plato); wisdom and its lovers
alternative conceptions of, 4
amorous style and, 189
attitude of loving, 177
becoming of a woman and, 113–137
beloved woman and, 11, 36, 89–90, 91–98, 162
body of woman and, 32
caressing gestures and, 109–111
carnal love and, 178
consciousness and, 107
daimonic conception of, x, 1, 153–156, 177–181, 205, 214*n*5
as dimension of existential style, 11
Diotima's account and, 149, 152
the divine and, 46, 79
dual perspectives and, 86

love and desire (eros) *(continued)*
  eros and, 177–181
  ethics and, 215*n*5
  Éthique and, 189–190, 197
  existential style and, 205
  fecundity and, 178
  female lover of wisdom and, 178
  the feminine and, 177, 195
  first-person expressions and, 61–62, 143
  fluid borders of, 10
  as forms of affections, 59
  generativity and, x
  hierarchies of, 143, 148, 152
  the hysteric and, 34, 35–36
  intentionality and, 60
  Irigaray's account and, 145–163
  Levinas's account and, 124–125, 189, 197, 216*ch*11*n*1
  male discourse on female bodies and, 61
  male lover and, 91–92, 139–143
  masculine style and, 139
  Merleau-Ponty's account and, 86
  "metaphysical" desire, 124–125
  the mystic and, 36–37
  objectivity and, 6
  phenomenology and, 105–108
  philosophical tradition and, 4
  'poverty' of, 143
  renewal and, 133–134
  Sartre's account and, 117–118
  self-love and love among women and, 99–104
  spirituality and, 126, 137
  Symposium and, 216*n*9
  transcendence and, 157–159
  transformation and, 188
  wisdom and its lovers and, 151, 194
love of same/love of other, 101, 136, 157–159
  see also sexual difference
love of self (feminine) and love among women
  beloved woman and, 92–93, 99
  difficulty of, 102
  disintegration of, 95–96
  feminine self-image and, 99–104
  flourishing and, 191
  Hegel and, 215*ch*6*n*1
  the hysteric and, 74
  infinity and, 103–104
  Irigaray's, 76
  language and, 103
  man's love of self and, 93
  multiple relations and, 194
love of self (masculine) and love between men, 91, 92, 93, 94, 135, 150, 171
love of wisdom. *See* wisdom and its lovers
lovers, female, 4, 41, 89, 102, 104, 113–137, 145–162, 168–169
  see also beloved woman; carnal love
lovers, masculine, 89, 93, 134–135, 139–143, 141–143, 188
  see also beloved woman; carnal love; desire, expectations and needs, masculine
Luce Irigaray and the Philosophy of Sexual Difference (Stone), 9

man's man, 202
man's woman. *See also* beloved woman; norms
  beloved woman as, 91–98
  carnal love and, 113–114
  differences between women and, 28, 83
  expression and, 33–34, 51
  female body and, 50–52
  first-person experience and, 86
  God and the Ideal and, 82
  the hysteric and, 34–36
  internalization of, 191
  Irigaray explication of, 30
  maternal-feminine and, 30–31
  mimesis and, 24–29, 40, 43, 84, 191–192
  the mystic and, 36–37
  narrow notion of sexuality and, 93–95
  philosophy and, 90
  question of, 54

sexuality and reproduction and, 53
transformation and, 201
Marine Lover of Friedrich Nietzsche (Amante marine) (Irigaray), 29, 32–33, 78, 97, 190, 191, 194
the masculine and masculinity. *See also* gender; sexual difference
  constitution of, 219*n*6
  dialogue with femininity, 11
  femininity and, x–xi, 7–8
  generic, 5, 202
  Ideal of, 28
  ideas and, 22
  norm of, 30
  transformation of, 201
masochism, 122
the material-elemental, 70
  see also the elemental
materiality. *See also* the elemental; matter
  anonymous, 100
  embodiment confused with, 186–187
  feminine lived body and, 71, 75
  of language, 75
  masculine self-representations and, 51
  maternal feminine and, 31–32
  Nietzsche and, 213*n*9
  philosophy and, 208
  Sartre's account and, 123
  writing and, 185, 186
the maternal. *See also* the mother
  beloved woman and, 91, 92
  desire and, 153
  as elemental, 100–101
  embodiment and, 137
  Levinas's account and, 131
  the masculine and, 201
  materiality and, 70
  as origin, xi
the maternal-feminine
  characterized, 31–33
  discourse and, 181
  homoerotic intersubjectivity and, 196
  Irigaray's work and, 45, 202
  Levinas's account and, 132
  male neutrality and, 45
  masculine subjects and, 65–66

mimesis and, 44
as "primitive," 90
projection and, 187
silence and, 48
singular body, feminine, *versus*, 100
the maternal-material, 43, 44, 70, 75, 101
matter, 33, 211*n*4, 213*n*12, 219*n*3
  see also materiality
Mazis, Glen, 124
meaning. *See also* language
  affectivity and, 59
  embodiment and, 22, 58
  feminine expression and, 73
  gestures and, 62, 75
  God and, 95
  intersubjectivity and, 156
  lived feminine body and, 49
  maternal-feminine and, 32
  Merleau-Ponty's account and, 61
  morphology of women and, 8
  Other and, 117
  shared, 86
  speech and writing and, 64
"La 'mécanique' des fluids" (Irigaray), 77
the mechanical *(le corps machinique)*, 83–84, 93, 96
Mechthild of Magdeburg, 46, 214*n*5
Menke, Anne M., 215*ch*4*n*1
mental illness, 48
"Mére de glace" (Irigaray), 172
Merleau-Ponty, Maurice. *See also* discourse (dominant masculine philosophical); phenomenology; phenomenology of the body
  on affectivity, 54, 59, 61, 77
  on carnal love, 146, 158
  on chiasm, 189
  Derrida and, 215*n*4
  on desire, 153
  on the elemental, 69
  on embodiment, 10, 215*ch*5*n*2
  on emotions, 60–61
  on essences, 28–29
  Éthique and, 190
  on expression and styles, 56, 60–62, 64–65, 73, 74

Merleau-Ponty, Maurice *(continued)*
  on flesh, 71
  on gestures, 60–61
  importance of, 23
  Irigaray's account and, 65–67, 146, 156, 158, 178, 197
  Irigaray's "mimetic" reading of, 43–46
  Levinas and, 196
  on love, true/mistaken, 157
  on love and desire, 86
  on loving madwoman, 106
  mimesis of beloved woman and, 97
  on neutral discourse, 186
  phenomenological method of, 54, 55
  on poetry, 73
  on reversability of bodies, 215n5
  sensible ideality and, 166
  on sexual difference, 66
  on sexual identity, 18–19
  on sexuality, 54, 59–60, 77–78, 79, 91, 158
  on soul–body unity, 82
  on styles and stylistic unities, 58, 64–65, 156, 158
  on subject-body, 57
  "texture of beauty" and, 24
metaphysics. *See also* abstractions, concepts and theoretical discourse; essences; essentialism of Irigaray's work; ideas, doctrine of (Plato); soul–body distinction
  Derrida and, 211n6
  desire and, 124–125, 153
  Diotima and, 148, 151
  the feminine and, 8, 10, 22–23, 30–31
  feminine self-definition as, 211n6
  feminine style and, 9, 17, 148
  forgetting and, 166, 203
  gender as style and, 211n4
  hierarchies of love and, 148
  as interchange between males, 196
  Irigaray's approach *versus*, 53, 132
  Levinas and, 124–126, 130, 152
  maternal-material and, 101
  phenomenology and, 3–4, 6–7, 56, 114, 132, 134, 166
  Platonism and, 114, 137, 148, 149, 213n8
  reproductive mimesis and, 25, 26–27
  Sartre and, 116–117, 117–118
  undecidability and, 196
mimesis. *See also* beloved woman *and other mimetic positions;* mimesis, productive; mimesis, reproductive
  amorous style and, 191
  author's interpretation distinguished, 212ch2n3
  auto-affection and, 94
  carnal love and, 146
  characterized, 25, 212ch2n3
  deconstructive readings and, 9
  of Diotima, 146
  discordant interpretations of, 207
  essence of Woman and, 21, 27–28, 30
  feminine authority and, 147
  as feminine existential style, 3, 14, 212ch2n3
  feminine lived body and, 69
  Ideal Woman and, 29–30
  index difficulty, as ∞
  Irigaray's style as, 40, 44, 45, 48–49, 75, 191, 193
  love and, 89, 90
  male desire and, 92
  man's woman and, 84
  masculine desire and, 91
  Merleau-Ponty's account and, 43–46, 64
  metaphysics and, 26–27
  non-unitary discourse and, 90
  opening and, 143
  philosophical discourse and, 48–52, 195
  Platonic background and, 212ch2n3
  quotations in Irigaray's writing and, 199
  relations and, 207
  reproduction and, 137
  sexual identity and, 19

strategic essentialism and, 8
transformation and, 89, 188
mimesis, productive
   Aristotle and, 212*n*5
   beloved woman and, 96
   carnal love and, 114
   characterized, 25, 40–41
   excess and, 21
   Irigaray's activity as, 38–52, 72, 84, 98, 165
   Irigaray's work and, 38–52
   lived feminine body and, 114
mimesis, reproductive, 21, 24–27, 30, 34–35, 39–40, 212*n*5
minds, 22
mirror image. *See* reflective surface (mirroring)
Moi, Toril, 7, 8, 30
morality, 116
morphology, women's, 8
mortality, 57
Mortensen, Ellen, 194, 211*n*2, 212*ch*1*n*2
(M)other, 94–95, 103, 124
the mother. *See also* the maternal; mother-daughter couples; reproduction (procreation)
   Eros and, 143
   the gaze and, 123–124
   Levinas's account and, 131–132
   man's woman and, 50–51
   misguided love and, 157
   as passage from nature, 82
   the philosopher and, 169, 172
   touch and, 109–110
mother-daughter couples, 100, 102–103, 219*n*4
mucous *(le muqueux)*, 77, 78, 83–84
multiplicity, 198–200, 207
music, 40, 64, 79
"La Mystérique" (Irigaray), 34, 37, 42–43, 46–50
the mystic (sorcerer). *See also* Diotima; Mechthild of Magdeburg; Teresa of Avila
   Beauvoir on, 213*n*13
   Diotima and, 148, 208

disturbance by, 35, 36–37
the divine and, 175
expression and, 33
as feminine, 177
feminists philosophers on, 46–50
fragmented expression and, 48
function of, 168
Irigaray's reference points for, 34
mimesis and, 26, 42–43, 46–47, 191
patriarchy and, 214*n*2
the rose and, 81

narcissism, 170
la narcissiste, 213*n*13
"natal bond" *(le lien natal)*, 56
nature. *See also* biology/physiology
   culture and, 213*n*12
   Diotima and, 175, 177
   as elemental, 70
   feminine existential style and, 5
   German philosophy of, 9, 213*n*12
   Nietzsche's account and, 213*n*9
   passage from, 82, 191
   as resource, xi, 70
   spirit and, 217*ch*13*n*2
nausea, 120, 122
needs, masculine. *See* desire, expectations and needs, masculine
Nesbitt Oppel, Frances, 211*n*6, 212*ch*1*n*2, 213*n*6
neutral discourse. *See also* perspectives (points of view)
   amorous style and, 166, 187, 188–189
   carnal love and, 114, 188
   detachment from embodiment and, 73
   differences and, 22
   disembodiment and, 186–187
   female discourse and, 3, 39
   femininity and, 122–124
   the hysteric and, 208
   Irigaray on, 183–184, 198
   Irigaray's style and, 161, 194
   Levinas and, 130
   Levinas's account and, 132
   maternal-feminine and, 45

neutral discourse *(continued)*
  omission of first-person perspective and, 187
  opening and, 209
  philosophers and, 55
  questioning of, 146
  readers and, 198
  reflective surface and, 30
  Sartre and, 120–124, 160
  the wife and, 169
the new. *See also* change and development; opening and openness; renewal; transformation
  Irigaray's style and, 191
  love and, 162
  mimesis and, 147
  radical reinterpretation and, 132
  readers and, 199
  readings and, 215*ch*5*n*4
  tension and, 11
New Testament, 47
Nietzsche, Friedrich, 23, 29, 211*n*6, 212*ch*1*n*2, 213*nn*6,9,10, 215*n*4
non-habitual, 152–153
the nonreflective *(irréfléchi)*, 118
non-worldly entities, 5
norms. *See also* abstractions, concepts and theoretical discourse; man's woman *and other norms*
  alternative, 52
  expression and, 33
  feminine style and, 19, 69
  feminine style as, 75
  of humanity, 27–28
  the hysteric and, 49
  Irigaray's account and, 207
  mimesis and, 25
  as pan-cultural, 92
  styles and, 16
  transformation and, 14
  of woman, 21, 22, 28, 29–30
nostalgia, 101, 131, 132, 154, 155, 161
nudity, 127–128
Nussbaum, Martha, 216*n*8
Nye, Andrea, 218*n*9, 219*n*11

objectivity. *See also* neutral discourse; truth and truthfulness
  descriptions by others and, 85
  dialogue and, 86, 179–180
  dimensions of existential style and, 11
  feminine sexuality and, 77
  Irigaray's style and, 191
  metaphysics and, 6
  philosophy and, 7, 56
  problematization of, 90
  writing and, 180, 184
objects. *See also* embodiment and bodies; persons; relations
  affectivity and, 59
  of desire, 107
  of exchange, 35, 92
  instrumentality and, 116
  of love, 89
  phenomenology and, 2, 54–55
  Sartre's account and, 115–116
  Sartre's examples woman as, 120
  seduction and, 116
  versus subject, 51
Oksala, Johanna, 219*n*2
ontology, 6, 21, 30–31, 54, 66, 217*ch*13*n*1
opening and openness. *See also* habits; the infinite; the new; transformation
  amorous style and, 189
  being and, 56
  the caress and, 107, 111, 128
  carnal love and, 113–137
  descriptions by others and, 85
  desire and, 153
  ethical relations and, 132
  expression and, 62
  of feminine style, 71–72
  feminine style and, 190, 200
  first-person experience and, 87
  fluidity and, 10
  gender and, 104
  the infinite and, 157
  Irigaray's style and, 193
  Levinas's account and, 131, 132
  lips and, 79, 81

lived feminine body and, 81
masculine subjectivity and, 202
mimesis and, 143
mother-daughter relations and, 100
objectivity and, 180
to others, xi
perspectives and, 190
readers and, 198
self-defined feminine expressivity and, 159–162
sexual differences and, 162, 209
of speech, 64
stylistic unities and, 104
tension and, 11
the wife and, 182
woman lover and, 89
writing and, 197
oppressive structures, 9
see also politics
the oracle/sorcerer, 26, 168, 176, 191, 208
see also Diotima
orgasms, 93
the Other
beloved woman and, 140
Levinas's account and, 105–106, 124–125, 126, 133–134
as lover of wisdom, 193–195
as radically transcendent, 121
Sartre's account and, 116–117, 122–123
transcendence of, 122
the other. See also difference and sameness; listening; relations; sexual difference
beloved woman and, 97
body of, 118
carnal love and, 141, 142
description by, 85
dialogue and, 179
eros and, 215n5
existential styles and, 18
feminine, 93
the hysteric and, 49
maternal, 70

of philosophical discourse, 48
"position" and, 50
Sartre's account and, 115, 215ch10n3
self-deception and, 21
sexually, 66, 148, 166, 182, 197
styles and, 58
L'oubli de l'air (Irigaray), 190, 198

pairing, 57
parent-child relation, 180
particulars. See specificity (particulars, singulars, uniqueness)
"passages," 82–83
Passions de l'âme (Descartes), 219n1
Passions élémentaires (Irigaray), 76, 78, 80–81, 97–98, 190, 191, 192
passive materiality and, 22
passivity, 31, 57
the past, 18, 132
see also history; nostalgia; temporality
patriarchy, 46, 214n2
pederasty, 150
Penia, 143
perception. See also the pre-conceptual and the pre-discursive; the sensible (sensual) transcendental (ideal); stylistic unities, perceptual
affectivity and, 5, 61
dialogue and, 179–180
doctrine of ideas and, 27
embodiment and, 57
the emergent and, 209
flesh and, 44
the hysteric and, 37
the ideal and, 47
love and, 96
masculine subjects and, 161
phenomenological method and, 54, 55, 56
pre-conceptual, 5
relations and, 56
stylistic unities and, 55
unity of, 55
perfection. See also the ideal; imperfection

perfection *(continued)*
  Diotima on love and, 151
  exclusion of femininity and, 22
  of feminine style, 188
  Levinas's Other and, 133
  the mother and, 95
  phenomenological description and, 2
  philosophy and, 165, 193
  Platonic forms and, 27, 29
  relations and, 198
  style and, 5
Perpich, Diane, 133, 215*n*6
personal growth, ix
persons and personhood. *See also* the face; human beings; subjects and subjectivity
  carnal love and, 129, 139, 140
  doctrine of ideas and, 27
  eros and, 127
  existential styles and, 17–18
  feminine expression and, 140
  as instruments, xi
  Irigaray's account and, 156
  Irigaray's writing and, 76
  Levinas's account and, 133
  love and, 91, 157, 180
  love of wisdom and, 180
  other, 76
  phenomenological method and, 55
  relations and, 179
  relations with world and, 59
  sexuality and, 60
  stylistic unity and, 58
  uniqueness of, 74
  the wife and, 169
perspectives (points of view). *See also* biases; first-person expressions/perspective; neutral discourse
  carnal love and, 159
  dialogue and, 199
  discourse and, 22
  embodiment and, 56, 57, 188
  feminine, ix, 90, 166
  Irigaray on, 214*n*1
  love and, 86, 89, 158
  man's woman as, 50–52
  masculine, 3, 30, 72, 77, 143, 187
  masculine discourse and, 24
  masculine lover and, 139
  new, 71–72, 87
  opening and, 190
  philosophizing subject and, 187
  Sartre's and Levinas's, 161
  style and, 5
perversity, 130–131
Phénoménologie de la perception (Merleau-Ponty), 62–65, 79, 156, 157
"Phénoménologie de l' éros" (Levinas), 45
phenomenology. *See also* Husserl, Edmund *and other phenomenologists*
  desire and, 105–108
  double touch and, 80
  existential styles and, 205
  the feminine and, 1–2, 10, 69
  forgetting and, 203
  inadequacy of, 113
  Irigaray's reading of, 6
  Irigaray's work as, 1
  of masculine being, 209
  mysticism and, 214*nn*3,5
  uniqueness of woman and, 105–108
phenomenology of the body. *See also* affectivity; Husserl, Edmund; Merleau-Ponty, Maurice; Sartre, Jean-Paul
  affectivity and, 5, 57, 59
  carnal love and, 105–108
  embodiment and, 87
  feminine interlocutors and, 146
  feminine style and, 10–11
  gestural unity and, 208
  Irigaray's rethinking of, 6–7, 53–54, 65–67
  language and significance and, 62–65
  lived body and, 55, 57–58, 69, 84–86
  maternal-feminine and, 32–33
  metaphysics and, 3–4
  method of, 54–56, 219*n*2
  objectivity and, 2, 7
  Platonic essences *versus*, 28–29, 162
  sexual bias and, 56, 69
  sexuality, holistic, and, 59–62
  Speculum and, 41
  style of another and, 18

Index   251

subjectivity and, 67
touch and, 109
philosophers, female, 4, 186, 195,
    197–198, 218*n*3, 218*n*7
  see also Diotima *and other feminine
    lovers of wisdom;* Pizan, Christine de
    and other female philosophers
philosophers, male. *See* discourse
    (dominant masculine philosophical);
    wisdom and its lovers (philosophers)
philosophers of religion, 46
the philosopher's wife. *See* the wife
    (philosopher's)
philosophy. *See also* discourse (dominant
    masculine philosophical); wisdom
    and its lovers
  carnal love and, 86, 113–137, 185
  de Beauvoir and, 214*n*14
  embodiment and expression and, 22
  as existential style (dynamic essence),
    185
  feminine, 201
  feminine subject and, 181
  Irigaray and, 212*ch*2*n*1
  Irigaray's style and, 43, 196–198
  mimesis and, 165
  readers and, 199–200
  styles and, 18, 19
philosophy of arts, 212*n*5
philosophy of nature, 213*n*12
Pizan, Christine de, 2–3
place, 50, 85, 214*n*6
  see also the here
Plato and Platonism. *See also* Diotima;
    discourse (dominant masculine
    philosophical); idea (form); *Symposium* (Plato)
  Aristotle and, 189–190, 196
  carnal love and, 114, 134–137
  the discursive and pre-discursive and,
    162
  doctrine of ideas of, 21, 22–23, 25,
    27, 175, 219*n*10
  on eros, 195, 197
  existential styles and, 205
  Irigaray's reading of, 3–4, 6–7,
    212*ch*2*n*1

Levinas's account and, 125, 134
loving and individual and, 216*n*8
meaning and, 61
metaphysical hierarchies and, 22
mimesis and, 25, 212*ch*2*n*3, 212*n*5
Nietzsche and, 29, 212*ch*1*n*2
Plotinos and, 219*n*3
radically transcendent Other and, 121
reproductive mimesis and, 40
"subject" and, 217*n*3
Plaza, Monique, 30
pleasure, 84, 93, 129, 140, 143, 170,
    215*ch*5*n*3
  see also enjoyment *(joissance)*
Plotinus, 23, 172, 212*ch*2*n*1, 219*n*3
plurality, 46, 85, 135, 194, 197, 207
poetry and the poetic, 11, 23, 63, 73,
    181, 193
politics, 23, 73, 213*n*12
  see also oppressive structures
Poros, 143
possessing. *See also* grasping
  Diotima's account and, 143, 149
  Irigaray's account and, 80, 154, 155
  Levinas's account and, 124, 128
  Sartre's account and, 107, 116–
    117, 118, 119–124, 128, 153,
    216*ch*8*n*1
potential, 158, 179
  see also becoming
'poverty of Eros,' 143, 145
the practical, 23, 168, 170, 212*ch*2*n*2
practice of breath, 192, 219*n*2
the pre-conceptual and the pre-discursive
  discordant interpretations of, 207
  discourse and, 49–50
  the discursive and, 3, 56
  feminine, 19, 21
  feminine being and, 6
  feminine gestures and, 95
  flesh and, 44
  Irigaray's style and, 192
  maternal-feminine and, 65
  mimesis and, 212*ch*2*n*3
  Plato and, 162
  style and, 18
  unity of, 5, 106

presuppositions, 2, 21, 54, 184–185, 194–195, 215*ch*6*n*2
  see also biases
the "primitive," 90, 115, 126, 193
"primitive" expression. *See also* crying; fragmentation (incoherence); singing; Xantippe
  beloved woman and, 36, 37, 48, 82, 95–96, 106, 109, 146
  the divine and, 82
  the hysteric and, 35, 106
  identities and, 45
  Irigaray's style as, 106
  Irigaray's transformation of, 146
  Levinas's account and, 129
  man's language and, 83
  masculine identity and, 140
  the mystic and, 37
  projection and, 187
  Sartre's account and, 122–123
  seduction and, 116
the private and the public
  amorous style and, 191
  beloved woman/mother and, 50
  Diotima and, 176
  essence of woman and, 7–8
  feminine amorous gestures and, 155
  feminine expression and, 75
  Irigaray on, 212*ch*2*n*2
  Irigaray's style and, 98
  Irigaray's style as, 147
  Irigaray's writing and, 145, 193
  Levinas's account and, 126
  philosophical writings and, 185
  the wife and, 171, 172
projective surfaces, 96, 100, 131, *141*, 157, 187, 218*n*8
the prostitute, 50–51, 213*n*7
Proust, Marcel, 215*ch*8*n*1
psychoanalytic theory, 8, 42
  see also Freud, Sigmund and psychoanalytic discourse; Lacan
the public. *See* the private and the public
public institutions, 212*ch*2*n*2
pure intuition, 5, 7

"Quand nos l èvres se parlent" (Irigaray), 76, 78
"Questions à Emmanuel Lévinas sur la divinité de l'amour" (Irigaray), 109
quotations in Irigaray's writing, 31, 71, 199

readers
  dialogue and, 199–200
  distancing and, 200
  embodiment and, 186
  first-person expression and, 10
  gender and, 76
  ideality and, 85
  Irigaray's choice as, 195–197, 201
  Irigaray's style and, 76
  multiplicity and, 198–200
  neutral discourse and, 198
  opening and, 190, 197, 198
  philosophy and, 165–166
  Plato and, 4
  Sartre's account and, 120, 160
  self-reflection and, 200
  undecidability and, 196
realist essentialism, 9
reality, 24, 39, 49
reason, 64, 219*n*10
reception of writing, 7
receptivity, 31
reductionism, 111
reflection (thought), 56, 65
reflective surface (mirroring). *See also* the nonreflective *(irréfléchi)*; self-reflection
  asymmetry of positions and, 45, 92
  beloved woman and, 37, 92, 188
  doctrine of ideas and, 27
  embodiment and, 31–32
  false neutrality and, 30
  the hysteric and, 35–36
  love and, 90, 98, 136
  masculine subject as, 209
  the mystic and, 37
  the nonreflective *(irréfléchi)*, 118
  productive mimesis and, 40

psychoanalysis and, 42
the wife and, 170
reflexivity of body, 57–58
relations. *See also* desire; embodiment and bodies; intersubjectivity; love and desire; wisdom and its lovers (philosophers)
    affectivity and, 59
    amorous style and, 155
    attitude of loving and, 177
    becoming and, 198
    beloved woman and, 97
    the caress and, 158
    change and, 4–5
    dialogue and, 156
    dimensions of, 19
    distancing and, 90
    the elemental and, 70
    embodiment and, 101, 186
    feminine embodiment and, 51, 75, 91
    feminine stylistic unity and, 84
    flourishing and, xi
    Irigaray's style and, 191
    Irigaray's writing and, 76, 192
    lips and, 79
    love and desire and, x
    love of wisdom and, 158
    masculine desire and, 92
    Merleau-Ponty's account and, 65
    mucous and, 77
    to nature, 70
    orgasms and, 93
    perception and, 56
    personal, 71
    personhood and, 179
    phenomenological method and, 55–56
    philosophers and, x
    Sartre's account and, 115, 123, 160
    self-reflection and, 19
    sexual difference and, 140, 198, 209
    structure of this book and, 11, 207
    styles and, 18
    stylistic unities and, 84
    subjectivity and, 18
    tension and, 11
    the wife and, 171
relaxation-discharge model (détente-décharge, tension-décharge), 93
religion, 43, 46, 148, 214n3
    see also the mystic
renewal. *See also* the new; transformation
    desire and, 153
    feminine style and, 190
    as human aim, 177–178
    Irigaray's style and, 191
    Levinas's account and, 133–134
    organic dynamics and, 198
    repetition and, 52
    wisdom, lovers of, and, 205
repetition. *See also* habits
    discourse and, 24
    disturbance of discourse and, 48–49
    embodiment and, 51
    Irigaray's style and, 43
    man's woman and, 51
    mimesis and, 25
    openness of speech and, 64
    renewal and, 52
    sexual identity and, 19
reproduction (procreation). *See also* fecundity; the mother; unborn child
    body of woman and, 32
    Diotima's account and, 150, 152
    fecundity and, 155
    feminine experience and, 76
    Irigaray's essentialism and, 8
    Levinas's account and, 126
    male self-love and, 94
    man's woman and, 51
    mimesis and, 137
    passive materiality and, 22
    sexuality and, 77, 93
responsibility, 10
roles, 3, 10, 11, 213n7
the rose, 81, 189–193, 198

sadism, 120, 122
sameness. *See* difference and sameness

Sandford, Stella, 133–134, 213*n*10, 215*n*5, 215*n*7, 216*ch*11*n*1, 218*n*5
Sartre, Jean-Paul. *See also* discourse (dominant masculine philosophical); phenomenology; phenomenology of the body
   the affective/sexual and, 57
   Beauvoir and, 217*ch*12*n*1
   on body of woman, 32
   on caress, 61, 97, 107, 120
   on carnal love, 115–124, 139–143
   on desire, 97, 115, 153
   on the elemental, 69
   on failure of subjectivity, 139
   homogeneity of discourse of, 114
   importance of, 23
   on intersubjectivity, 101
   Irigaray's style and, 159–161
   Levinas's account and, 196
   on loving embodied consciousness, 106–107
   man's woman and, 90
   mimesis of beloved woman and, 97
   neutral discourse and, 120–124, 160
   on nudity, 127
   the Other and, 215*ch*10*n*3
   Platonism and, 134
   on possessing, 215*ch*8*n*1
   on seduction, 97, 115–116, 115–118, 121, 122–123, 215*ch*10*n*1
   style of writing of, 114
Schor, Naomi, 212*ch*2*n*2, 212*ch*2*n*3
science, 2, 19, 23, 24, 54, 71, 73, 85, 118
   see also biology/physiology
Second Sex (de Beauvoir), 34
seduction
   the hysteric and, 41
   Levinas's account and, 129, 131
   man's woman and, 95–96
   Sartre's account and, 97, 115–118, 121, 122–123
   self-sacrifice and, 169
   writing and, 215*ch*10*n*1
self, internal alterity of, 57
self-affectivity, 80
self-deception, 21, 182

self-definition (self-image). *See also* identities
   Derrida on, 211*n*6
   the elemental and, 69
   feminine, x, 99–104
   feminine sexuality and, 78
   first-person expression and, 40
   Irigaray's style and, 191
   lips and, 80
   masculine, 202, 218*n*8
   as metaphysics, 211*n*6
   mimesis and, 212*ch*2*n*3
   philosophical discourse and, 167–168
   sexuality and, 78
   touch and, 160
   the wife and, 182
   writing and, 181
self-development, 28
   see also change and development
self-expression, ix, 31
self-knowledge/self-understanding, 30, 31, 51, 161, 166, 185, 202
self-love, 126
   see also love of self (feminine) and love among women; love of self (masculine) and love between men
self-perception, 28, 96, 104
self-realization, essences and, 33
self-reflection. *See also* first-person expressions/perspective
   amorous style and, 194
   being and becoming and, 11
   dialogue and, 157, 199
   embodiment and, 61–62
   Éthique and, 191
   habits and, 18
   Irigaray's style and, 199–200
   masculine subject and, 149
   neutral discourse and, 186
   relations and, 11, 19
   Sartre and, 160
   writing and, 180
self-sacrifice, 169
self-understanding/self-knowledge, 30
the "senseless," 11
senseless speech, 91

the sensible, 55, 76, 81–83, 134, 139, 140, 156, 166, 213*n*9
the sensible (sensual) transcendental (ideal), 5, 47, 162, 166, 175, 176, 177, 208
  see also style, existential (dynamic essence)
Sexes et parentés (Irigaray), 188–189
sex/gender distinction, 211*n*4, 212*ch*1*n*3
sexual acts, 155–156
sexual difference. *See also* difference and sameness; the feminine *(le féminine)*, femininity and woman *(la femme)*; gender and gendered being; hierarchies; love of same/love of other; the other, sexually; style, feminine *(la style féminin)* and woman's style *(le style de la femme)*
  actualization of, xi
  amorous style and, 190
  carnal love and, 89
  Ce Sexe and, 202–203
  concepts and, xi
  daimonic origins of eros and, x
  de Beauvoir on, 213*n*13
  discordant interpretations of, 207
  discourse and, 53
  dualisms and, 197
  intersubjectivity and, 214*n*1
  Irigaray's characterization of, 15, 209
  love and, 90
  lover philosopher and, 160
  Merleau-Ponty's account and, 77, 146
  non-hierarchical, 200
  opening and, 162, 209
  the other and, 66, 133
  possession and, 155
  realist essentialism and, 9
  realization of love and, 162
  relations and, 140, 198, 209
"Sexual difference" ("*La différence sexuelle*") (Irigaray), 189
sexual identities, 19
  see also gender and gendered being; identities; style, existential (dynamic essence)

sexuality. *See also* eroticism
  body of woman and, 32
  expression and, 61
  as expression of existence, 60
  freedom and, 85
  Freud's account of, 42
  holistic conception of, 59–62, 77–81, 91, 104, 109–111, 156
  joy and, 215*ch*5*n*3
  masculine (narrow notion of), 78, 93–95, 153
  passivity and, 57
  phenomenology of the body and, 53–54
  Sartre's account and, 107, 115
  significance of, 27
  styles and, 60
  writing and, 72
Shapiro, Lisa, 3
sight, 77
significance, 60, 62–65
"sign of becoming," 9
signs, 60, 61
silence, 44, 48, 49, 64, 111, 117, 168, 213*n*7, 218*n*8
  see also the maternal
simultaneity, 16
singing, 72–73, 80, 83, 91, 97–98, 106, 192
"a single transcendence" *(une même transcendence)*, 115
singulars. *See* specificity (particulars, singulars, uniqueness)
the sister, 172
smiling, 61
social constructivism, 9
Socrates. *See* Diotima; Plato and Platonism; *Symposium* (Plato)
solidity, 31, 83, 84, 101
solipsism, 66
solitude, 43, 66, 126, 133
the son, 103, 126, 130, 131–132, 133, 140, 169, 218*n*4
Songe-Møller, Vigdis, 3, 136–137, 218*n*9
Song of Songs, 47, 214*n*5
the sorcerer. *See* the mystic (sorcerer)

"Sorcerer Love: A Reading of Plato, *Symposium*, 'Diotima's Speech'" ("L'amour sorcier. Lecture de Platon. Le Banquet, 'Discours de Diotime'") (Irigaray), 135, 189, 195, 218n9
soul–body distinction, 21, 22, 23, 120–121, 123, 137, 166, 175
souls, feminine, x, 5, 79, 81–84
space, 58, 59, 71, 100
specificity (particulars, singulars, uniqueness). *See also* individuals; stylistic unities; substitution
  anonymous materiality and, 100
  body of woman and, 32
  carnal love and, 29–30, 113–114
  desire and, 153
  discordant interpretations of, 207
  doctrine of ideas and, 27
  essences and, 28
  essentialism of Irigaray and, 7–9
  existential style and, 5
  female body and, 51
  feminine-embodied and expressive, 9
  feminine style and, 84–85
  Irigaray's account and, 7–9, 156, 159
  love and, 157–158
  masculine, 56
  norms and, 29–30
  phenomenologists' promise of, 105–108
  Sartre and, 115, 118
  the teacher and, 208
the specular feminine, 212n4
specularization, 90
Speculum, de l'autre femme (Irigaray). *See also* "L'incountournable volume"; "Mére de glace"
  Diotima and, 218n8
  Éthique and, 4
  feminine embodiment and, 53
  feminine style and, 190
  on generativity, 213n10
  generativity and, 47
  the hysteric and the mystic and, 33, 37, 41, 47, 191–192
  Jones on, 219n3
  lips and, 78
  man's woman and, 30, 191–192
  on masculine subject, 191
  the maternal and, 101
  mimesis and, 40–41
  the mystic and the hysteric and, 33, 37, 41, 47, 191–192
  organization of *Éthique* and, 219n3
  Platonism and, 27
  quotations in, 31
speech. *See also* expression; language; listening
  Éthique on, 191–193
  the face and, 125
  gestures and, 73–74
  incarnate, 123
  Irigaray's account and, 156
  lips and, 80
  love and, 189
  masculine bias and, 6
  reason and, 64
  senseless, 91
  as sexual act, 156
  sexuality and, 77
  the wife and, 171–173
Spinoza, Baruch, 23, 189, 190, 196
spirituality. *See also* consciousness; the ideal and ideality; soul–body distinction; transcendence; wisdom and its lovers (philosophers)
  beloved woman and, 36
  carnal love and, 82, 137, 145, 146
  as dimension of existential style, 11
  embodiment and, 4, 5, 75, 81, 87, 107, 114, 147, 166, 200
  eros and, 113, 178
  female embodiment and, 52
  first-person expressions and, 49
  incarnate beings and, x
  Irigaray's essentialism and, 8
  love and desire and, x, 143
  man's woman and, 51
  masculine discourse and, 82
  maternal-feminine and, 32
  phenomenology and, 87
  Speculum and, 41

woman and, 82
women's perspectives and, ix
Steinbock, Anthony, 2–3, 214n3
stereotypes, 28, 104
Stone, Alison, 9, 187, 213n12
Strasser, S., 215ch4n3
strategic essentialism, 8, 9, 19, 39, 53
style, existential (dynamic essence). *See also* affectivity; embodiment and bodies; gestural unity; relations; the sensible (sensual) transcendental (ideal); spirituality; stylistic unities, perceptual; writing
   characterized, 5, 15–18
   embodiment and, 187
   eros and, 178
   gender and, 4–5, 10, 18, 211n4
   masculine, 209
   metaphysics and, 211n4
   mimesis and, 3, 212ch2n3
   openness and, 158, 197
   as organizing principle of this book, 10–11
   philosophical tradition and, 205
   philosophy and, 165
   the pre-conceptual and, 18
   seduction and, 96
   singular and generic, 5
   unity of, 1, 5, 10, 14, 58, 76, 84, 85, 104, 106
   variety and, 86
style, feminine *(la style féminin)* and woman's style *(le style de la femme)*. *See also* amorous style; expression, feminine; the feminine *(le féminine)*, femininity and woman *(la femme)*; first-person expressions/perspective; fragmentation (incoherence); the generic feminine; Irigaray's style (writing); mimesis, productive; mimesis, reproductive; "primitive" expression; repetition; silence; style, existential (dynamic essence)
   this book as example of, 10
   carnal love and, 114
   characterized, 5, 15–19
   Derrida and, 212ch1n2, 212n6
   Diotima and, 147–159, 149, 150–151, 176
   diversity of expression and, 104
   the elemental and, 70
   embodiment and, 5
   expression and, 56
   feminine lived body and, 71
   gender and, 18–19
   generic, 190, 195
   gestural unity and, 105
   jouissance and, 79
   Lacan on, 212ch1n1
   language and, 63
   Le Dœuff's, 217ch13n1
   love of, 157
   man's love for himself and, 101
   masculine style and, 202
   masculine subject and, 95
   of men, 5
   Merleau-Ponty's account and, 63
   Nietzsche and, 212ch1n2, 212n6
   as norm, 75
   opening and, 200
   phenomenological method and, 55
   phenomenology and, 69
   philosophical, 188, 201
   philosophical writings and, 64–65
   prevailing discourse and, 15–16
   relations and, 18
   renewal and, 190
   the rose and, 81
   sensible transcendental and, 162
   sexual difference and, 58
   sexuality and, 60
   singulars and, 84
   Socrates and, 151
   spiritual bodily persons and, 159–162
   "styles" *versus*, 16
   touch and, 16–17
   unities and, 58, 104
   unity of, 70, 75, 81
style, masculine (writing). *See also* discourse (dominant masculine philosophical); the masculine and masculinity; neutral discourse

style, masculine (writing) *(continued)*
  change in the feminine and, 10
  disturbance of discourse of, 9
  essence of woman and, 7–8
  feminine style and, 202
  love and, 139
  Merleau-Ponty's account and, 58
  Sartre's account and, 120
  sensible transcendental and, 162
"style of (all possible) styles" and "texture of beauty," 24, 55, 179, 205
  see also the world
stylistic unities, perceptual. *See also* holistic attitude
  beloved woman and, 106
  embodiment and, 58, 85
  essences as, 55
  feminine, 208
  feminine becoming and, 14
  first-person expression and, 202
  fluid ideality and, 76
  of lived, expressive body, 5
  masculine, 202
  Merleau-Ponty and, 156, 158
  openness and, 104
  relations and, 84
  the teacher and, 208
  temporality and, 55
  the wife and, 171
  the world and, 179
subjects and subjectivity. *See also* dialogue; identities; intersubjectivity; persons and personhood; style, existential (dynamic essence); subjects and subjectivity, feminine; subjects and subjectivity, masculine; wisdom and its lovers (philosophers)
  affectivity and, 59, 198
  carnal love and, 95, 139–143, 159, 184
  embodiment and, 57, 62, 71
  ideal of, 54
  Irigaray on, 214*n*1
  Levinas's account and, 124
  love and, 90
  love of wisdom and, 179–180
  man's woman and, 31, 50
  materiality and, 70
  maternal-elemental and, 100–101
  objects distinguished from, 51, 65
  of perception and experience, 5
  phenomenological description and, 2
  phenomenology and, 67
  philosophical, 137
  Plato and, 217*n*3
  relationships and, 18
  Sartre's account and, 115, 116
  seduction and, 96
  sexuality and, 80
  speech and, 156
  transcendence of the Other and, 95
  writing and, 10, 74
subjects and subjectivity, feminine. *See also* becoming, feminine; fragmentation (incoherence)
  Antigone and, 218*n*2
  Irigaray on, 214*n*1
  Irigaray's work and, 11, 76
  Levinas's account and, 133
  man's woman and, 30
  masculine subjects and, 200
  metaphysical hierarchies and, 22–23
  mimesis of Diotima and, 146
  phenomenology and, 56
  philosophy and, 181
  pre-discursive experience and, 56
  stylistic unity and, 85
  wisdom and, 165–166
subjects and subjectivity, masculine, 85, 90
  see also disembodiment of male philosophical subject; neutral discourse; reflective surface (mirroring); wisdom and its lovers
  beloved woman and, 208
  carnal love and, 95, 139–143, 184
  embodiment and, 85
  feminine subjects and, 200
  hierarchies and, 22
  the ideal and, 153
  maternal-feminine and, 65–66
  reproductive mimesis and, 26

Index 259

self-deception and, 21
Symposium and, 141
transformation of, 202
substitution. *See also* specificity (particulars, singulars, uniqueness)
  beloved woman and, 140–141
  carnal love and, 113–114
  the face and, 130
  female body and, 32, 33, 51
  Levinas's account and, 131–132, 133
  (M)other and, 94–95
  mother-daughter relations and, 103
  other's body and, 57
  positions of woman and man and, 180
  Sartre's account and, 115–118, 122
  sexuality and, 107
Symposium (Plato). *See also* Diotima; Plato and Platonism
  amorous style and, 4
  beloved woman and, 90, 135–137
  body of woman and, 32
  on carnal love, 139
  carnal love and, 139–143
  consistency of Plato's views and, 219n10
  eros and, 6, 216n9
  on failure of subjectivity, 139
  on fusion of sexes, 216n9
  the Ideal and, 134
  Irigaray's account of, 134
  mimesis and, 45
  prologue to, 217ch12n2
  souls and, 22
  the wife and, 171
  woman and, 31
system building, 197–198

the teacher, female. *See also* Diotima
  amorous style and, 191
  Beauvoir as, 85
  carnal love and, 114, 208
  desire and, 207–208
  as feminine lover, 146, 147
  Irigaray's style as, 146, 148–153
  Levinas's account and, 132

masculine discourse and, 145
masculine subject of philosophy and, 184
mimesis and, 26, 89, 143, 165, 191, 193, 208
as "passage," 82
the teacher, male, 218n4
teacher-pupil relation, 180
telos (end-point), 5, 50, 52
see also instrumentality
temporality. *See also* time and space
  amorous style and, 155
  beloved woman and, 91, 140
  the caress and, 107
  cyclical, 70–71, 81
  embodiment and, 56, 188
  essences and, 55
  Irigaray's account and, 156
  Levinas's account and, 131
  linear, 70
  man's self-love and, 94
  mucous and, 83
  objectivity and, 180
  perception of lover and, 96
  philosophical discourse and, 185
  sexual identity and, 19
  sexuality and, 77, 78, 79
  stylistic unities and, 55
  subjects and, 158
  woman's being and, 70–71
Temps et l'autre (Levinas), 105–106
tension, 11, 93
see also dualisms
tension-décharge, détente-décharge, (relaxation-discharge model), 93
tension, 199
Teresa of Avila, 34, 46, 79, 214n3
"textual strategy," 43
"texture of beauty" and "style of (all possible) styles," 24, 55, 179, 205
see also the world
"texture of duration" ("le 'tissu' de la déploiement de la durée"), 83
theoretical discourse. *See* abstractions, concepts and theoretical discourse; metaphysics

the There, 57
thinking and thought. *See also* abstractions, concepts and theoretical discourse; the ideal
  alternatives and, ix–x
  Diotima and, 148
  disembodiment and, 184
  habit/openness and, 11
  illusion of, 63–64
  limits of, 44–45
  mucous and, 77
  philosophical expression and, 166
"Thinking Life as Relation" (Irigaray), 56
Thinking with Irigaray (Rawlinson, Hom and Khader, eds.), 200
third-person perspective, 84
the threshold, 81
time and space, 58, 60, 74, 83, 85, 100, 153
  see also temporality
"le 'tissu' de la déploiement de la durée" ("texture of duration"), 83
Totalité et infini (Levinas), 97, 127, 159–160, 216*ch*11*n*1, 218*n*6
touch and tactility
  dialogue and, 157
  feminine style and, 16–17
  flower figure and, 80–81
  lips and, 79–80
  the mother and, 109–110
  phenomenology of the body and, 109
  Sartre's account and, 119
  self-definition and, 160
  sexual difference and, 78
  solipsism and, 66
  writing and, 198
traditional woman, 30
"traditional woman," 207
transcendence. *See also* the ideal and ideality; the sensible (sensual) transcendental (ideal); spirituality
  the caress and, 215*n*6
  desire and, 153
  the Ideal and, 134
  Irigaray's account and, 160
  Levinas's account and, 126, 134
  love of same/other and, 157–159
  reflection and, 56
  Sartre's account and, 115, 117, 121, 122, 123
  single, 115
transcendental reduction, 54
transformation. *See also* change and development; the new; opening and openness; renewal
  beloved woman and, 89, 91
  carnal love and, 90
  cultural imagination and, 3
  dialectics of dependency and integrity and, xi
  Diotima's account and, 179
  feminine being and, 8
  first-person expressions and, 87
  forces of, x
  gestural unity and, 74
  Irigaray's style and, 195–196, 200, 201–202
  love and, 188
  love of self and, 74
  of the masculine, 201
  of masculine subjectivity, 202
  metaphysical tradition and, 3–4
  mimesis and, 89, 188
  of oppressive structures, 9
  of "primitive" expression, 146
  readers and, 200
  of Western philosophical tradition, 3–4
  the wife and, 172
transparency, 76, 77
truth and truthfulness. *See also* neutral discourse; objectivity
  beauty and, 135
  bodies and, 71
  carnal love and, 129–130, 141
  dimensions of existential style and, 11
  Diotima's account and, 136, 149
  discourse and, 49, 84
  the face and, 129
  Irigaray's style and, 6–7, 9–10, 160–161, 191, 197–198
  masculine subject and, 139
  new, 147

perception of other and, 158
phenomenology and, 29
as way of life, 6
the wife and, 170

unborn child, 50, 67, 78, 110
the unconscious, 218n9
une même transcendence ("a single transcendence"), 115
the ungraspable. *See also* grasping
   the caress and, 107, 110, 158
   the elemental as, 70
   experience (this index) as, 18
   the feminine and, 9, 17, 142
   lips as, 80
   philosophy and, 56, 136
   place and, 58
   the world as, 179
uniqueness. *See* specificity (particulars, singulars, uniqueness); substitution
unities. *See also* deconstructive readings; essences; gestural unity; stylistic unities, perceptual
   beings and, 49
   beloved woman and, 36
   discourse and, 86, 90
   of embodiment and expression, 79
   of existence, 59
   of existential style, 1, 5, 10, 14, 58, 76, 84, 85, 104, 106
   expressive, 49
   of feminine expression, 98
   feminine "style" and, 81, 84
   instrumentalities and, 100
   language and, 51–52
   love and, 107
   masculine, 84
   materiality and, 185
   metaphysics and, 8
   of philosophical tradition, 196
   of "primitive" expression, 82
   soul–body, 82
   soul of woman and, 83
   spiritual-embodied, 75
usefulness, 50, 78, 79, 111
   see also instrumentality

value, 10
Vasseleu, 211n2
the virgin, 213n7
virginity, 128, 170
the visible, 61, 67
Le Visible et l'invisible (Merleau-Ponty), 43–44, 55, 156
Vlastos, Gregory, 216n8
voluptuousness, 110, 126, 128, 129, 130

Waithe, Mary Ellen, 218n9, 219n10, 174218n9
Weed, Elisabeth, 42
Welton, Don, 58
Whitford, Margaret, 3, 92, 172, 200, 215ch5n4
the wife (philosopher's). *See also* mimesis
   amorous style and, 191
   female students and, 218n4
   function of, 168–171
   Irigaray's style and, 172, 194
   Le Dœuff on, 218n3
   Le Dœuff's example, 218n5
   masculine subject of philosophy and, 184
   mimesis and, 26, 171–173, 191
   philosophical style and, 176
   stylistic unity and, 171
   transformation and, 89
   writing and, 208
wisdom and its lovers (philosophers). *See also* discourse (dominant masculine philosophical); the Ideal; neutral discourse; philosophers, female; philosophy; Sartre, Jean-Paul *and other male philosophers;* spirituality; thinking and thought; the wife (philosopher's)
   amorous expression and, 185, 188–195
   authority and, 23
   canonized, 219n2
   carnal love and, 141–142, 147
   conclusions, 205
   as dialogue, 135, 157–158, 195–196
   dialogue and, 179

wisdom and its lovers (philosophers) *(continued)*
   as dimension of existential style, 11
   Diotima and, 145
   female, 178
   female subject and, 165–166, 200–203
   feminine, 177
   the feminine and, 212*ch*2*n*1
   feminine first-person expression and, 167–181
   feminine style and, 165
   the Ideal and, 136
   Irigaray's style and, 146, 161–162, 185, 188–195, 197–200
   love and desire and, 151, 194
   love for persons and, 180
   masculine subject and, 141–143, 184
   the mystic and, 36
   the oracle and, 168–169
   the other and, 193–195
   relations and, x, 55–56
   relations between persons and, 158
   renewal and, 205
   sensual-transcendental relations and, 208
   Socrates and, 174
   soul-body dualism and, 4
   transcendent other and, 159
   transformation and, 90
   writing and, 185–188, 200–203
witches, 175
Woman, 7
woman's man, 202
woman's style *(le style de la femme)*. See style, feminine *(la style féminin)* and woman's style *(le style de la femme)*
woman-woman relations, x
   see also love of self (feminine) and love among women
wonder *(étonnement)*, 54, 159, 189, 217*n*4, 219*n*1
the world, 18, 55, 100
   see also relations; "style of (all possible) styles" and "texture of beauty"
writing. See also discourse; expression; fiction; Irigaray's style (writing); language; poetry; style, feminine; style, masculine
   as acts of love, 162
   alternatives and, ix–x
   detachment from body of, 74
   embodiment and, 10, 186–188
   as emergent in perceivable, 209
   feminine lived body and, 84–86
   illusion of inner life and, 63–64
   love of wisdom and, 180
   materiality of, 9, 186
   openness of, 190
   Sartre's account and, 215*ch*10*n*1
   seduction and, 215*ch*10*n*1
   as sexual act, 156
   sexuality and, 77
   Socrates on, 148
   style distinguished from, 16, 19
   touching and, 198
   the wife and, 208
   wisdom and, 183–203, 184–185
Wyschogrod, Edith, 125, 129, 132

Xantippe, 169–170

www.ingramcontent.com/pod-product-compliance
Lightning Source LLC
LaVergne TN
LVHW041216280426
837443LV00033B/182